W9-ABE-675

ADD-Friendly Ways to Organize Your Life

Acclaimed professional organizer Judith Kolberg and Dr. Kathleen Nadeau, renowned ADHD clinical psychologist, are back with an updated edition of their classic text for adults with ADD. Their collaboration offers the best understanding and solutions for adults who want to get and stay organized. Readers will enjoy all new content on organizing digital information, managing distractions, organizing finances, and coping with the "black hole" of the Internet. This exciting new resource offers three levels of strategies and support—self-help, non-professional assistance from family and friends, and professional support—allowing the reader to determine the appropriate level of support.

Judith Kolberg formed FileHeads Professional Organizers in 1989. She is the founder of the National Study Group on Chronic Disorganization, the precursor to the Institute for Challenging Disorganization (ICD), a popular international speaker, and widely recognized as an industry thought leader. Chronically disorganized people of many stripes have embraced her non-traditional organizing methods as described in her five books, which have sold nearly a half million copies worldwide. Her latest book, *Getting Organized in the Era of Endless*, addresses the complex area of digital disorganization. Judith has held several leadership positions in the National Association of Professional Organizers (NAPO) and has been awarded the organizing industry's highest honors. Judith resides in Atlanta, where she takes care of her mom, sees clients, writes, and blogs.

Kathleen G. Nadeau, Ph.D., is a clinical psychologist and director of the Chesapeake ADHD Center in Silver Spring, Maryland, where she continues to practice and provide supervision and training related to ADHD. She has been a leader in the field for the past 20 years, publishing over a dozen books on topics related to ADHD. In 1999, she received the CHADD Hall of Fame Award for her ground-breaking work on women and girls with ADHD. Dr. Nadeau is a frequent lecturer both nationally and internationally and is known for her solution-focused, integrative approach to treating ADHD. She has focused for many years on issues relating to organization, planning, and daily life management challenges faced by individuals with ADHD and first approached professional organizer Judith Kolberg in the late 1990s about the need for an organizing book that specifically addresses the particular challenges faced by adults with ADHD.

"When you notice yourself silently shouting, 'Ah-ha!' and 'Oh, yeah!' as the book unfolds, you know you've found yourself a winner. If you have ADD and want to get control of your life, prepare for lots of this kind of response to the insightful and practical writing of Kolberg and Nadeau. While reflecting their years of successfully helping ADD clients, they manage to make their up-to-date information not only useful but FUN. Thanks a bunch, you two. It's good to know somebody understands —and can help. This book does both."

—Sandra Felton The Organizer Lady®, Author of *5 Days to a Clutter Free House*, and Founder of Messies Anonymous

"As a professional organizer, I really appreciate the three levels presented in this book. It requires an active and optimistic approach from the client. The levels are like a navigation system, each level showing new roads and shortcuts, but the client is always responsible for the next step or the engagement of the next level. That's what I love about this book most of all: there is no more 'waiting to be rescued', no more excuses to sit back or give up. The simple and attainable strategies will boost our clients' self-confidence and will help them prosper."

—Hilde Verdijk, CPO-CD®, MRPO®, Yourganize Professional Organizing

"*ADD-Friendly Ways to Organize Your Life*, 2nd Edition offers even more practical ADHD approaches on paper, digital, and time management situations. The chapter on decision-making has especially valuable insights into ways to move into action."

—Ellen R. Delap, CPO®, President-Elect, National Association of Professional Organizers

"Judith Kolberg has done it again. This pioneer in productivity still leads the vanguard as the landscape changes. Packed with practical solutions and illuminating anecdotes, this new edition of *ADD-Friendly Ways to Organize Your Life* is a must-read for those who have ADD and those who work with them."

—Casey Moore, CPO, ACC, The Productivity Coach

"The new edition of *ADD-Friendly Ways to Organize Your Life* by Kolberg and Nadeau is simply wonderful and I will highly recommend it to all my clients!"

—Sari Solden, MS, LMFT, Psychotherapist and Author of *Women with Attention Deficit Disorder* and *Journeys Through ADDulthood*

ADD-Friendly Ways to Organize Your Life

Strategies That Work from an Acclaimed Professional Organizer and a Renowned ADD Clinician

Second Edition

Judith Kolberg and
Kathleen G. Nadeau, Ph.D.

Routledge
Taylor & Francis Group

NEW YORK AND LONDON

Second edition published 2017
by Routledge
711 Third Avenue, New York, NY 10017

and by Routledge
2 Park Square, Milton Park, Abingdon, Oxon, OX14 4RN

Routledge is an imprint of the Taylor & Francis Group, an informa business

© 2017 Taylor & Francis

First edition published 2002 by Routledge

Library of Congress Cataloging in Publication Data
A catalog record for this book has been requested

ISBN: 978-1-138-19073-3 (hbk)
ISBN: 978-1-138-19074-0 (pbk)
ISBN: 978-1-315-64067-9 (ebk)

Typeset in Sabon and Frutiger
by Keystroke, Neville Lodge, Tettenhall, Wolverhampton

Contents

Contents

Foreword by Ari Tuckman

When I was starting out in the field of ADHD, I read the first edition of this book intensively and it taught me *a lot*. It taught me all sorts of great strategies that I could suggest to clients to help them better manage the various aspects of their lives that brought them in to see me. More importantly though, it taught me how people with ADHD process information—where things work and where things fall through the cracks. I'm a fan of having a large repertoire of possible strategies so you have plenty of good options at your fingertips when a situation comes up, but I think it's more important to have this deeper understanding which explains why certain strategies will work better than others. The better you understand how the ADHD brain works, the better you can tailor your approach to the specific situation, whether you're an adult with ADHD, parent of a child with ADHD, clinician, coach, organizer, or educator (or, likely, more than one of those).

The first edition of this book was so accessible and packed with useful ideas that it was really easy to recommend it to clients. I probably should have just ordered a couple of cases and sold them at cost. But in all the years since that first edition came out, the world has changed. On the plus side, we understand ADHD better than we used to, so we can target our strategies and treatments more effectively. In many ways that are less unambiguously positive, the world itself has also changed radically—the digital explosion was in its infancy then and *a lot* has happened since. All those great concepts from the first edition still apply to our ever more distracting, increasingly connected, Internet-enabled world, but I was really glad to hear that an updated edition was being released (and honored to be asked to write this). You can still learn a lot from the first edition, but this second one is even better.

As a psychologist, I spend all day working with clients in my office. They come to me because ADHD is negatively impacting their life. Things that should be easier are frustratingly harder. Things that should be pretty straightforward too often become disappointingly unpredictable. Clients have tried all the obvious solutions (and some less obvious ones) but still aren't getting the traction that they hope for. People don't come to see me because of the symptoms of ADHD; they come to me to help them reduce the *suffering* of ADHD. It's the impact on their daily life that matters. No one reads out of the diagnostic manual and says, "I often have difficulty organizing tasks and activities." Instead, they talk about how they're scattered at work and it's making them chronically stressed out, feel like they're less capable than their coworkers, and worry that they would get fired if their boss really knew how crazy things got sometimes.

This is where this book comes in—on the surface, it's just teaching you to be more organized in various ways. It's about systems and strategies to stay more on top of your life. This is all good stuff, but don't underestimate what's really going on here. More importantly, this book helps you feel better about yourself and more optimistic about your future because these are the ultimate reward for better managing your ADHD. Not being able to find your keys is annoying, but doubting your basic competence (or even sanity) when this happens regularly cuts far deeper. I think of ADHD as the Colorado River that gradually wore away the mighty Grand Canyon. It wasn't a volcanic explosion that moved billions of tons of rock and dirt all at once, but rather a slow washing away over many years. This book will stop that slow erosion of your quality of life and the gradual undermining of your self-esteem.

So buy this book and work really hard at it. Mark it up. Dog-ear the pages. Scribble in the margins. Rip pages out and tape them up on your wall. Scream out "Yes!" when you find an especially fitting part. Give it the energy that your life and happiness rightfully deserve. This is the thing that will make the difference.

Ari Tuckman, PsyD, MBA, author, presenter, and ADHD expert

Foreword by Sue West

"The red book," as so many of my clients with ADD have called the original edition of *ADD-Friendly Ways to Organize Your Life,* is *life-changing.* But wait, isn't this book "just" about organizing? That **is** what this book is about, but that's only the beginning, and the new edition is even more of a treasure. Here's the thing about organizing strategies and the person with ADD: We can't live well without them.

Without our organizing strategies, our days go off the tracks and end up in chaos. We miss appointments. We forget commitments to people, lose things, and can't consistently remember what we were supposed to do when we need to do it. Our finances are typically not healthy and cause stress. Work is a struggle. Relationships are fraught with issues as ADD becomes a third wheel. Research supports these experiences; the risk for all kinds of life chaos is much higher for those with ADD than those without.

You may have thought or been told: "Why is it so difficult? It should be easier. It must be me." When you understand your ADD, you will finally know that it's not *you.* It's very likely your ADD. And *you are not your ADHD.* Where can you start? *Right here,* with an industry leader in the professional organizing field and a nationally renowned psychologist who specializes in ADD, writing *together* for you.

Organizing our things, thoughts, and time *requires* executive functioning, which is at the heart of ADD differences. Without organizing strategies that work with your ADD, life is not what it can be, should be, or what you are *capable of.*

This wonderful, practical book walks you through how to make changes in your daily life, *ADD-friendly changes.* As you practice using the strategies, and read about involving support and creating structure, you will discover strengths and advantages to your way of thinking. Your confidence and your self-esteem will start climbing to where you'd like them to be. As psychologist, author, and leader in the field Dr. Ari Tuckman has said, "Competence breeds confidence."

And that is why organization matters so much to those with ADD.

A key aspect to this book is Kolberg and Nadeau's pyramid of Strategies, Support, and Structure. At the top is Organizing Strategies, with Support and Structures forming the pyramid's base. With ADD, you will need *all three* to make a difference in your life.

The Support and Structures assist you in remembering to consistently use your Strategies. You can build your own "base" by relying on yourself first. My clients call it "gaming their ADD mind" to ensure they stick to what they know works for them. At a next level, the authors will show you how to ask for what you need from family and friends and keep your pride and independence intact. It's not about rescuing or nagging!

At the third level of Support and Structures, you may choose to interview and work with professionals, such as professional organizers, organizer coaches, ADD coaches, and therapists, among others. Sometimes you *know* what to do and can't get yourself to actually do it. The professionals will create Strategies, Support, and Structure with you in ADD-friendly ways.

Remember to select professionals who are educated and, preferably, credentialed in ADD. It is a specialty area in organizing, coaching, and in the therapy and counseling worlds. Numerous clients have left their therapist or organizer because there was not enough understanding, education, or compassion for ADD. They need to "get it" or the relationship and results suffer.

Where to find the professionals? The National Association of Professional Organizers (NAPO) is the largest industry association of organizers. The Institute for Challenging Disorganization (ICD) is primarily made up of organizers with specialized education and certification to work with clients who typically have a lifelong history of organizational challenges including ADD.

If you are choosing to read this book, then you already know that ADD cannot be stepped over or ignored; it is a part of your life and of your human essence. Whether you start with the practical, organizational strategies or with the emotional and psychological strategies, you'll end up knowing so much more about *your* ADHD and how it shows up in *your* life.

And *that life* is much easier to manage with these ADD-friendly organizational strategies in your court. Finally, you are not simply living *through* each day, but enjoying the days and experiences you deserve.

In her organizing and coaching practice, Sue West specializes in adults with ADD and ADHD. She is a Certified Professional Organizer in Chronic Disorganization® as well as a Certified Organizer Coach®. She has held leadership positions at both the ICD and NAPO, and is a member of the ADHD Coaches Organization. Sue is a published author, blogger, and presenter. She designed and co-led "Collaboration: Creating the Best Team to Support Your Adult ADHD Self" at CHADD's international conference in 2014, and in 2015 addressed the Japan Association of Life Organizers as the ADHD organizing expert. Sue came to her organizing career after 18 years in corporate America. She is a graduate of Smith College and has an MBA in Marketing from Babson College, U.S.A., www.organizeforafreshstart.com.

Foreword by Sandy Maynard

Disorganization is synonymous with chaos in the life of any adult with ADHD. Many adults report that trying to get organized on their own feels so painful, so it gets avoided at all costs and the problems just grow. Organizational projects that do get started often never get finished. Systems that are put into place to assist in managing our time and space are briefly used and then forgotten about. The ADHD organizational dilemma is not just what to organize and how to organize it, the dilemma involves actually doing it and maintaining what has been done. This book expertly and wisely presents solutions to this problem. Strategies are given that thwart overwhelm and prevent shutdown so organizational tasks actually get completed.

Judith Kolberg and Kathleen Nadeau provide the reader with motivational strategies that enable adults with ADHD to get started on boring, repetitive, and uninteresting tasks. They give the reader the tools that are needed to conquer their fears of failure in trying to get organized. As explained in this book, getting organized is not an event; it is a process and the reader is guided gently through this process with sage advice, understanding the need for frequent rewards that are meaningful, predictable, and immediate to promote and sustain healthy maintenance behaviors once the project is done. All this is presented in steps that are "do-able" so successful results are achieved. As the authors have noted, "Success leads to confidence and confidence leads to success." As a coach I know this to be true and have seen this book's approach work in many of my client's lives. Using the authors' approach has given my coaching clients the tools and confidence needed to make healthier, less impulsive decisions that thwart confusion and chaos.

The authors not only present a multitude of organizational tips and tactics that help the reader understand the true meaning of "less is more and simple is best," but the book is also a road map that guides the reader over and around their own ADHD pitfalls. Each and every suggestion is based on what has been empirically demonstrated to be effective for those with inattention, impulsivity, and executive functioning challenges. Self-regulation is required to do the hard work of getting organized and staying organized, yet extremely problematic no matter what "flavor" of ADHD you have or what behavioral symptoms are present. The authors of this book get it. Period. They know that a multidisciplinary approach is needed and provide ADHD-friendly solutions that utilize rational and resourceful strategies, structures, and support systems that address disorganization on all fronts.

The gem of this new edition is the section on "Getting Organized in the Digital World." In today's fast-paced, digitally connected culture with immediate access to everything and anything with the click of an icon, Kolberg and Nadeau have come to the rescue. Managing digital distractions is ever-increasingly problematic for the population in general and presents a severe handicap in both the personal and the professional lives of adults with ADHD if not recognized, understood, and dealt with.

This section of the book explains with laser precision how technology has introduced a whole new set of "impulsivity buttons" that further reduce one's ability to self-regulate and avoid impulsive decisions and behaviors. The effect these distractions have on working memory and what to do about it are presented with clarity and humor. Kolberg and Nadeau's expertise in helping the reader recognize and fully understand each problem while providing the appropriate solution is unmatched. After reading the many insightful suggestions in this chapter, I have crafted a "personal technology policy" for myself and will start encouraging all my coaching clients to do the same. This book is a must-read for adults with ADHD, whether the clutter is on the kitchen table or swirling around at lightning speed in their minds.

A pioneer in the field of ADHD Coaching, Sandy Maynard holds an MS in Health Psychology and has established herself as one of the country's preeminent coaches. Ms. Maynard was instrumental in the development of the Attention Deficit Disorder Coaching Guidelines and was a founding member of the Institute for the Advancement of ADHD Coaching. She has lectured internationally and is a regular contributor to ADDitude magazine. Sandy has been helping adults with ADHD lead happier, healthier, and more organized lives for over 20 years.

Preface

This revised version of our original book is long overdue and we are excited to update our recommendations to include the explosion of digital supports (and distractions) that now play such a major role in the lives of adults in this twenty-first century. Sadly, however, our book remains one of the few books that deals directly and exclusively with the challenges faced by adults with ADD—getting things done, dealing with clutter, developing more functional daily life management habits, learning how to prioritize, and managing time.

We've learned so much more about ADD as the years have passed since the first version of this book was published. We've moved away from a concern with hyperactivity and inattention toward a focus on what are called the "executive functions" of the brain—the cognitive skills we need to plan and execute tasks, to get things done, to meet our goals. Moving away from a focus on hyperactivity, distractibility, and impulsivity, more recent research suggests that executive functions are the primary challenges of adult ADD.

ADD is a disorder that affects us to varying degrees throughout our lives. It doesn't go away but evolves and can look quite different as we grow older. As we move from childhood, through adolescence, and into adulthood, expectations of us change. Once we are adults, the world expects us to take charge of and manage our lives. And taking charge requires learning all of the executive functioning skills we discuss throughout this book.

Our lives are much more complex today than even a half-generation ago. With the advent of the Internet, the world is at our fingertips—for good or for ill. The great challenge for many adults, especially those with ADD, is learning how to manage the instant accessibility of the Internet. News, social media, sexually oriented sites, gambling sites, and countless commercial sites beckon to us—encouraging us to spend time we don't have and money we can't afford. And it's all too easy to succumb. In this new edition, we focus on the "Internet Black Hole" and how to manage its seductive lure.

The Internet also becomes the source of countless communications and requests. Work for many has become a 24/7 enterprise, with supervisors and coworkers expecting instant responses, even after work hours. This information and communication bombardment makes it even more challenging for adults with ADD to stay on track and focus on their priorities.

Money management has become both easier and more challenging to those with ADD. The boon of the Internet is that now we can conduct our financial lives online and go paperless. In our last edition, we spent a great deal of time focusing on how to manage paper—paper filing, paper bill paying. Now our financial lives can be conducted online, eliminating the need for elaborate filing systems. Records are at our fingertips from our brokers, our bankers, and all of the vendors that we do business with. And yet money management has also become a greater challenge. We can spend money in the unreal environment of the Internet with the click of a button, making it ever more challenging to resist impulsive spending.

Another great challenge for those with ADD comes with the ever-increasing choices we are offered. One man lamented the complexity of buying a pair of blue jeans. In the past, he related, he just needed to know his waist size and inseam measurement. Today, the range of choices is so great—the cut, the color, the fabric, and the size—that he finds it an overwhelming task to make what used to be a simple purchase. This man's sense of overwhelm is experienced by all of us as we search online for the goods and services we need. Everywhere we turn, a decision must be made from among increasing choices. And he who hesitates is lost. Procrastination can result in facing a growing mountain of decisions, creeping clutter, and missed deadlines. Even time itself has changed. Everyone agrees that there simply seems to be less of it.

The appearance of 24-hour grocery stores and gas stations has eliminated the natural rhythm to the 24-hour cycle. We can eat, shop, fill up the car with gas, or obtain cash at any time of the day or night, during the week or on the weekend. We're forced to either create our own patterns or fall into unplanned chaos.

In the world of work, profound changes have occurred and continue to occur that can make work life more challenging for adults with ADD. Many of the hands-on, physical jobs that have always existed in the past have been taken over by machines, leaving an abundance of jobs in the service, communication, and technology fields—jobs that require less physical activity and more mental concentration, more sustained focus on details, and more information to be classified and organized.

Stress is particularly high for women with ADD. Despite the sexual revolution, studies show that women continue to be responsible for more than their share of childcare and household management. Commutes are long as families move further from their jobs to find affordable housing. And children are caught up in the rat race as well, being overscheduled in organized sports and other after-school activities most days of the week. This has led to the gradual demise of the family dinner hour and the increase in fast-food meals as parents race from work to children's activities with no time between for meals at home. All of these factors combine, resulting in greater than ever challenges for adults with ADD.

This book is focused on helping rushed, stressed, and disorganized adults with ADD learn to prioritize, focus on what's important, and develop daily routines that can reduce the daily chaos. In this book, we (Judith Kolberg, a professional organizer with a great sensitivity to the organizing needs of ADD adults, and Kathleen Nadeau, a nationally recognized authority on adult ADD) join together in addressing the challenges faced by today's adults with ADD in a simple, straightforward fashion.

While other books on organizing have been written, none have been focused on the particular challenges and dilemmas of adults with ADD. We hope that our readers will find that this book can help them organize their lives, allowing them to spend their time and energy on what's important rather than floundering in daily disorder.

Acknowledgments

I would like to acknowledge the contribution of my co-author, Dr. Kathleen Nadeau. Kathleen's commitment to people with ADD never falters, and it was her vision that led to the publication of this book, and her leadership in this second edition. My thanks to the Institute for Challenging Disorganization, specifically members Denslow Brown, Sue West, and Cris Sgrott-Wheedleton for their support of this second edition. I am especially grateful to all my ADD clients for the real world education they provided me. My admiration goes out to Dr. Ned Hallowell, Ari Tuckman, and Sandy Maynard for the innovative ways they convey organizing advice to their clients, which have been an inspiration to me. A special thanks to the associate members of the National Association of Professional Organizers who provided graphics for this book. I deeply appreciate the commitment of our editor, Chris Teja, for tirelessly working to create a book Kathleen and I know the ADD community deserves. And finally, my thanks to my mom who continues to support my career even at age 94.

Judith Kolberg

First and foremost, I would like to acknowledge the countless adults with ADHD that I have worked with over many years who have taught me so much about the struggles that they face on a daily basis as well as the creative solutions that they have found to surmount them. They have been my teachers, in sharing their struggles and triumphs along the path to taking charge of their lives. I would also like to thank my long-time co-author, Judith Kolberg. She and I first began working on the concept for this book in the late 1990s. I thank her for her patience, her perseverance, and her impeccable attention to detail as she has shepherded this new version of our book through each stage of revision. Our differing skills have dovetailed very nicely, leading us to accomplish this revision almost seamlessly. I would also like to thank our editor, Chris Teja, for his encouragement, enthusiasm, and flexibility. It's been a pleasure to work with an editor that understands the needs of the ADHD reading community and has allowed us the leeway to create a very ADHD-friendly presentation for our book. And finally, I want to express much appreciation to my family, many of whom also live with these wonderful, creative, and sometimes challenging brains called ADHD, for their input, patience, and encouragement along the way.

Kathleen G. Nadeau

Getting Started

ADD-Friendly Organizing

A Different Organizing Approach

For many adults with ADD, life feels overwhelming and chaotic. Their homes are cluttered; laundry and dishes go undone; unread newspapers and magazines pile up. Their cars are filled with junk and debris—clothes to take to the cleaner's, misplaced athletic shoes, and half-eaten, dried-out fast food. And many spend hundreds of dollars each month on storage units because they can't decide to throw away long-unused items. Because decision-making is often difficult for adults with ADD, the default decision is to keep everything. Time rushes by and they don't notice, leading them to miss some events and arrive late to many others; bills and important paperwork are buried under piles. Their finances are often in overdraft; charge cards are up to their limits; frequent late fees are assessed; tax returns are filed late, often several years late. And when they make an effort to get organized, their clutter seems to magically reappear shortly after it has been cleared away because they haven't developed the habits required to keep their belongings put away. The skills to manage the demands of daily life, to make plans, and to execute those plans all come under the term "executive functioning skills." In this book, we will teach you many strategies to build and support better executive functioning skills—the skills you need to manage your time, your tasks, and your belongings.

If you are an adult with ADD who struggles with organizing the many aspects of your life, this is the book that can put you on a path to finally create order. Other organizing books often aren't helpful because their approaches aren't well designed for people with ADD who need simple solutions and more structure and support while they implement those solutions. The advice in other organizing books may be too detailed, for example suggesting a complex paper filing system when most adults with ADD would be thrilled simply to see the surface of their dining room table again. Also, in most other organizing books, there is an assumption that readers will be able to follow the book's suggestions and put their home or office in order, without any support from others.

You've probably tried to "get organized" many times before—buying organizing books, day planners, organizing apps, and electronic gadgets—but nothing in the past has worked. You start out with the best intentions, only to find that each new organizing system falls apart very quickly. This doesn't mean that getting organized is a hopeless quest, but it does mean that you need special approaches designed for adults with ADD. That's what this book offers, ADD-friendly ways to organize your life. In this book, you'll find stories about adults with ADD, describing the organizing dilemmas they've encountered and the ADD-friendly approaches that worked for them—and that can work for you as well.

How is this book different?

- It's written by two experts: an expert on ADD, Kathleen Nadeau, Ph.D., and an expert on organizing, Judith Kolberg.
- The tips and tools in this book are specifically designed for adults with ADD.
- Not only is our advice ADD-friendly, but the book's format is ADD-friendly too, with clearly outlined topics, bold headings, readable print, an open page design, and a reader-friendly writing style.

Dr. Nadeau

Problems with planning and organization are among the biggest challenges for adults with ADD. Planning and organizing challenges can be especially difficult for women with ADD who are often in charge of organizing not only themselves but their families as well.

Years ago, I began to realize that most organizing tools and training didn't work well for adults with ADD. For example, daylong seminars on time management or organization require people to listen effectively for six to eight hours at a time. Listening for that long is difficult for most, and next to impossible for adults with ADD. Also, typical organizing books and seminars assume that you will be able to put their organizing ideas into action on your own, without structure or support—the "just do it" school of organizing. If it were that simple, adults with ADD would have gotten organized long ago!

On top of unrealistic expectations, many organizing approaches suggested in other organizing books are ludicrously inappropriate for adults with ADD. Someone whose garage resembles a landfill, or whose dining room table is permanently covered with piles of papers, isn't likely to benefit from detailed advice on record-keeping or filing systems.

Other organizing systems don't take into account the ADD stumbling blocks of inconsistency and forgetfulness. For example, day planners (yes, even in this digital age, some people find that pencil and paper are more helpful) and digital calendars on laptops, iPads and smartphones can be helpful for adults with ADD. However, without developing strategies to counteract patterns of inconsistency and forgetfulness, these tools can't be used effectively.

To use a planner or digital calendar successfully, you must first learn to use it consistently—to write necessary information about schedules and tasks in the planner on a daily basis, and consult your planner regularly throughout the day. And even those adults with

ADD who enter information and consult their planner on a daily basis must also develop strategies to keep their planner with them at all times, and to avoid misplacing or losing it. The standard training seminars on the use of day planners don't even begin to address these typical ADD challenges.

After repeated failed efforts to take charge of your life, you may be convinced that the task is impossible. Instead, the problem may lie in the approaches that you've tried. In this book, we'll help you learn to better understand yourself and how you are affected by ADD, so that you can develop successful strategies to manage the organizing tasks of your life. The keys to ADD-friendly organizing success involve:

- Strategies (ADD-friendly strategies, of course!);
- Support; and
- Structure.

We'll come back to these "three S's" again and again throughout the book, as we describe ADD-friendly organizing approaches.

Judith Kolberg

The difference between the organizing needs of people without ADD and those of people with ADD could not have been more apparent to me than when I began to do organizing work with Olivia. What an education! Olivia is a mini-whirlwind, a swirl of dangling purses, bags of groceries, car keys, and odd papers. Always in motion (mainly because she is often late and hurrying), Olivia whirls to answer the phone, spins around to yell out to the children, frees a hand to pet the dog as she simultaneously opens the door. Her desk and dining room table are buried beneath unopened mail, newspapers, and loose papers. "I tend to disorganize spontaneously," she explains. It's true. I watch her turn a clear space on the kitchen counter into a clump of clutter in no time at all.

I am a good professional organizer. Olivia is a successful career woman. With patience and a can-do attitude, I figure we can organize Olivia's life. But few of the approaches I used with other adults seem to work for Olivia. I try putting her papers in file folders with titles, stacking them neatly in her in-box. But Olivia can't find anything. Two weeks later, her desk is overflowing again with heaps of papers. I teach her the time-honored "A place for everything and everything in its place" proverb as we put things away and try to clear out the clutter. But these approaches are thwarted by her forgetfulness. She leaves her cell phone behind, and the dog's leash is nowhere to be found. We work on her time management skills and, with my support, Olivia agrees to plan her week in advance; however, her plans deteriorate into a rush of semi-emergencies and unplanned surprises.

Eventually Olivia explained to me that she had attention deficit disorder. At first I was convinced that even a neurologically based organic disorder like ADD would eventually yield to the logic of standard organizing approaches. What I learned through working with Olivia was that these standard approaches couldn't work for her—and don't work for many others with ADD.

Here's what *did* work. Instead of filing papers in plain old manila file folders assembled into a filing cabinet, we bought a colorful milk crate and stuck casters (wheels) on it. Inside we used multicolored file folders with lettering on the tabs and, instead of using many file folders, her papers were filed into a few simple categories. Everything was easy to see and simple to retrieve. Olivia learned to develop the habit of filing a little every day instead of letting it accumulate into a big, overwhelming stack. She kept the filing crate underneath the dining room table so it was an easy transition from piling papers on top of the table to slipping them into a few files in the crate under the table.

We liberated the dining room table from the tons of junk mail that had imprisoned it. This was accomplished by turning on some of Olivia's favorite music and teaming her up with a "clutter companion." Simply a friend, and not a critic, Olivia's clutter companion provided moral support and another set of hands while she kept her on task. To counteract some of her forgetfulness, we had a good time putting up reminder signs in logical spots such as on the door, on the bathroom mirror, and in the car. And we learned to be more realistic. Maybe Olivia wasn't quite ready to plan an entire week at a time. We planned a day at a time instead, until she got the hang of managing her days more realistically. Then we moved on to planning a week.

Many of the approaches suggested in this book were developed through my work with Olivia and others with ADD. They speak directly to the organizing issues people with ADD confront: distractibility, variations in attentiveness, hyperfocus, and stimulation issues. Like Olivia, by learning ADD-friendly approaches, you can organize your life. It just takes a different perspective, one with more creativity, more support and structure, and less self-criticism!

Organizing your life is a custom-ordered task. Although all of the strategies we describe are designed with the ADD adult in mind, not every approach suggested in this book will be a good fit for you. As you read this book, select and adapt those approaches that best match your lifestyle and temperament.

Start with the most basic and important ADD-friendly organizing concept:

> **Don't fight *against* your ADD; work *with* your ADD to take charge of your life.**

In the following chapters, we'll teach you ways to do just that.

Review

- Standard organizing approaches often don't work for adults with ADD.
- Organizing techniques that work are those that help you compensate for your ADD-related struggles such as forgetfulness, distractibility, and difficulties with time management.
- Your best organizing strategy is to work *with* your ADD instead of fighting against it.
- The "three S's"—*strategies, support,* and *structure*—are the keys to ADD organizing success.

ADD-Friendly Strategies That Work *with* Your ADD

If you're like many adults with ADD, you put "getting organized" on your list of odious and impossible tasks—like a starvation weight-loss regime, or a predawn daily exercise plan—something requiring impossible iron will and perseverance. There may be a person in your life who seems to embody all the organizing virtues—"early to bed, early to rise," combined with "a place for everything and everything in its place." Modeling your behavior after someone who is very controlled, perhaps over-controlled, can rarely work if you're an adult with ADD. Those few adults with ADD that are super-organized, who probably also have some degree of obsessive compulsive traits, typically consume every waking moment in their organizing efforts. Most adults with ADD should not set their sights on being perfectly organized, but rather on reaching a level of organization that helps them function with more productivity and less stress as they go through each day.

Work *with* Your ADD to Get Organized

"Shoulds" and "oughts" rarely motivate adults with ADD in the long run. To stay motivated, you need something that will focus your attention, engage your interest, and stimulate you.

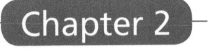

If you want to get organized, get *focused, engaged, and stimulated!*

Our goal in this book is to teach you how to work *with* your ADD to take charge of your life. Following are some techniques to get "hooked" on ADD-friendly organizing.

Make It Fun

Think it's impossible to have fun while decluttering? Think again! Get the whole family involved. Competition often makes things more interesting. For example, give everyone a "five-minute challenge." Set a timer for five minutes. The game is for each player to enter his or her bedroom and spend five minutes stuffing items into a bag to throw away or give away.

The person who gathers the most *appropriate* items in a five-minute period wins the round. We insert the word "appropriate" because some children may become carried away and indiscriminately stuff items into the bag, including perfectly good items of clothing, game parts, or school supplies.

Five minutes is painless, and this can be a daily event until rooms are cleared out—with a special dessert or other small prize going to each day's winner.

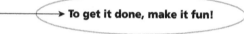

To get it done, make it fun!

Catch the Mood

Adults with ADD can catch a mood and ride it as effortlessly as some surfers catch a wave. Working *with* your mood often works better for adults with ADD than trying to schedule a task. Being in the mood to organize may catch you by surprise. You may be looking in the back of the closet for your snow boots, and, before you know it, you're madly tossing galoshes, mismatched gloves, and old winter jackets out into the hallway.

Impulses can lead either to chaos or decluttering depending upon how you handle them. Chaos ensues if you leave the mess in the hallway, only to later toss it all back, pell-mell, into the closet. But significant decluttering can take place if you organize yourself just a bit—long enough to grab a throw-away and a give-away bag, toss the items inside one or the other, and haul the bags to the garage or other storage space awaiting trash day or pick-up days scheduled by your local charity.

Organize for Reasons That Matter to You

Don't try to adopt someone else's organizing values. If being "tidy" or "organized" has negative connotations for you (tedious, boring, uptight, perfectionist), motivate yourself by organizing according to your own values.

For example, if you value social service, put together coordinated outfits from clothing that you want to discard, then donate these complete outfits to a local homeless shelter or shelter for victims of domestic abuse. Your castoffs can be transformed into job-interview outfits for women with limited income. With this goal in mind, you're not engaged in tedious tidying—you're making a positive difference in the life of someone less fortunate.

If you value creativity, imagine an art project—a collage, a quilt, a sculpture, or a braided rug. Then, just as some artists collect objects at the local dump, or collect discarded clothing at a thrift store for their art projects, go around the house with a collection bag looking for items for future art projects. You've had fun collecting materials and have decluttered your environment at the same time.

To Get Organized, Get Energized!

Many adults with ADD can move from a couch potato state to one of high energy in response to the right kind of stimulation. Think about what stimulates you best. For some it's physical movement. For others it's companionship. Singing can make time melt while you're engaged in uninteresting chores. Lively music is often a good motivator. You may need to create a beehive of activity to get motivated and stay motivated while you organize.

Divide the Dreadful into Micro-moments

If the activity is something you truly dread, divide the activity into micro-moments. For example, if you detest filing or processing papers, set a low limit for each filing exercise. Decide that each time you enter your office (at home or at work) you will process the first ten paper items that you happen to pick up. Some you may immediately toss, others you may need to file, still others require an action such as completing a form or writing a check. If you're lucky enough to grab ten papers that can be tossed, you'll be done in seconds! Rarely should you need to process papers for more than 10 or 15 minutes if you use this rule. You'll be amazed how quickly the paper chaos melts when you use this micro-moment approach to drudgery.

Grab Unplanned Organizational Moments

Organizational moments are times when you take advantage of unplanned opportunities to organize. An example is filing a paid bill and then, while you're at it, flipping through the file folder and throwing out any obsolete junk. Or it might be taking the opportunity to empty out your glove compartment when you're stopped at a traffic signal. Or cleaning out your purse while you search for your nail file buried at the bottom.

Think like a Restaurant Server

Many restaurant servers have ADD tendencies and are attracted to the work because it is active, social, and allows them to maintain their long-established night-owl tendencies. Think like a restaurant server when you're in your own environment. A busy restaurant never allows the tables to remain cluttered. Dishes are quickly removed as soon as a menu item is eaten. A server is constantly in the process of decluttering and reorganizing. Have you ever watched a restaurant table cleared and reset? The table is wiped, a new tablecloth put down, and salt, pepper, flower vase, whatever items that belong on the table are instantly reorganized so that the table looks fresh for the next set of diners.

A server learns that creating clutter (by serving diners) and removing clutter (by taking plates away) is one integrated process.

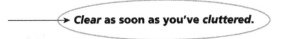
Clear as soon as you've *cluttered.*

ADD-Friendly Strategies That Work *with* Your ADD

When you think like a restaurant server at home, you get into the habit of tidying as you go. Hang up the robe on the hook as you leave your bedroom. Scan each room for cups or glasses as you pass from one room to the next, and automatically take them to the kitchen.

So often our clutter gets the best of us because we think of "straightening up" as a separate, distinct, and dreaded activity that we put off as long as possible instead of one that is integrated into each moment of the day.

Be a Sprinter, Not a Long-Distance Runner

Remember the old story of the tortoise and the hare, whose moral is that "slow and steady wins the race"? That story was obviously written by a tortoise! If you have ADD, you'll operate better as a hare, going as fast as you can to the finish line. The key is to make the race short, so that you'll be able to cross the finish line without stopping. For ADD-friendly organizing, be a sprinter not a slow and steady walker.

In practical terms, being a sprinter means dividing up organizing projects into small pieces that can be completed, from start to finish, in one dash. That way, you're less likely to be interrupted, to tire of the project, or to become distracted. Sprinting is stimulating, and keeps your interest high. No matter how large the organizing project, it can be broken down into short sprints.

ADD Patterns and Disorganization

In the preceding paragraphs, we've described ways to work *with* your ADD to organize. It's equally important to recognize common ADD patterns that lead to disorganization. Then you can learn strategies to counteract those patterns.

Heading "EAST"

People with ADD often head "EAST," trying to do Everything At the Same Time (EAST). They may begin multiple organizing projects with great enthusiasm—purchasing storage boxes, shelving, and paint but months later the shelving hasn't been taken out of the boxes and the paint cans are still unopened. To change this self-defeating habit, remember:

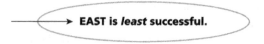

In your enthusiasm, you overextend yourself in the beginning, and then complete few if any of the projects that you started. Instead, it's better to:

Getting off Track

ADD brains tend to be reactive—that is, they react to whatever comes into their immediate vicinity—making it harder for adults with ADD to stay on track with projects. "Sprinting to the finish line" is one ADD-friendly approach to staying on track—by not giving yourself a chance to dawdle and look at other things. Another ADD-friendly approach to staying on track is to have a "body double" in the room. We'll talk more about this in the next chapter, but basically a body double is someone who simply hangs out with you as you do your organizing task—to make sure you stay on task. With the added support of another person in the room, you're less likely to start a diversionary tactic—such as reading a magazine article that you come across in your organizing efforts.

If there's no one else to provide structure or support for you, self-talk can help. For example, set the timer on your smartphone when you're engaged in your organizing task. Reset it repeatedly at ten-minute intervals. Each time it goes off, ask yourself, "Am I doing what I'm supposed to be doing?" If so, congratulations! If not, reset the timer and get yourself back on track.

Going into Micro-focus

Adults with ADD often tend to slip into micro-focus when they're organizing—they get lost in the details instead of focusing on the larger task. For example, if your task is to declutter your family room, but you find yourself organizing photos in your photo album, you've slipped into micro-focus, instead of keeping your focus on the "macro" task of clearing the family room. Going into micro-focus is often tempting for adults with ADD because it allows them to block out the "overwhelm" they feel when dealing with macro issues such as a large, clutter-filled room. Levels of focus—from macro to micro—will be discussed in detail later. A body double can help you avoid micro-focus, just as they can help you stay on track.

Underestimating

One of the effects of ADD is often a poor sense of time. Typically, adults with ADD grossly underestimate the amount of time a task will require. If you lose track of time, this can negatively impact others in your life who may be expecting you to meet them, or to meet another commitment.

To combat your poor time sense, instead of saying, "My goal is to clear out and organize the family room," set your goal in terms of time expenditure. For example, set a timer for one hour (or six ten-minute intervals if you tend to slip into micro-focus) and stop working at that point.

Getting Stuck

Adults with ADD seem to both underdo it and overdo it, as paradoxical as this seems. Underdoing occurs when we don't stick to a task we've set for ourselves because we're drawn away by something more interesting. Overdoing can also cause significant problems, and is related to a well-known ADD tendency to "get stuck" and resist moving on to the next task of the day. Staying stuck on one task can lead to other organizing challenges—you may be spending too much time on your current task at the expense of others. For example, spending hours on the computer designing a business card or brochure, while ignoring the undone dishes and laundry. Setting a time limit rather than a task limit can help avoid getting stuck.

Overcomplicating

Another ADD-related pattern that may interfere with organizing is to complicate a task. For example, you might decide to install a time management program on your computer—a potentially very useful approach to making better use of your time. However, if you're like many other adults with ADD, you might find that you've spent hours on your computer, customizing calendars, color-coding time blocks, and programming reminders—time that could have been better spent on another task. By making it overly complicated, you don't get down to the actual organizing.

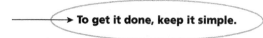

To get it done, keep it simple.

Adding without Subtracting

Adults with ADD often add things to their life—objects, activities, commitments—without doing the subtraction that's necessary in order to make sure they stay within their time budget, space budget, or financial budget. That's how ADD lives become so jam-packed—closets are packed with unworn clothing, bookshelves packed with unread books, schedules packed with too many activities. All this addition increases the chronic stress in the lives of many adults with ADD. Many adults repeatedly convince themselves that they'll "find the time" or "make the room" for their latest addition, despite all the evidence to the contrary.

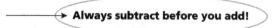

Always subtract before you add!

If you struggle with too much addition and too little subtraction, you may need to set very structured limits for yourself. To limit the addition of commitments, make a rule for yourself that you will not add a new commitment until you either finish or eliminate a prior commitment. Similar rules can be helpful for reading material (no new books or magazines until I read and/or give away unread books or magazines) or purchases (for every new article of clothing, at least two rarely worn articles will be put in the give-away bag).

As you begin to explore this book, remember:

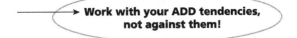

Work with your ADD tendencies, not against them!

Learning to organize in ADD-friendly ways is your key to success.

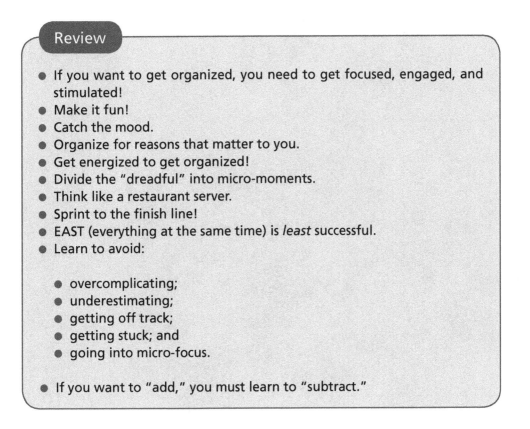

Review

- If you want to get organized, you need to get focused, engaged, and stimulated!
- Make it fun!
- Catch the mood.
- Organize for reasons that matter to you.
- Get energized to get organized!
- Divide the "dreadful" into micro-moments.
- Think like a restaurant server.
- Sprint to the finish line!
- EAST (everything at the same time) is *least* successful.
- Learn to avoid:

    - overcomplicating;
    - underestimating;
    - getting off track;
    - getting stuck; and
    - going into micro-focus.

- If you want to "add," you must learn to "subtract."

ADD-Friendly Strategies That Work with Your ADD

Structure and Support

Creating the Framework for Success

We introduced many ADD-friendly organizing strategies in the preceding chapter. But without *structure* and *support*, those strategies are less likely to be successful. Structure and support provide the underlying framework for organizing success, a framework that will help you implement ADD-friendly strategies in a *consistent* and *persistent* manner. Think of the three "S's"—structure, support, and strategies—as a pyramid, with structure and support at the base, supporting the strategies above. The abilities to initiate a project, to behave in a consistent manner, and to persist until the project is completed are all critical executive functions. As we are building these executive functioning skills, we will need more support, but as these skills become habitual, your need for this "scaffolding" will lessen.

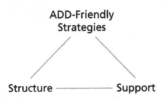

ADD-Friendly
Strategies

Structure ———— Support

Structure and support can be introduced at different levels, depending upon how challenging an organizing task is for you. Throughout the rest of this book, ADD-friendly strategies or solutions are suggested following each ADD organizing challenge. These solutions all involve structure and support. **Level One** structure and support is the kind you can provide for yourself. Examples of structure and support that you provide for yourself are cues, timers, and reminders. At **Level Two** a higher level of structure and support can be provided by family and friends. Examples of Level Two supports are asking a friend or family member to help you plan or execute a project. At **Level Three** we suggest strategies and solutions that involve professional assistance from professional organizers, ADD coaches, or, in some cases, psychotherapists.

Match the Level of Support to the Challenge of the Task

For simpler organizing challenges, you may want to start with support that you can provide for yourself. If you find yourself unable to follow through on your own, then it's time to consider enlisting friends or family members to provide Level Two structure and support. Some of your organizing challenges may feel so overwhelming that you'll need to engage the support of a professional from the outset. Of course, as you learn techniques and build habits, you may be able to reduce the level of support that you need to maintain organization in a particular area of your life.

Level 1: Creating Your Own Structure and Support

When you choose to organize independently, you still need to think in terms of creating structure and support for each organizing challenge.

Structure

You can structure yourself in a variety of ways:

- **Create a schedule.** (From now on, I'll do my laundry every Saturday, rather than waiting until I have no clean clothes to wear.)
- **Break down the task into do-able bits.** (Instead of tackling my entire closet, I'll just organize these two shelves today.)
- **Establish a step-by-step plan.** (This weekend, I'll purchase the shelving for my home office. Next weekend, mount the shelves and after that I'll use the shelves to neatly store the books and periodicals piled on the floor around my desk.
- **Develop habits and routines.** (A habit or routine is, by definition, structured—an activity that you do in a certain sequence at a certain time.)

ADD-Friendly Habit-Building

If you're like many other adults with ADD, you have difficulty developing and maintaining habits. Probably, when you've consciously tried to build a habit, you've gone about it in an ADD-*unfriendly* way. For example, if you want to change your bedtime habits, it would be very ADD-*unfriendly* to simply get into bed at 11 p.m. and turn out the light, willing yourself to go to sleep when your standard bedtime has been 2 a.m. for years. As an example of ADD-friendly problem-solving and habit-building, let's think through how to approach a very common ADD challenge—staying up too late and being chronically sleep-deprived.

1. *Change your evening routine* so that you have at least an hour to relax and calm down before turning out the light.

2. *Move your bedtime earlier by 15-minute increments week by week.* In that way, you will gradually work toward a bedtime that allows you to get adequate sleep each night.

3. *Give up night-owl habits on weekends* to achieve your goal during the week. If you stay up until 2 or 3 a.m. on Saturday night each week, you've reset your biological clock back to the old pattern.

4. *Introduce other supports* into your life to achieve your goal—such as an "artificial dawn" device that slowly lights your bedroom at a preprogrammed time each morning to help you get up, or a relaxing meditation tape to listen to as you fall asleep at night.

5. *Set an alarm on your smartphone to remind you to begin your bedtime routine.*

6. *Change your routines so that your bed is not used for* answering e-mails, surfing the Web, playing video games, working on the computer, online shopping or watching television. Research strongly supports only allowing yourself to stay in bed if you are sleeping and to require yourself to get up and go to another location if you are unable to sleep (the only exception to this is reading in bed which can be very relaxing.) That way, a strong association is developed between being in bed and sleeping. Many adults with ADD engage in so many stimulating habits while in bed that sleep becomes less and less likely.

7. *Eliminate a pattern of sleeping in places other than your bed.* Many adults with ADD, for example, have developed a habit of falling asleep on the couch in the evening while watching television, then waking at some point in the night and going to bed, only to find that they are unable to fall asleep again.

8. *Eliminate any caffeine after your morning coffee or tea.* Many adults with ADD are chronically sleep-deprived and keep themselves awake during the day by drinking caffeinated beverages, not realizing that they are perpetuating their night-owl tendencies with caffeine.

You may need to institute changes in your sleep habits one at a time, slowly building a good sleep routine to gradually get a full and restful night's sleep. Changing your sleep habits can be very challenging at first, but the payoff is huge. Regular restorative sleep is one of the most powerful ways to reduce ADD symptoms.

Other habits may not be as difficult to change as sleep habits and may not require as much structure and support to achieve. This discussion of altering your sleep habits is a good way to introduce the concept of ADD-friendly approaches to changing and building habits. The "just do it" approach to habit change rarely works. Create the structure and support you need for each habit change and your chances for success are strong.

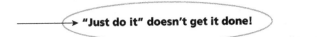

"Just do it" doesn't get it done!

Habit-building is a powerful way to introduce structure into life-long organizing tasks—especially *maintenance* organizing. Maintenance organizing is the type of organizing that needs to be done on a regular, routine basis in order to maintain organization once it has been established. A professional organizer may help you work wonders in your environment. But without maintenance organizing, your new orderly environment will rapidly descend into chaos again. That's because old habits remain firmly ingrained.

New habits take time. Don't be discouraged if you're not successful at first. Following are ten steps that make habit-building more successful for people with ADD. Just like all of the

Structure and Support

other organizing approaches that we suggest, you may find that you need support from others when you're in the early stages of habit-building. Working with an ADD coach or professional organizer, who can help you stay on track as you build new habits, can be very effective.

It's also important to work collaboratively with the people you live with. If you are trying to improve your sleep habits, while your partner has no desire to make changes in their sleep habits, your process will be much more difficult and perhaps doomed to fail. For example, one woman who tried to develop better sleep habits was actively discouraged by her husband who wanted to continue his night-owl habits and wanted his wife's company as he watched television late into the night. Everyone in the family must understand the need for change and the importance of supporting you in making changes, if you want to succeed in building better life management habits.

Ten Steps to ADD-Friendly Habit-Building

1. **Tie a new habit to an old one.** Most of us have some ingrained habits. It's easiest to develop a new one if it's tied to an old one. For example, place your vitamins next to your toothbrush to better remember to take your vitamins each morning.	2. **Make the habit as easy as possible.** For example, pick a convenient, visible place to put your keys, a place that makes sense, such as by the door through which you leave the house.
3. **Make the reminder hard to ignore.** Put bells on it, put it in a place where you'll trip over it, make it impossible to leave the house without it (tie your car keys to it).	4. **Put reminders everywhere.** When you are first starting out, put sticky notes where you are sure to see them that remind you to act on your new habit.
5. **Visualize yourself doing the new behavior.** For example, if this is a morning habit, imagine yourself going through your morning routine, including your new habit at the appropriate point in the routine.	6. **Practice "instant corrections."** If you forget to practice the new habit, go and do it the *instant* you remember it, if at all possible, even if it's not convenient.
7. **Get back on the horse and ride.** Habits take time. Forgetting is *not* failure; it is part of developing a habit.	8. **Problem-solve if it's not working.** Maybe you need a different reminder. Perhaps you need to tie it to a different habit. Perhaps it would fit better into a different time of day.
9. **Practice the habit for at least 30 days in a row.** Make a calendar in the kitchen and check off the days.	10. **Reward yourself.** Celebrate when you reach your 30-day goal.

Habit-building can be aided by apps because an app is an excellent way to automatically track your activities toward a preset goal and remind you to engage in those activities no matter where you are. Over time, those activities become hardened into habits. Habitclock. com is a great app designed specifically to support your morning routine. Habitbull.com and Wayoflife.com can be customized to create all kinds of habits. Both require the input of data, sometimes on a daily basis over a period of time, so they're not for every person with ADD.

Support

You can support yourself in many ways as you organize:

- Set *reasonable* goals—avoid perfectionism.
- Use positive self-affirmations—replace critical, negative messages in your head with encouraging ones. *I'm getting better. I've remembered to check my e-mail three days out of five.*
- Recognize your progress—instead of always focusing on the disorganization that remains to be tackled. *Look at how much better the breakfast table looks! I'll tackle the dining room next week. Or, I deleted 50 old files on my computer. Next week, I'll delete another 50.*
- Reward yourself for progress! *As soon as I have finished folding the laundry and putting it away, I'm going to sit down and watch a new Netflix movie. (or) As soon as I finish my expense report, I'm going to try that new coffee shop across the street.*

Organize for Yourself, Not for the Approval of Others

Many adults with ADD, especially women, approach organizing with feelings of failure and shame—failure to meet their mother's standards, their spouse's standards, society's standards, or standards they impose on themselves. It's important to define organization realistically. Your goal should be to meet your own needs, to create an environment that works for you, one that feels good to inhabit. You may need to examine more than once whether you are measuring your success against some external "should" instead of your own needs and desires.

Be Open to Fresh Ideas

Supporting your own organizing efforts also means trying new ideas and not doing the same old things over and over again. If you've tried to file papers in file folders and failed, give it up and try something different like baskets or bins. If you can't use a running to-do list, there are alternatives such as a stubby to-do lists (more about this later). This book gives you many fresh, new ideas. Look for something you have not yet tried even if it seems a little unusual to you. Have some fun. Break out of old patterns that don't work for you.

Level 2: Structure and Support from Friends and Family

One of the biggest struggles for many adults with ADD is to admit that they need help— perhaps more help than some other adults may need. Coming to terms with this may be difficult at first. You may tell yourself, "I'm smart, I'm capable. Cleaning, getting to meetings on time, and organizing my desk aren't rocket science. I don't need help. I just need to *decide* to do it." The challenge is that distractible ADD brains have difficulty staying on task, especially on mundane, uninteresting life-maintenance tasks. Adults with ADD also have more difficulty with unstructured tasks such as household maintenance. Women with ADD, especially, may have trouble admitting and accepting that such tasks are not their strong suit. Society puts subtle and not-so-subtle pressure upon women to take major roles, at home and in the workplace, in creating and maintaining order.

Give Yourself Permission to Get the Help You Need

Don't let other women make you feel guilty or inadequate for needing a higher level of support. One woman's mother (a mother *without* ADD) frequently questioned her daughter's choice to have household help after school each day when her middle-school-aged sons were home and she was still at work. "That costs so much money," her mother admonished. "The boys are old enough to be home by themselves for a couple of hours." Fortunately, the woman with ADD had confidence in her own decision and knew that having after-school household support allowed her to have energy and time for herself and her family after she arrived home from work. Don't let family members or friends talk you out of the support you need to have a less stressful life.

Once an adult with ADD gives himself or herself permission to ask for help, half the battle has been won. Although you may prefer to begin with independent organizing strategies, if you find that your solo efforts are not successful, then it's time to build in more structure and support by engaging the help of family members or friends. One potential source of support can come from others with ADD. An adult ADD support group, for example, decided to support one another in tackling organizing projects at home. As we all know, it's easier to organize someone else's space because you are not enmeshed in their belongings and their habits. Members of this ADD support group exchanged "dig-outs" in which one member would come to the home of a fellow-member to assist in an intensive dig-out of a specific area of the home. Then, later, they swapped roles to help dig out the other's home. This became an enjoyable and mutually supportive process with no need for embarrassment or explanation.

Benefits of Help from Friends and Family

- Your morale will be higher.
- You won't be as distracted.
- You'll organize faster.
- You'll stay at it longer.

Working with Family Members

Family support can be very powerful when tackling major organizing challenges. For example, one family, in which both husband and wife had ADD traits, played "hot potato" for years, tossing recriminations back and forth, each claiming the other was primarily to blame for the chronic disorganization of their home. When they finally decided to join forces to attack their disorder, the mutual structure and support allowed them to make headway on tasks they had each avoided for years. Instead of assigning blame, they began to look for solutions. Instead of avoiding each other and the tasks at hand, they began to make "organizing appointments" with one another. As they came to recognize their need for structure, they began to interact differently with their children regarding chores, introducing schedules, structure, and support for them as well. Nagging and resentment decreased, while encouragement and camaraderie lightened the load. They had transformed from an ADD-challenged family to an ADD-friendly family.

ADD-Friendly Family Organizing

- **Let your family know specifically how your ADD affects you:** your ability to organize, your time management difficulties, your difficulty with follow-through, or your problems in keeping track of things. The more your family understands ADD, the better they'll understand the reasons underlying your disorganization. Then, instead of blaming and criticizing, they can join you in finding solutions that work.
- **Don't use ADD as an excuse.** Make it clear that you are working to improve your organization and that you need their understanding and support.
- **Share information with your family**—the ideas, books, methods, or organizing advice you are following—so that they know what it is you are attempting to achieve.
- If other family members face organizing challenges too, **make it a joint project to develop better organizing habits together.**
- **Family members often make the best "maintenance organizers."** Once you've organized a closet, kitchen, or garage, family members can be great at helping you maintain your organizing effort. When you are disorganized, it's hard for other people, even well intentioned people, to know how you want things or where to put things. But when you are organized, you have a system that your family can more easily help you to maintain.

Structure and Support from Friends

Friends can play a very constructive role as organizing support. They are less invested in your organizing progress than your family is and can be more objective and less judgmental. A friend can keep your morale up and help the work go faster, making the organizing work more satisfying. Having the support of a friend while you're organizing is not only warm and fuzzy, it is also very useful in counteracting distraction, one of your key concerns.

Many adults with ADD find that another adult with ADD can provide the best structure and support of all—support that can be reciprocal. Help me dig out my kitchen this week, and I'll come over and help you next week. Or help me clean out my garage this week and I'll help you with yours next week. But even when your friend does not have ADD, help can be reciprocal. For example, one man with ADD bartered technical computer support to a friend in exchange for assistance with organizing and tracking his financial records.

Organizing Roles That Family and Friends Can Play

Look for a support person who is patient, supportive, noncritical, and understanding of the organizing challenges that are part of having ADD. Ideally, they will bring enthusiasm and a sense of humor to the task. These can even be other people with ADD. Often, though they can't focus alone on their own organizing tasks, they can be focused and helpful when it's *your* stuff that's being organized. Friends or family can play a number of different support roles. These roles can include Clutter Companion, Paper Partner, Body Double, Time Tutor, Habit Helper, and Tech Tamer.

Getting Started

If you have friends and family that fit into the roles of Clutter Companion, Paper Partner, Time Tutor, Body Double, Habit Helper, and Tech Tamer that would be ideal. These do not have to be six separate individuals. Perhaps you know someone in your family or among your friends who is great at organizing papers *and* residential clutter. This one individual can perform the dual roles of Clutter Companion and Paper Partner. And remember this important fact: if you come up short on any of these roles, a professional organizer can step in to perform them.

To help guide you through areas of organizing that might be accomplished best with the support of a Clutter Companion, Time Tutor, Paper Partner, Body Double, Habit Helper, or Tech Tamer, we've added a small picture of each everywhere they occur in the text.

Clutter Companion

Choose someone who is good at organizing possessions, clutter, closets, and storage areas in the home as your Clutter Companion.

Time Tutor

Your Time Tutor should be someone who gets to places on time, seems to have a reasonable schedule, and accomplishes pretty much what they need to in the course of a day.

Paper Partner

For your Paper Partner, look for someone who is strong on organizing papers and filing.

22

Body Double

Sometimes all you need is the presence of someone else—a Body Double—in order to start organizing and keep organizing. A Body Double doesn't have to do anything but keep you company while you organize. Their presence is a support and a reminder that you are there to focus on a particular organizing task.

Habit Helper

Your Habit Helper should be a partner, roommate, or family member that is good at friendly reminders to help you stay on track as you build a new habit. For a Habit Helper to be helpful, you should remain in charge of whether and when you want to be reminded. You're asking for helpful reminders while building habits, not nagging or criticism!

Tech Tamer

There are so many technical or digital supports that can be helpful to you in becoming better organized, but not all of us are equally equipped to take advantage of them without additional support. If you have a friend, neighbor, or family member that is technologically savvy, they can serve in the role of Tech Tamer to help you learn to use the organizing tools that can then provide structure and support for you in organizing your tasks and your time.

Level 3: Structure and Support from Professionals

There are many benefits to using a professional for support in getting organized. Professionals are skilled and objective. They have a great deal of experience helping adults with similar organizing challenges. Although family and friends can be helpful, their time and/or motivation may have limits. Family and friends may also not be objective because they are impacted by your organizing difficulties and may sometimes feel annoyed and frustrated with you.

There are several different approaches to organizing challenges that can be provided by professional organizers, ADD coaches, and psychotherapists who specialize in working with adults with ADD. You will need to decide which approach and what level of help will benefit you the most.

Professional Organizers

Sometimes adults with ADD need a level of support more intensive than family, friends, or coworkers can provide. A professional organizer (PO) provides hands-on help. The support of a professional organizer at your side may be what you need to get started, especially when the level of clutter feels overwhelming.

Later, when clutter has been reduced and storage shelves and containers are in place, the adult with ADD can begin to implement new habits and make decisions that will prevent the return of complete disorder. The needs of each adult differ. Some may benefit from working with an ADD coach to succeed in the maintenance phase of organizing. Some may need periodic "dig-outs" with a professional organizer; others can get support from family or friends to do maintenance tasks once a professional organizer has helped to create an ordered environment.

The kinds of services available from professional organizers include:

- helping to create solutions custom-designed to work for *you*;
- providing hands-on support as you implement these solutions; and
- helping you to select products and services to enhance your organization.

The attitude of an organizer is just as important as the practical solutions they suggest. A good organizer is encouraging, supportive, and nonjudgmental. No matter how big your mess, they've seen worse! The presence of an organizer can help you overcome your procrastination and reach decisions more quickly as you decide to give away, throw away, or store your belongings and papers. Most important, an organizer is respectful of your feelings and should never insist that you rid yourself of objects that you want to keep.

Choosing a Professional Organizer

The process of hiring a professional organizer is similar to that of choosing any consultant or independent contractor. You should ask:

- How long have they been in business?
- What is their area(s) of expertise?

- Do they have experience with ADD?
- Do they have references you can contact?
- Do they have a certificate of study or certification in working with adults with ADD?

Sometimes you can tell from an initial phone call if the PO is someone you would feel comfortable working with, but often it takes one or two organizing sessions to determine if you've found a good match.

Not all professional organizers are good at working with adults with ADD. It's critical, if you decide to work with an organizer, that you find one who is very experienced and comfortable working with ADD issues. You might also ask if the organizer is familiar with this book, or other ADD organizing books. If they are, that's a positive sign that they understand that ADD organizing differs from standard organizing approaches. Some organizers have had specific education about ADD and have a certificate or certification proving they are up on ADD and how it affects organizing. You can find one by contacting the ICD at www.challengingdisorganization.com or NAPO at www.napo.net.

ADD Coaches

An ADD coach offers a different kind of organizational support. Coaching can be very effective in helping you to build and maintain habits, to set goals, and to stay on track as you work toward them. A coach typically works by phone (although your first contact may be in person), and you may have periodic in-person meetings with a coach. Some coaches use Skype or other Web-based video teleconferencing.

While a professional organizer can work with you on-site, providing hands-on help to get your desk cleared off, a coach may be most effective in helping you to develop the habits that will *keep* your desk cleared off, once order has been established.

A coach can help you:

- **Analyze daily habits that create disorder.** Do you leave unfinished projects on your desktop? When you've completed a task, do you fail to file papers away before you move on to the next task? Do you avoid filing and simply start piling again?
- **Problem-solve to build new habits.** Perhaps you tend to leave your desk cluttered at the end of the day because you're tired and running late. A coach might talk with you about developing a new morning habit of spending ten minutes reading e-mail before you dive into the day's work, or building a habit of putting clean dishes away before bed. Another approach might be to hire support staff or a virtual assistant to help you maintain your new system.
- **Provide structure and support as you work to strengthen new habits,** so that they become integrated into daily life.
- **Help you with time management habits** to make sure you're leaving time (and energy) each day to keep your daily life organized.

Organizer-Coach

The field of professional organizing is always evolving to respond to the needs of people facing organizing challenges. A new professional called the Organizer-Coach might also be a good choice for ADD adults. The Organizer-Coach is a professional organizer with special coach training into the "why" of disorganization as well as the "how." Coupled with organizing, the Organizer-Coach is trained in communication skills, collaborative problem-solving, life goal visioning, and a variety of accountability structures. Find out more about the services of an Organizer-Coach at www.napo.net.

Psychotherapists

You may already be seeing a counselor or psychotherapist if you've been diagnosed with ADD. A therapist who is experienced in working with adults with ADD uses many problem-solving strategies that are also used in coaching. However, unlike a coach, who may contact you briefly many times throughout the week, your psychotherapist may see you once a week or even less often. Therapy and coaching can often work very effectively hand-in-hand. You may decide upon a new strategy or habit in therapy, and then use your coach to support you with more frequent contacts while you build that habit into your daily routine.

Emotional Issues Leading to Disorganization

Psychotherapy can also address other sorts of emotional or psychological issues that may get in the way of organization.

- *Unrealistic self-expectations*, for example, may lead you to judge yourself too harshly or set your organizing goals at an unrealistically high level. This is the sort of issue that is best dealt with in therapy.
- *Depression* can be a strong deterrent to improving organization in your life. If you're depressed and tired, the organization of your daily life tends to fall apart. Beds go unmade, bills go unpaid, and laundry goes undone. Without treatment for depression, all the organizing help in the world can't be effective.
- *Anxiety* can drain you of energy and focus, allowing daily tasks to go undone and clutter to pile up around you. The longer you go with unfiled taxes or piles of papers and magazines, the more impossible the task may seem. Even looking at the task can then create waves of anxiety you might seek to escape by avoiding the prospect of working on getting organized.
- *Obsessive-compulsive disorder* (OCD), one form that anxiety takes, may cause you to overfocus on tiny details. You may spend hours obsessively reordering your CD collection while much higher-priority items go undone. You may be so perfectionistic that you can't unpack your books because you haven't found the perfect bookcase to put them in. If you struggle with OCD issues, you may feel that you are constantly "organizing" without ever getting organized.

A psychotherapist who specializes in treating ADD in adults can also work with you as you learn more about yourself and exactly how you are affected by ADD, as well as help you develop strategies to counteract these tendencies. For example, if you are very easily distracted from the task at hand, you and your therapist can develop techniques to reduce or eliminate distractions so that you can succeed in completing your organizing task.

Conclusion

The organizing approaches outlined in the rest of this book will suggest strategies that take many aspects of ADD into account, helping you to break down huge projects into do-able bits, helping you learn to develop and maintain new organizing habits, providing many levels of external structure and support that will help you get started and keep going. So, start small, get the support you need to keep going, and learn how you can work *with* your ADD to get your life better organized.

Review

- Organize independently by providing yourself with structure and support.
- Give yourself permission to ask for help.
- Ask for help from family and friends.
- Engage professional organizing help.
- Decide on the level of support that you need for each organizing task.

Structure and Support

Part 2

Taking Charge of ADD

Streamline and Simplify

Counteracting Complications

Simplify, simplify, simplify. The more simple the task, the lower the demands on executive functioning skills. This should be the mantra for adults with ADD. Simplification is one of the strongest stress management and life management tools that an adult with ADD can learn. The more complex the task, the more overscheduled the day, the more chances there are for confusion, forgetfulness, and careless error.

Let's take a look at Karen's life before she begins to introduce the concept of simplification into her daily life.

Karen, a married mother of two, has been in treatment for ADD for several months. The medication has been helpful, and she's asked for accommodations at work. That has taken some pressure off, but now that the school year has begun again, Karen is feeling overwhelmed. "It feels like I just can't keep up. I ran late today because I couldn't find anything to wear. And I just realized that I am wearing navy pantyhose instead of black! So I'll be running around all day mismatched unless I take even more time out to stop and buy black hose. Why can't I seem to do even the simplest things, like get dressed for work in the morning?"

Karen's two children are in elementary school and she works full time. Her children are in multiple after-school activities including soccer practice, dance lessons, and martial arts. Many evenings her kids are eating fast food in the car as she ferries them to or picks them up from an activity. She and her husband juggle the after-school pick-ups and are also in a carpool for soccer practices and games. Even on evenings when she doesn't have to take the kids somewhere, she feels rushed. On her way home in heavy traffic, she stops to pick up last-minute groceries, or takeout from a fast-food place, fully aware that she'd rather have a more nutritious meal for her family. She never seems able to work out a menu, shop, and cook. And even when she has shopped for groceries, she may forget to thaw the chicken she's planned for dinner. "I should buy stock in Domino's Pizza!" she jokes.

"My husband and I feel as if we never see each other we're so busy with work and the kids. I am always drowning in piles of unopened mail, unanswered e-mails, voicemail messages, and text messages. My friends and work colleagues frequently complain that they haven't received a response from their communications to me. And my social life? Ha! Who has time for friends? When would I find the time to clean the house, plan a dinner, and invite people over?" She feels out of touch with friends and overwhelmed by the often competing demands of work and home.

Is This Your Story?

It is if you:

- feel overwhelmed by the demands of home, kids, and work;
- find that forgetfulness and lack of planning add to your daily stress;
- feel that daily life is too complicated; and
- can't seem to find time to relax or enjoy life.

Today's busy lifestyles tend to place more demands on us than we can possibly meet. Karen, like most women today, is chronically stressed, trying to juggle work and family commitments. Her ADD makes this juggling act even harder because she has greater difficulty developing streamlined routines for herself and her family. In addition, she has difficulty organizing her day, a common problem for adults with ADD. So, on top of an overly busy schedule, she's frequently pinch-hitting. To cut down on stress and the complications of disorganization, Karen needs to find ways to streamline and simplify her life.

Do a Stress Analysis of Your Daily Life

The first step toward simplifying your life is to do a "stress analysis" by making a list of the things that have become regular sources of stress in your life, and then start problem-solving to look for ways to simplify your life to reduce those stresses. Karen is married with two children, so her stress analysis needs to take the needs and activities of her family into account. Here's what Karen's stress analysis looks like:

Morning Stressors

- Can't figure out what to wear—clothes are dirty, at the cleaner's, don't fit any more, and what's clean doesn't go together—clean tops don't go with skirts that are clean.
- Kids can't find what they need to wear—laundry hasn't been folded and put away; clothes aren't organized in their rooms; can't find their shoes.
- Breakfast is chaotic—never enough time.
- Kids can't find everything they need for school—homework, backpack.
- Lunches aren't packed.

- My husband and I are both trying to get out the door at once with no time to help the kids get organized.

Evening Stressors

- Often running late due to traffic.
- Confusion over who's supposed to pick up the kids.
- Dinner rarely planned—have to go by the store or pick up fast food.
- House is a mess—no time to straighten up.
- Arguments over homework while kids watch TV or use their digital devices.
- Bedtime always late—no one is getting enough sleep.
- No time with my husband in the evening.
- Mail piles up on the table, no routine for paying bills.
- Can't keep up with e-mail and text messages.
- No time for myself.

As stressed out as Karen's weekday sounds, her story is not unusual. Adults with ADD that don't have children often have other stressors. They may tend to work later, neglecting things that need to be done at home. Or they may take on after-work commitments that leave them little time for rest, exercise, or time with their partner. Other adults may not be in a relationship but feel stressed every day due to poor sleep habits that leave them feeling tired and rushed most mornings. Or they may be trying to complete a graduate degree while working full time. The fact is that many adults with ADD, regardless of family structure or lifestyle, need to find ways to simplify and streamline their lives.

Let's go back to Karen's list of morning and evening stressors and think about ways that she can simplify her life. Initially, Karen didn't see any significant changes that she could make. She and her husband both need to work, and they want their kids to be involved in sports and other activities, so she couldn't see any way out of the high-stress lifestyle she led until she started working with an ADD coach. The coach helped her review her stressors and consider changes, both large and small, that might bring more peace and order to the flow of her days. Some of the changes the coach suggested could be made by Karen and her husband with no support from others, while other changes might be more easily implemented with some greater level of support.

LEVEL ONE SOLUTIONS: WAYS TO HELP YOURSELF

First, let's look at the changes and decisions that Karen and her husband were able to make on their own. Here are solutions that Karen and her husband came up with after doing their stress analysis:

Karen Can't Find Anything to Wear in the Morning

Karen simplified her wardrobe so that choices could be made quickly and easily. She decided to buy dresses or suits from now on so that it was clear what "matched" with what, and chose a simple color palette for her spring/summer work wardrobe and her fall/winter work wardrobe so that her accessories could coordinate well with most of her weekday outfits. She hangs scarves and blouses or sweaters that go together on the same hanger so that it's a breeze putting a coordinated outfit together for the next day's work. Karen now takes a couple of minutes while preparing for bed to lay out her clothes for the next day.

Keeping up with Laundry

Karen talked with her husband about a better division of labor in the evening. They decided that she would spend time helping the kids with homework, while her husband washed the dinner dishes and then took care of the laundry so that it was dry, folded, and back in the appropriate drawers. He did one load of laundry each day, putting it in the washer in the morning, then popping the load in the dryer when he came home from work. That way, each day's load could be folded and put away in a few minutes. No more mad dashes to the laundry room for socks or underwear in the morning as everyone was dressing for work.

Everyone Feeling Tired and Rushed in the Morning

Karen and her family had a family meeting to talk about how to make the mornings go better. They decided that it would be best to do as much as possible the night before—preparing lunches, gathering everything that was needed for school and work, and putting it on the "launching pad" (more about this later) so that there was no frantic search for shoes, car keys, glasses, or checks and forms needed for the school field trip. The whole family had developed night-owl tendencies and decided as a family to change the bedtime routine so that the kids went upstairs to shower and go to bed at 8:30 p.m., lights out at 9. The "no TV during the week" rule they established made it much easier to get the kids to bed on time.

No Time for Breakfast

"We're just an ADD family," laments Karen. No matter how hard we try, we can never get up early in the morning. Instead of continuing to feel guilty about the sweets her kids eat as they run out the door, Karen rethought the morning meal. "Why don't I just accept that we won't have a sit-down breakfast and plan something nutritious that the kids can grab and go?":

- yogurt with fruit on the bottom;
- individual containers of 2 percent milk or skim chocolate milk;
- cheese sticks and crackers;
- fruit of any kind;
- frozen breakfast sandwiches that can be heated in the microwave;
- multigrain muffins;
- bagels and jam; or
- peanut butter and jelly sandwiches (the kids' suggestion).

Getting out the Door with Everything We Need

Karen and her family created a "launching pad," a place, conveniently located near the door, where all items are kept that family members need to "launch" into their day. Laundry rooms, mudrooms, or a corner of the kitchen can often serve the purpose. Karen created a launching pad near the kitchen door that led to the garage. Each child has his own colorful plastic crate in which athletic cleats, sports equipment, or sports bags were placed. Two shelves on the wall are labeled—one assigned to each child—to provide a place for musical instruments, art projects, or anything else that needs to be taken to school the next day. On the wall, each child is provided with two hooks—one for his backpack, the other for a jacket or sweatshirt. A third, higher shelf serves as Karen's launching pad. On it she places clothes to take to the dry cleaner's, purchased items to return, and anything else she needs for the next day. Her laptop briefcase is placed on the floor, while two wall hooks are used for her coat, umbrella, scarf, and purse.

Making Lunches

Karen asked her kids to help her create a list of healthy lunch items that she would keep on hand so that packing lunches would be easy and streamlined. The kids agreed that they were old enough to make a sandwich for themselves and then pack a few healthy snacks to go with their sandwich. Their lunch snack list was:

- small bags of almonds;
- mozzarella cheese sticks, individually wrapped;
- small boxes of raisins;
- healthy, low-sugar protein bars;
- carrot sticks with small container of Ranch dressing;
- cherries, grapes, or blueberries (fruit that wasn't drippy and didn't need to be peeled)

The kids made their lunches every evening right after supper, before they sat down to do their homework. Lunch bags had been washed and dried by Dad, ready for repacking, so making lunches was a five-minute task. Mom organized a shelf in the pantry and a shelf in the refrigerator door that was dedicated to lunch items, so it was easy to see what she needed to buy at the store to replenish the lunch items.

No Time as a Couple

The new evening routines meant that Karen and her husband had time to talk and to relax from 9 p.m. until they went to bed at 11. Karen reported that it's amazing how different things are now. "The kitchen is clean, the laundry is folded and put away, the homework is done, and the kids are in bed by 9, which means we have time to talk."

Streamline and Simplify

No Time to Keep up with the Mail and the Bills

Karen and her husband divided the mail into two categories: 1) bills to pay and 2) paperwork that required a response—insurance claims to file, forms to complete, etc. Karen's husband, Dan, agreed to reserve one night each week for paying bills—which became a very manageable task after he set up online bill paying through their local bank. Karen agreed to take responsibility for filling out school forms, camp forms, insurance claims, etc. They decided to do their paperwork tasks on the same night each week. That way they were less likely to forget because they could remind each other. And by doing it on a weekly basis there wasn't that much to keep up with, so they still had some time to relax before bed at 11.

No Time to Keep up with Personal E-mail

Karen decided to use her lunch hour at work as personal time to e-mail friends and family or to respond to their e-mails. She was more relaxed during her lunch hour than she was at home when there were competing demands and multiple interruptions. She found that she could keep up with personal e-mail easily and still have time to take a walk or run an errand several days each week.

Frantic Afternoons Shuttling the Kids to After-School Activities

Karen and her husband decided to take different parenting "shifts." Dan was naturally an early riser and agreed to head into work early, arriving at 7, which allowed him to leave work at 3 p.m. Meanwhile, with clothing and lunches more organized, Karen felt she could easily be in charge of shepherding the kids through their morning routine and getting them and herself out the door on time. She could be relaxed at work knowing that Dan was picking up the kids and getting them to sports practices and lessons. That way, on the way home she could pick up the dry cleaning, go by the bank, get gas for the car, or do some random errand, without worrying that she'd be late picking up the kids.

Dinner Preparation

Karen and her family sat down together and created a list of weekday dinners that were simple, quick, and nutritious. They wrote them down on meal planning cards—five meals for week one, five meals for week two, with the necessary ingredients for each meal on the back of the card. Meals were planned in an order that reduced cooking time. For example, the family all liked spaghetti, chili, and tacos, so these meals were all planned for the same week. That way, Karen or her husband could cook a huge batch of ground turkey with tomato sauce on Sunday evening (the first night of the weekday cycle). Sunday night, the family enjoyed spaghetti. The second night, more of the ground turkey with tomato sauce was seasoned with taco seasoning and enjoyed as a taco meal. The third night, they ate the last of the ground turkey with tomato sauce by adding black beans and chili powder to enjoy a meal of hot chili. They followed a similar pattern in week 2, using chicken strips one night in a stir fry, another night in fajitas, and a third night simply pan-seared and served with microwaved rice. Pre-packaged salads and frozen vegetables that can be microwaved were always kept on hand to accompany each meal. Karen cooked on nights that her husband arrived late bringing the kids home from after-school activities. Her husband cooked on nights when everyone arrived home sooner. The family looked forward to "pizza night" on Friday—a night when both Karen and her husband were tired from the busy week. Saturday night dinner was more flexible. When the day was filled with kids' activities, the family often ordered carry out, but on less busy Saturdays Karen and her husband enjoyed cooking on the grill and having a more relaxed meal, sometimes inviting friends to join them. Once this routine was established, grocery shopping and meal preparation were simple and smooth.

Keeping the House in Order

Karen and her husband paid for a cleaning service to come every other week to do the heavy cleaning of the kitchen and bathrooms. In the past, there was an exhausted and frantic effort to straighten up the house the night before the cleaning crew was expected. But their new regime worked much better. After a family meeting to discuss the clutter in the house, everyone agreed to do a nightly pick-up before heading for bed. One parent was responsible for kitchen cleanup, while the other parent supervised the kids picking up in the common areas of the house. By doing it on a daily basis, the pick-up time was never more than ten minutes and often only five.

Whatever you place on your list of daily tasks or routines that frequently go wrong or that frequently cause stress, your next step is to ask yourself how you might streamline or simplify them. Many adults continue with routines that don't work well, never stopping to strategize, to create a simpler approach. Here are some strategies that worked for Karen.

Spending Too Much Time Searching for Keys, Phones, and Other Critical Items

Despite her launching pad, there are certain things that Karen still scrambles to find. For example, she can never seem to find her cell phone when she is ready to leave in the morning. It's a small frustration that nearly drives her crazy every day. Now she keeps her cell phone in a bright yellow leather case. From her kitchen phone, she can call her cell phone and locate it by its ring tone.

Another daily frustration for Karen is her difficulty in quickly finding essential items in her purse. Karen solved this problem by choosing a different bright color for her wallet, change purse, pens, and comb. Before, most of her accessories were black. Now, a quick glance for the right color ends her search. Karen eliminated her searches for her keys by purchasing a large metal clip to attach her key ring to her purse strap. The clip allows her to tuck the keys inside her purse, but prevents them from falling into the abyss.

Keeping the House Stocked with Groceries

Make a sweep through your supermarket and see what is in each aisle. Then arrange your shopping list in categories roughly parallel to the way your supermarket is organized. Use your list to shop by aisle and you'll shave up to 35 percent off your shopping time.

Streamline and Simplify

37

Create a master list of standard grocery items on your computer and add to it as new items become family staples. Create this list in categories related to the layout of your grocery. Then print that list and check off needed items. Voilà! There's your grocery list, with much less chance that you'll forget items you've run out of. The list will remind you to check what you need before heading to the store.

Buy in quantity. With her eight rotating meals in mind, Karen was soon able to stock up on sales items that fit into her biweekly routine, saving both time and money. The prepacked lunch routine and the "grab and go" breakfast routine also helped structure her grocery shopping and allowed her to buy in bulk.

No Time for a Social Life

Before they had kids, Karen and her husband loved to organize dinner parties several times a year, go out to nice restaurants regularly, as well as attend plays and concerts. Although regular entertaining and money for nice restaurants, plays, and concerts are out of the question for now, Karen began to look for ways to be in touch with friends on a more regular basis.

- **Call a friend while doing routine tasks.** Now that her dinner preparations are more streamlined, she has developed a regular routine of calling a friend for a chat as she cooks.
- **Plan low-key, low-effort social events.** Instead of going without social contact altogether, Karen and her husband make regular plans to meet friends at a local restaurant or to catch a movie together on a Saturday night. They joined a babysitting co-op in the neighborhood, which not only saved them lots of money, but also allowed them to become friends with people in their neighborhood.
- **Socialize *with* your kids.** Karen and her husband were among the first in their social group to have children, so in the early days of parenthood they didn't have many friends in the same boat. Now, several years later, most of their friends have kids. Instead of making plans for babysitters and restaurants, often now they call another couple or two, arrange a spontaneous potluck, and cook burgers on their grill. The kids love socializing together while their parents have time to get together with other adults.
- **Introduce regular, automatic social gatherings.** Now that she understands the important roles that *structure* and *support* play in creating an ADD-friendly life, Karen applies that to her social life as well. She has joined a book club with a friend. This gives her a regular routine that ensures she'll have friendly social interaction on a monthly basis, without having to initiate and schedule it herself. The structure of the book group has an added advantage. Karen is now finding time to read a book each month—an enjoyable activity that she had neglected after the kids were born.

No Time for Exercise

Every working parent has a right to the stress-releasing and physical benefits of exercise. Parents of ADD children and parents who also have ADD need to regard exercise as part of their lifelong plan to manage ADD. To simplify your exercise routine, choose a program that requires little or no equipment to remember, maintain, store, or purchase. Walking, running, stretching, yoga, swimming, and many other exercises qualify. Another way to simplify exercising is to build it into other aspects of your day—making a routine of taking the stairs at work, or parking a distance from your office and then walking to and from your car each day.

Spending Too Much Time on Digital Devices

Karen and her husband decided to set limits on technology use for the whole family. They realized that one of the big reasons they hadn't had time for meal preparation, couple time, and household maintenance tasks was that they had both fallen into the habit of spending several hours each evening online or watching shows and movies. They were also setting a bad example for their kids, who had to be pulled away from their tablets or phones to do homework or chores. They created a rule of no digital devices on weeknights for the kids, and limited their own use of digital devices after the kids were in bed. For more information about managing technology, see Chapter 20.

LEVEL TWO SOLUTIONS: HELP FROM FRIENDS AND FAMILY

Problem-Solve as a Family

The solutions that Karen and her family developed to streamline and organize their days worked well because everyone in the family, including the kids, participated in the problem-solving. That way, everyone was on board and helping each other to remember their new routines.

Don't Shop Alone

Bring along a friend—or your Clutter Companion who is less likely to be thrown into confusion if you shop at stores that are not well organized, such as discount or outlet stores. While these stores can save you money, their inventory is not as well organized as in a regular department store. Sizes are jumbled. Styles are mixed. The jumble and confusion of searching for a bargain may cause ADD patterns to intensify to such an extent that you forget what you came for and begin to shop in a reactive or impulsive mode. A Clutter Companion is a friend or family member you can call upon to help you organize your things, clutter, and possessions because they are good at it themselves. Your Clutter Companion can help you cope with the confusion of outlet store chaos.

Exercise with a Friend

Simplified, streamlined exercise is more likely to fit into your busy schedule, but doing that exercise with a friend adds structure and support, so you're likely to exercise more consistently. Look for a time of day that is convenient, and support each other in getting more regular exercise. Many adults find it convenient to take a brisk walk during their lunch hour. While jogging requires a shower and change of clothes, walking requires only comfortable shoes.

Create an ADD-Friendly Closet with the Help of a Clutter Companion

Many adults with ADD make better and faster wardrobe choices when the choices are easier to see, when there are fewer choices, and when outfits are preassembled. The answer is to create an ADD-friendly closet. A Clutter Companion or PO can help you organize an ADD-friendly closet. Hang your clothes in your closet by complete outfits. Match a skirt to a blouse or a pair of slacks with a top and jacket. You can even preselect jewelry or accessories; put them in a plastic bag and hang them all together on the same hanger.

Take the clothes out of your dresser drawers, fold them neatly, and stack them on your closet shelves. Or put the clothes in attractive see-through boxes and stack the boxes on the shelf. Retire your dresser.

Keep a large plastic bag in your closet. If you find anything you can give away, put it in the bag. Take the bag to a women's shelter or a thrift store when it's full.

LEVEL THREE SOLUTIONS: HELP FROM PROFESSIONALS

Use a Personal Shopper

Better department stores are staffed with personal shoppers. You tell them what you want and your size and they make the selections for you. Then all you need to do is go to the store, look over the selections, and choose from among them.

Personal shoppers are paid a percentage of the cost of the clothing that you purchase, so be sure to set a clear budget for them. Cut out magazine and catalog pictures of outfits you like. Hand them over to your personal shopper with your color preferences and sizes and wait for a phone call to see your options.

Other Personal Services

Increasingly, as our lives have become busier, many other personal services have become available, especially in urban areas. If such services are in your budget, you can find companies that will run all sorts of errands, help with common chores, and do other sorts of shopping for you. If such services are not affordable, think of creative ways to barter with friends, exchanging errands that are convenient for you to accomplish for other errands that may be more convenient for your friend.

Simplicity Partners

If you are in therapy with an ADD specialist, he or she can serve as a partner for reviewing your daily life and discussing the things that routinely overwhelm you. It may be difficult for you to see ways to simplify and streamline your daily life. ADD coaches and professional organizers are typically very experienced in simplifying and streamlining—helping you to streamline not only daily routines, but also your environment to support those new routines. You may find that you need professional support in the beginning, as you learn to streamline your life. It's important to develop the habit of streamlining and simplifying all aspects of your daily life. It's a powerful ADD-friendly organizing strategy to build into your life.

How is this book different?

- Simplify, simplify, simplify.
- Simplify your meals, wardrobe, social life, and exercise.
- Create a launching pad.
- Solve problems as a family.
- Simplify your technological life.
- Work with others to simplify and streamline.

Streamline and Simplify

ADD Decision Dilemmas

June looks out her window at the pouring rain and the water gushing from her gutters. She calls several contractors from among the mass of business cards she has acquired. Each contractor provides June with ever more detailed information, and all their quotes are wildly different. "I guess I need more information," June thinks. She is no closer to replacing her gutters now than she was two months ago.

Tommy, June's son, is ten years old and looking forward to going away to camp this summer. It's mid-April, and June's dining room table is overrun with brochures, newspaper clippings, and Internet printouts about summer camps. Selecting a camp has turned into a very time-consuming project. June wants to be sure she makes the best choice possible, but the camps are filling up fast.

Paradoxically, the more June tries to make the perfect decision about every aspect of her life, the more out of control her life feels. Time slips away as time-critical decisions are not made. Deadlines are missed, not due to procrastination but because her anxious perfectionism prevents her from reaching decisions.

Alicia, another woman with ADD, also struggles with decision-making. The process overwhelms her. The more information she gathers, the more choices she has, the more frustrated and confused she feels. In her attempts to plan a family vacation, for example, she has trouble managing and organizing the number of possibilities and a kind of paralysis sets in. Should we go to the beach or the mountains? Should we visit nearby family members, or fly to Florida to see the grandparents? In the end, having made no decisions, she and her husband pile the kids in the van and take off, picking a route almost at random, deciding to "sight-see" along the way. Alicia feels immense relief—the burden of deciding was lifted—but she is disappointed in the vacation that results.

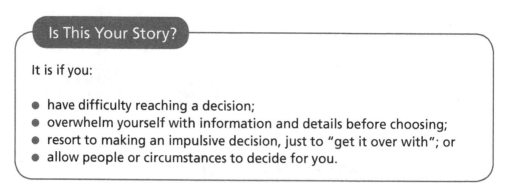

Is This Your Story?

It is if you:

● have difficulty reaching a decision;
● overwhelm yourself with information and details before choosing;
● resort to making an impulsive decision, just to "get it over with"; or
● allow people or circumstances to decide for you.

John's ADD-related decision-making struggles are different. John tries to avoid decisions altogether. He never feels sure of the correct decision, so he prefers to let people and events chart his course. His strategy in life has been passivity. By avoiding decision-making, he believes he can also avoid responsibility for the outcomes of decisions. Not surprisingly, John is married to a take-charge woman—someone who has always made plans for John, and who organizes his life.

Large Decisions

Most of the decisions we've focused on so far are relatively small ones—where to go on vacation, which summer camp to choose for your child. But we all face large decisions as well, and they can feel so difficult to make that we may be even more likely to let "fate" decide what we do. Let's look at a couple of large decisions that were difficult for two individuals with ADD at different stages in life.

Alex was a college junior. He'd been a bright, successful high school student, getting by on sheer ability. When he went away to engineering school as a freshman he had no idea how to discipline himself to study. He'd never had to study before. After three semesters, he was home again, leaving engineering school on academic probation. His big decision was "what's next?" Because Alex had no idea how to go about making a choice that suited his strengths and interests, he relied on his father, a successful CPA, to guide his choice. His father, not surprisingly, suggested that Alex study accounting as he had. "Alex, you're certainly smart enough, and the world will always need good accountants." Alex followed his father's advice and found himself miserably unhappy a few years later, feeling restless and bored in his job at a large accounting firm. In this case, Alex didn't have the tools to make an informed decision and relied upon his dad to make the choice.

Catherine was a mid-career professional in a public relations firm. She'd felt stressed at work and chronically unhappy. "I'm constantly overloaded and have no time for a personal life," she related. However, just like Alex didn't know how to figure out what he would be happy doing, Catherine couldn't see a way to make a good career change and remained in her job despite her unhappiness. The consequences of quitting her job seemed too large, and she had no guarantee that she'd be happier in her next job anyway. While Alex let his father decide, Catherine was letting fate make her big decision. If she was fired or if her husband was transferred to another city, then she would leave her job. Otherwise, she remained stuck, unable to decide what her next move should be.

Perfectionist Indecision

June's efforts toward perfectionism can be the result of several ADD issues. For some, perfectionism is a way to compensate for the disorganization, distractibility, and impulsivity of ADD. This type of adult with ADD is a "compulsive compensator." The compensations they've developed have become so strongly ingrained that they seem compulsive. For example, one man with ADD became compulsively neat because, when his surroundings are cluttered, things seem to "disappear" all the time. For years, he has arranged his keys, wallet, cell phone, loose change, and even the tie he has just taken off neatly on his night table. To the outsider, this behavior may seem fussy and overly tidy. He has learned from experience that when he lets these carefully developed habits slip, he won't be able to find his car keys or wallet.

For others, perfectionist tendencies may have developed in response to criticism. In some adults, especially in women, persistent negative feedback results in chronic anxiety. For example, June's mother was very controlling and demanding, a former schoolteacher who had stayed home to focus all of her energies on her daughter. June anxiously learned to double- and triple-check herself, expending most of her emotional energy trying to gain her mother's approval. Now, in adulthood, she has internalized her mother's harsh criticism and feels compelled to do everything perfectly.

June's attempts to be perfect come at a very high cost. She expends too much energy on unimportant decisions, and even misses deadlines in her driven approach to gathering every possible bit of information.

Impulsive Decision-Making

Another ADD pattern, impulsivity, can also unduly influence decision-making. Impulsivity is the tendency to act without fully considering the possible consequences; in other words, leaping before you look. For some adults with ADD, decision-making occurs on impulse. They act on emotion instead of reason, and often later regret their actions. For impulsive adults with ADD, decisions can greatly improve by resisting the impulse and taking time to think it through.

For many others, though, what may appear to be impulsivity is actually a reflection of a difficulty with thinking things through and considering the options. Such an adult may think about a decision for a long time, speaking to many people in the process, only to make an impulsive decision in the end, just to "get it over with." In other words, the ADD difficulty with executive functioning—with information gathering, evaluating, considering possible consequences, and ranking the choices—is so challenging for them that they resort to metaphorically flipping a coin or throwing a dart.

Decisions by Default

Others with ADD, like John, deal with their difficulty making decisions by avoiding them altogether. For example, one young man with ADD felt overwhelmed by the college application process. Despite prodding and nagging from his parents and high school guidance counselor, he continued to procrastinate—never writing his college essay or mailing his applications until most deadlines had passed. In the end, he was admitted to a local state school that had a rolling admission policy and no college essay requirement. His college decision was made "by default"—after many opportunities had passed him by as he avoided making choices and acting on them.

LEVEL ONE SOLUTIONS: WAYS TO HELP YOURSELF

Solutions to Perfectionist Decision Blocks

If you are a "hunter," always seeking the perfect answer, choice, or solution, your expedition can take you almost anywhere—to the Internet, the library, into many discussions with many people, on a search through magazines, newspapers, and into your own world of needs, wants, preferences, and ideas. This search for the perfect choice is very time consuming. But, if you "fence in" your hunting ground, it will set an objective limit to your hunt, reducing choice and increasing the prospects of succeeding in your hunt for a good decision.

The Time Limit Fence

The search for a perfect summer camp is meaningless if the camp application and payment arrive late. June might first look at the camp application deadlines. They are likely within a week or two of each other. To be conservative, she could choose the earliest deadline from any camp. On her calendar or day planner, June should enter the camp decision deadline as if it were an appointment with herself. Then, because there is so much reading material and Internet research to do, it would be best if she actually blocked time out on her calendar or day planner to achieve this.

Butting up against a time limit fence will not ensure that June will make the perfect choice. Truth is, she can only make her best choice. No choice is perfect. But a time limit will ensure that a choice does get made, that it is as well informed as time permits, and, most important, that it is timely. Tommy might not think his summer camp is perfect, but he sure will like it better than missing out on camp altogether. Make the best decision you can, given the time you have.

The Budget Limit Fence

Use your budget limit as a fence, and your choices will automatically be reduced. With her budget limit in mind, June is able to discard out of hand many of the gutter repair offers and the summer camp options. June observes, "I am not frivolous financially, but it is easy for me to not pay much attention to my budget when I look at glitzy brochures of summer camps, or alluring pictures of beautiful houses. The fewer choices I have, the better. Once I set a budget limit, it is easier to get past the glitz to the bottom line of cost." Make the best choice, given your budget.

Create a Physical Limit as Your Fence

If you tend to be a perfectionist, it is likely that the internal signal that says "Stop! Enough is enough" may not go off. You need an external signal to compensate for the lack of an internal one. Set up an external physical signal that tells you when to stop when your internal signal does not.

Find a physical container for your choices, options, and possibilities, for instance a basket for vacation brochures, a cubbyhole for credit card offers, a box of decorating ideas, or the entire surface of the dining room table for summer camp information. When that container is full, you have reached your limit. It does not matter how much new material you come across. The fullness of the physical container is your signal to stop and make a decision.

Create a Numerical Limit

Decide to obtain three estimates for a household repair. Then go with the best option.

Dealing with Decision Overwhelm

The Impulsive Escape

It's important for you to distinguish *true* impulsivity from impulsivity as an escape from overwhelm. For those with ADD who are truly impulsive, important decisions may be made on the spot, sometimes in the heat of the moment. If impulsivity causes you to leap now and look later, you'll probably need professional help in learning to overcome these patterns, and may possibly need to consider stimulant medication as part of this process. In this instance, however, we are not addressing *true* impulsivity, but the kinds of impulsive decision—"what the heck" decisions—that result from frustration with indecision. These impulsive decisions are often a reaction to too many choices. For example, Alicia's impulsive decision to take off on a driving vacation followed months of indecision. She didn't make an impulsive decision off the bat, but only after she'd been unable to reach a considered decision. Too many options were on the table; too many family members disagreed about what should be done.

The Passive Escape

When you let people and events decide for you, you're probably feeling decision overwhelm, but your escape is passivity rather than impulsivity. Most likely, you haven't liked the outcomes of many decisions in life that were made *for* you, but at least you could shrug and tell yourself, "It wasn't *my* choice." But, in fact, the choices *are* yours! They're just not very well controlled choices. When you choose to let circumstances decide, the outcome is more risky.

In certain circumstances, passivity is relatively cost-free. Pizza or Chinese? Go to the movies or stream a video? Perhaps you don't really care and would prefer that your companion do the work of deciding. But what about important decisions? Stay here or move to L.A.? Go to college or get a job? Accept a promotion or keep doing the same old thing? The cost of passivity becomes much higher.

Solutions to overwhelm

When overwhelm leads to either impulsive decisions or passive decisions-by-default, look for ways to reduce overwhelm. Overwhelm can occur when you're overstimulated (for example, in a crowded, loud, or noisy environment), when you have too many choices, or when you're trying to please too many people. The best way to avoid decision overwhelm is to limit the input.

- Shop in smaller stores with fewer displays.
- Limit the number of options to consider before you decide.
- Identify the most important issue (price, convenience, practicality, and so on) and then focus on that factor to make your decision.

Use Your Own Yardstick: Value-Based Decision-Making

Decision-making often feels overwhelming if you're not using your own values as a yardstick. For example, one young woman with ADD was considering the purchase of her first home. She felt completely overwhelmed by the number of factors to take into account. Should she move to the outer suburbs, where she could purchase a larger house for the same price? Should she think about resale value, or go with her personal preferences? How much should she be willing to pay for a shorter commute? Everyone gave her differing advice. Instead of enjoying the prospect of owning her own home, she felt stressed and frustrated. Ultimately, she realized that the advice she received from her parents, her realtor, and her friends shouldn't cloud her own values and preferences. Once she trusted her own feelings and reactions, the decision-making process became clearer. "My father kept telling me, 'Look for the least expensive house in an expensive area.' But I didn't really like any of the homes that filled that bill. One weekend, I walked into a house and just *knew* that it felt right—for me."

Paradoxical Decision-Making

Sometimes, when we can't seem to make a decision that will help us reach our goal, it can help to try the paradoxical approach. Here's how it works. Dan wanted to retire in two to three years, but he could never seem to figure out when he could "afford" to retire. He drew up lots of numbers and figures, but kept putting off the decision. Then, someone suggested the paradoxical approach. "Why don't you write down what you need to do to never be able to retire? Once you figure that out, turn the process on its head and you'll figure out how to retire." So Dan thought, "Well, in order to never be able to retire I should stay in my large home where we raised our family, spend money on expensive home renovations, pile up consumer debt taking vacations and going out for expensive meals, and make risky investments on the stock market that would take years to recover from if they went bad." Dan made a game of figuring out what to do so that he could *never* afford to retire. "I could buy a very expensive car with huge monthly payments. I could take poor care of myself so that I incur large medical expenses."

Then Dan turned this paradoxical problem-solving on its head. So that means, Dan thought, that maybe I should stop putting money into our big house, and sell it so that I can reduce my housing costs. If I'm smart, I could downsize and end up without a mortgage payment. Next, I should practice never putting any purchases or expenses on credit cards and pay off all of my consumer debt. I should live below my monthly income to prepare for living on a reduced income when I retire; I should talk to an investment advisor about shifting retirement savings to secure stable investments; I should trade in my car for a less expensive, more fuel-efficient model; and I should start to eat a healthier diet and exercise regularly so that I can enjoy a healthy retirement and reduce out-of-pocket medical expenses. Suddenly, Dan had created a path toward retirement through his paradoxical decision-making.

Supports: Rewarding Yourself

You can support your efforts by rewarding yourself when you have passed a decision-making milestone. Rewards along the way can reduce the frustration of delayed gratification and are essential to keep you going on any long-term project.

LEVEL TWO SOLUTIONS: HELP FROM FRIENDS AND FAMILY

Honor the Difference between Small and Large Decisions

If you are in doubt about the difference between a small and large decision, consult with your Time Tutor (or PO, therapist, or ADD coach). From a time management point of view, the preoccupation with the hunt can be a real time waster, especially if the decision is small but the hunt is large. Choosing a summer camp is a bigger decision than choosing Tommy's T-shirts for camp. Don't spend the same amount of time on each. Finding a good gutter contractor is a bigger decision than finding the perfect beige gutter. Keep your hunt appropriate to the size of your decision. Time is precious. Spend it wisely.

Prioritize Decisions and Spread Them out over Time

What is more important, a mother's self-care or caring for her children? Her commitment to the community or needed home repairs? Attending a school meeting or an environmental task force meeting? All of these things are important, but they are not all equally important at the same time. And that is the key. People who manage their time well have a natural instinct for not only the relative importance of things to each other, but also what is important when. But many people try to do all the important things with the same intensity at the same time.

A Time Tutor can be of great help in putting priorities in order and phasing decisions in over a period of time. "I decided that my health (teeth) and my son's homework come first right now," June decided. She notified the community group that she would finish the project she was currently working on, but could not attend meetings again until Tommy left for summer camp. She let the environmental group know that her child's academic needs were her priority at present. For now, she would send them a larger donation than usual and read their newsletter to keep informed. Spread your important decisions and commitments out over time.

Use a Stop Coach

If you have difficulty knowing when enough is enough, you might want to ask someone without ADD to help you determine when you are finished. For instance, June is writing an article for her church on religion and the Internet. But the article never seems to end. She's missed one deadline already but hopes to make the next one. A church member who writes could tell June when the article is finished, when it has said enough to the reader to inform them but not overwhelm them with everything there is to say on the topic. We call this person a stop coach. Stop coaches can help you end writing and research projects, bring renovating and decorating to a conclusion, and add closure to organizing projects.

Use a Decision Coach

Often, it can be very helpful to talk through a decision with someone who can help you gain a different perspective. Alicia, in struggling to make a vacation decision, was stuck in the ant's perspective—running here and there, looking at details: airline schedules, brochures, input from multiple family members. She never stopped long enough to step back and think about her values and objectives. Alicia jumped from one possibility to the next, never deciding, never clear on her priorities.

Clarify Your Thoughts with a Decision Coach

Talking with a decision coach—a friend or family member—can frequently clear the way to making a decision that feels "right." A decision coach is not just one more person who offers you their opinion, but rather someone who can help you clarify your own thoughts and feelings—by asking questions you've been too distracted to ask yourself. A decision coach could have asked Alicia questions such as: What are your goals in choosing a vacation? Do you want to expose your children to new experiences to broaden their horizons? Or does your family need a relaxing vacation, with time to reconnect, while doing low-stress, familiar things? Or is connecting with far-flung family members at the top of your list? Had Alicia been asked these questions, and thought about them, she would probably have made a more satisfying choice than the ill-planned road trip that was the eventual result of her indecision.

Turn Black-and-White Decisions into Gray Ones

Working with a decision coach can help you to think things through. Again, the role of a decision coach is not to give his or her own opinion, but to help you think things through and break things down. Some choices are all or nothing, once in a lifetime. We grab at the brass ring or we don't, and that's the end of it. But most choices are not that black and white, although they may seem so to you.

A decision coach can help you think of ways to turn a black-and-white choice into shades of gray. For example, you may have been offered a job opportunity in a distant location. Although this may be presented as a "yes or no" decision, perhaps it need not necessarily be so.

Explore Options with a Decision Coach

A decision coach can help you explore options you're not aware of. Is there a possibility of a temporary assignment? Is there a possibility of returning if the job doesn't work out? How about visiting the area for a number of days to gather information? What is the possibility of postponing reassignment until your oldest child graduates from high school next year? Do I negate future opportunities if I turn down this one?

Even if you decide against this opportunity, talking your decision over with a decision coach may open up new ideas for you. For example, this opportunity may make you more aware of the value of advanced training. Perhaps you'll decline this offer but decide to return to school for more training to increase your chances of future offers that are a better fit for you or your family.

LEVEL THREE SOLUTIONS: HELP FROM PROFESSIONALS

Decision-Making and Reaching Goals

Many decisions are necessary in order to meet a goal. You must decide upon:

- an appropriate, realistic goal;
- an ADD-friendly plan for reaching your goal;
- the steps required;
- the level of structure you need to succeed in your goal; and
- the supports you'll need to keep your motivation high.

Your PO, an ADD coach or an Organizer-Coach can help you make decisions at each step—from goal selection to goal completion—keeping the three S's—strategies, structure, and support—in mind.

Structure: Setting Milestones

Milestones provide structure in the course of a long-term effort. Your PO or coach can help you establish milestones to measure and mark your progress.

ADD-Friendly Strategies

Your PO or coach can help you set goals and use strategies to reach those goals that work *with* your ADD.

Right-Brain Approaches for Right-Brain People

Many adults with ADD are right-brain thinkers. Everyone uses both sides of the brain simultaneously, but each hemisphere serves different functions. The left-brain is oriented to traditional organizing strengths like sequencing, ordering, and analysis. But if you are right-brain dominant, you'll tend to be a visualizer, and more intuitive instead of a goal-oriented planner. Dr. Lynn Weiss, in her book *A.D.D. and Success* (p. 35), writes of right-brain tendencies among her clients with ADD:

> Cesario . . . "goes with the flow" . . . often effectively using feelings as a guide. To Cesario, the journey tends to be more important than the goal. It is not that he doesn't have or reach goals . . . it is just that he reaches them in his own way, frequently creating an experience in the process.

Let the goal choose you

Dr. Jane Petrick, the director of Informed Decisions International, advises: "We are most effective, not when we choose the goals, but when we let the goals choose us." Letting goals choose you is a very right-brained process. However, planning, by its nature, is left-brained, using logic and sequence. If you are right-brained, a completely left-brained planning process is unlikely to work well because it does not use your creativity or access your intuitions. When a plan doesn't "feel right" to you, it's not likely to work. It's critical that you find a PO or coach who understands your right-brained approach to the world, and who can help you develop strategies that are compatible with your style.

Give up getting it right

"In the common daily life most of us lead, 'getting it right' is a cultural obsession," notes Dr. Fred Newman in his book *Let's Develop!* "Our culture is a culture of getting. Perfectionism is taken as a sign of how good we are as getters. This preoccupation with rightness is a fanaticism . . . and it produces one of the quintessential postmodern diseases: stress" (p. 170).

A better philosophy than "getting it right" is doing your best. If you have given something your all, that is the best you can do. Even the best information is filtered through our imperfect desires, wants, and preferences. There is no perfect outcome, only the best effort.

After many struggles, June finally reached this conclusion: "I realized that no matter which of the final two camps I decided to choose, Tommy was going to have a great time. And if for some reason he turned out to be unhappy, we'd deal with that when it happened." June had spent her life anxiously gripping the wheel, trying to avoid every pothole in life. Finally, she realized that she could cope with the bumps if they occurred. June was working on another essential executive function—shifting actions as needed when circumstances change.

When Psychotherapy May Be Necessary

If you find that decision-making fills you with dread or anxiety, you may need to see a therapist. Also, you might not be the best judge of how injurious your brand of perfectionism, or your need to be right, is. You might not cause yourself emotional pain, but if you see that it distresses others, like your spouse or coworkers, it might be wise to consult with a therapist, if only to hear an objective opinion.

> ## Review
>
> - Set time, budget, and physical fences to limit perfectionist hunting.
> - Reduce decision overwhelm.
> - Use your own yardstick to make value-based decisions.
> - Honor the difference between small and large decisions.
> - Prioritize decisions and spread them out over time.
> - Use a stop coach.
> - Use a decision coach.
> - Turn black-and-white decisions into gray ones.
> - Set decision-making milestones to structure the process.
> - Reward yourself, and seek supportive encouragement from others.
> - Consider setting right-brain goals.
> - Give up getting it right.
> - Consider psychotherapy if decision-making causes you great anxiety or dread.

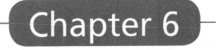

B-o-r-i-n-g

Managing Stimulation Hunger and Hyperfocus

Jerry is a very bright but bored certified public accountant. He struggled with ADD issues throughout high school and college, switching from a science major to accounting after a "crash-and-burn" freshman year at college. Jerry's ADD and basic lack of interest in accounting have resulted in a checkered career path. At age 30 he is on his third job. "Even if a job interests me, after a short while I feel bored and want to move on. I just can't seem to settle into anything," Jerry says.

Because he gets such little gratification from his job, Jerry is engaged in all kinds of activities at night to compensate for his boring days. He belongs to an investment club, plays cards regularly, and gets lost for hours in video games. He also loves late-night TV and, with a tablet in bed with him, rarely gets enough sleep before his alarm rings in the morning. Jerry's mornings look like a juggling act. He checks his e-mail and cannot resist responding to some of it as he gulps down cereal standing up. He takes a quick look at his investments online as he heads for the shower. Dressing is always complicated by the state of his laundry and whether he remembered to pick up his dry cleaning. Sometimes he resorts to buying more socks and underwear because he hates doing laundry. It's so boring.

Jerry watches Internet TV on his tablet, catching the morning news and carrying it around with him as he dresses. As he gazes at his tablet, Jerry is unaware of time slipping away. He is so captivated that if he never had to go to the bathroom, he might still be standing there! He glances at his watch, realizes he's running late, grabs his briefcase, scrambles for his cell phone, and searches for his keys. His chronic lateness is affecting his performance reviews at work, and he's in danger of losing his job.

Marge doesn't seem to resemble Jerry on the surface. Although they both have ADD, Marge goes through her life at a much slower pace. Single, Marge lives alone and works as a paralegal in a downtown law office. Marge is very bright. Attorneys in the firm sometimes joke with her that she can do legal work better than they can. The truth is, Marge *is* as bright as the attorneys, but a spotty academic record and lack of role models precluded her from gaining acceptance to law school. Often she feels frustrated and bored by her paralegal work, but with little else going on in her life she works long hours, sometimes on weekends when a big case is pending. She is able to focus and organize at work, but her personal life is a different story. Her apartment is extremely cluttered and rarely cleaned. Housework bores her to death. At home she resorts to online shopping late at night or she escapes into romance novels, often missing sleep if she gets hooked on a story. And meanwhile her weight has climbed steadily over the years as she stimulates herself with late-night eating. Marge is hyperfocused on work. Neglected friendships have faded away. Her only regular social contact has been reduced to lunch with coworkers, conversations with the checkout cashiers at the local cafeteria, and attending church on Sundays.

Executive functioning (EF) issues are involved in managing hyperfocus. Both Jerry and Marge are prone to hyperfocus and tend to be unaware of their hyperfocus, leading them to lose track of time. The EF skills of self-monitoring and self-management come into play here. Hyperfocus can be a great gift if you can hyperfocus on something at work or at home that is a constructive, productive activity. But hyperfocus needs to be managed through self-awareness (catching yourself) and self-management (stopping yourself) when you are hyperfocused on something that interferes with important daily activities at work or at home.

Is This Your Story?

It is if you:

- cannot tolerate boredom;
- crave stimulation;
- tend to develop addictive stimulation-seeking patterns;
- let "escape" activities interfere with responsibilities; and
- tend to hyperfocus and lose track of time.

Stimulation Craving and ADD

Many people with ADD crave stimulation. In fact, some researchers hypothesize that some ADDers have a "risk-taking gene." Although we don't really understand the neurological mechanism, the ADD need for stimulation is well known. It is more obvious among hyperactive/impulsive ADDers because their stimulation seeking is quite observable, from fast driving and fast talking to skydiving. But even quiet, inattentive-type ADDers stimulate themselves through daydreaming, social media, escape novels, and overeating if the events around them aren't interesting. Some ADDers are so intolerant of boredom that they start an argument or create a crisis to avoid understimulation with little or no awareness that they are creating these problems in order to feel more engaged and alive. Stimulation-seeking behavior can be either your key to success or your undoing, depending upon how it is managed.

How do EF skills come into play when you experience stimulation craving? Self-control is a critical executive functioning skill. If we don't develop and exercise self-control, our stimulation craving can become a very destructive force in our lives. We can't wish our stimulation craving away, but we *can* learn to manage it and use it for good by actively seeking forms of stimulation that are positive and constructive.

Destructive Stimulation Craving

While Jerry seeks stimulation in a very active, sometimes hyperactive fashion, Marge's stimulation seeking is more passive, but equally destructive. Stimulation for Marge comes in the form of romance novels and over-eating and watching favorite shows online late into the night. Her finances are always on the edge due to almost nightly online shopping. Her credit cards are all charged up to the limit and she struggles to make minimum monthly payments on them. Now in her late thirties, Marge has let her weight balloon to over two hundred pounds. No matter how many diets she tries—and she has spent a fortune on them—she has never been successful in maintaining weight loss.

Because Jerry cannot tolerate boredom, he seeks stimulation—from Internet games, constantly checking e-mails, incessantly checking his online investments, and watching Internet television on all his devices. Even lateness is a stimulant for Jerry. Jerry may not *want* to be late, and he tries not to be, but the short-term effects of the stimulation generated from lateness are undeniably engaging. There is the stepped-up whirl of external commotion. There is the brain engaged in simultaneously remembering where things are, processing information from the TV, thinking about his investments, internally creating an excuse for being late, and so on. Things may be chaotic, but they certainly are not boring! At least not until he gets to the office. However, lateness is a destructive source of stimulation with numerous negative effects.

LEVEL ONE SOLUTIONS: WAYS TO HELP YOURSELF

Save Stimulating Recreational Activities as a Reward for Doing What You Need to Do

As Jerry engages in multiple activities during his morning routine, he predictably loses track of time. A "minute" checking his e-mail becomes 15. A quick glance at the TV turns into full engagement as he listens to the latest crime or disaster. With a morning routine that is so stimulating and distracting, it's no wonder he's usually late.

The solution? Limit the distractions until after he's completed his morning routine. Only the threat of being fired motivated Jerry to go "cold turkey" with his morning distractions. On the advice of his therapist, he avoids the Internet altogether in the morning; no TV, no e-mail, and no online investments. His new morning routine is to get up, shower, dress as quickly as possible, and leave for work immediately. With an earlier departure, he arrives at his office building way *ahead* of schedule. He can purchase a muffin and a cup of coffee in the deli on the ground floor and be at his desk, enjoying his breakfast and checking his e-mail and investments online, when his surprised but very pleased manager arrives a half-hour later.

Managing Stimulation Hunger and Hyperfocus

Look for Constructive Sources of Stimulation

One of the driving forces behind Marge's compulsive overeating patterns was stimulation hunger. Women with ADD who crave stimulation often satisfy their craving in passive ways—television, shopping, and eating.

Instead of focusing on trying to eat less, Marge began to pay attention to her need for stimulation. Because initiating and scheduling are typically difficult for those with ADD, Marge increased her participation in groups and activities that met at regular, scheduled times. First, Marge joined a singles discussion group at her church that met on Sunday evenings. A few weeks later, an online ad caught her eye for a master's program in business management that offered evening classes for adults who work full time. She enrolled in a couple of fall classes. She noticed a flyer for yoga classes at the local coffee shop and she signed up for a ten-week class.

Within a few months, Marge's work was no longer the center of her life, and her compulsive overeating patterns began to lessen as her evenings filled with more interesting and stimulating activities.

Manage Hyperfocus

Jerry, like many people with ADD, tends to hyperfocus on activities that are highly engaging. Hyperfocus has to do with the disregulated attentional system of the ADD brain. Most adults with ADD find that they are prone to attention difficulties at both ends of the continuum. In some situations, they are highly distractible; in other situations, they hyperfocus to the point that it is very difficult to shift their attention. One woman with ADD reported that she was so involved in working on writing a paper that she didn't know her building was on fire until firemen burst into her room, amazed to find her at her desk!

When you are hyperfocused on a book, TV program, or favorite activity, you may find that it is very difficult to pull yourself away—to "transition" to another activity—because you are so involved. Often, it requires a strong signal—hunger, fatigue, or a ringing phone—before you can unplug from hyperfocus. For Jerry, hyperfocus on morning distractions caused lateness. At night, hyperfocus on escapist activities prevented him from getting to bed on time.

One pitfall of hyperfocus is losing track of the passage of time. This full engagement creates a kind of outside-of-time experience; time seems to be adrift. When engaging in hyperfocus, you need to arrange for external reminders so that you don't become oblivious to life's other commitments.

Hyperfocus, when it occurs, is involuntary, but typically it's quite predictable. Most likely, you hyperfocus on select activities. Typical hyperfocus activities include:

- work;
- television;
- reading;
- Internet games;
- online investing;
- gambling;
- online or live shopping;
- social media.

Hyperfocusing becomes problematic when it causes lateness because you've lost track of time, or when your difficulty shifting out of hyperfocus leads you to neglect responsibilities and relationships. It's important that you develop ways to snap out of hyperfocus when it's time to turn to other activities. Make a list of the activities during which you get stuck in hyperfocus. Then plan ahead and problem-solve so that you can move on to what's next.

- Set an audio or vibrating alarm on your smartphone or use an alarm watch.
- Program your computer to send you a "Stop" reminder.
- Engage in your hyperfocus activity in an environment where there will be multiple external cues that it's time to stop—where there are other people and activities around.
- Don't start a hyperfocus activity at a time and place where you're most likely to ignore reminders and extend your period of hyperfocus—for example watching a favorite movie or checking Facebook a few minutes before you should be going to sleep.

Using Hyperfocus Constructively

Like many ADD traits, hyperfocus can become a very positive force in your life if you use it strategically. So don't just think in terms of *controlling* your hyperfocus, but also in terms of using it to your advantage. Some of the most spectacularly successful people are those with the ability to hyperfocus. The key is that they have crafted a life in which they hyperfocus on constructive career-related activities. Do what you love, and you can put your hyperfocus to work.

Many adults hyperfocus only on leisure or escape activities and never think in terms of constructing a career that allows them to focus on their interests. Some interests may not work as a career focus, but if you think creatively about what aspects of your leisure activities draw you into hyperfocus, you'll be surprised at how many career paths involve similar activities.

LEVEL TWO SOLUTIONS: HELP FROM FRIENDS AND FAMILY

Help from Others in Managing Hyperfocus

You may find that when you're engaged in certain activities, your own efforts to end hyperfocus are not successful. When this happens, you'll need to strategize with others to manage your hyperactivity.

When your hyperfocus is extreme, extreme measures may be necessary. For example, one computer analyst tended to become so hyperfocused on his work (using his hyperfocus constructively) that all of his efforts using alarms and reminders were ineffective. He had missed or arrived late to so many meetings that, finally, he requested that the administrative assistant for his group come to his office door, grab his attention, and remain there until he pulled himself away from his computer to attend the meeting. His wife learned a similar technique, calling him on his cell phone to pull him away from work at the end of the day. Just as with the administrative assistant, his wife's efforts were successful only if she kept his attention by keeping him on the phone as he reported, "I'm standing up, grabbing my briefcase, turning out the light, shutting the door, and heading for the car." Only when he'd started his car engine was she sure she'd succeeded in her goal.

Friends, colleagues, and family members can help manage your hyperfocus in a variety of ways.

- Ask them to tell you when "time's up."
- Engage in hyperfocus-type activities with another person. You're more likely to be able to shift from hyperfocus when they shift.
- Arrange for someone to call you on the phone to snap you out of hyperfocus. Depending upon the strength of your hyperfocus, they may need to keep you engaged in conversation while you "snap out of it."

Don't abuse the structure and support provided by others, however. You need to develop strategies for avoiding hyperfocus at critical times. For example, don't kid yourself and begin a hyperfocus activity half an hour before it's time to go home for the day, or half an hour before bedtime. You may need help with hyperfocus, but you can't completely shift responsibility to others or your support system will begin to fold.

Using Your Time Tutor to Manage Hyperfocus

The Internet is a place perfectly designed for hyperfocusing. You can get stuck in it like the prey of a spider. Jerry invests online and though his philosophy is to invest for the long term, he feels compelled to check his investments several times a day. There are colorful charts to see, graphs to track, research to conduct, intriguing information, and the opportunity to chat with others.

With the help of his Time Tutor, Jerry says, "I've put myself on an 'Internet diet.' I restrict myself to one hour online, three days a week, and set an alarm to tell me when my time is up." Internet games are another of Jerry's hyperfocus traps. Instead of playing them alone, he now plays games online with other people. Now the games are entertainment, a chance to socialize with friends instead of being purely an escape. And his friends, who don't have ADD, are more time aware and able to stop playing in order to attend to other commitments, a perfect cue for Jerry to stop also.

LEVEL THREE SOLUTIONS: HELP FROM PROFESSIONALS

You may find, especially if your stimulation hunger plays a very destructive role in your daily life, that you'll need a higher level of support at first—from an ADD coach, PO, or ADD therapist— to build new habits and to find constructive ways to use your hyperfocus and manage your stimulation hunger.

Use Your Stimulation Hunger for Career Advancement

Jerry's need for stimulation, especially in the morning, had led to problems in meeting daily responsibilities. Even at work, Jerry frequently resorted to Internet activities and surreptitious gaming when he became bored with his routine accounting work. A plan that required Jerry to ignore his stimulation hunger could never have worked for long.

Instead, Jerry and his therapist developed a plan to *use* his stimulation hunger to become more successful in his career. Instead of continuing to do the repetitive, uninteresting accounting and tax work that he found so mind-numbing, Jerry went to his supervisor and expressed an interest in conducting seminars to train other accountants to use a very complex new software that the firm had purchased. A whiz at the software, Jerry was the ideal choice, and a much less costly choice than hiring outside consultants to do the training. Jerry's ADD-related traits of being very active, both physically and verbally, made him well suited to training others. Finally his interest in computers could be used to his advantage at work, rather than as an escape from work.

The Cutting It Close Game

In the Cutting It Close Game, the PO suggests a strategy that appeals to many hyperactive adults with ADD because it introduces a fun challenge to the task of getting to work on time, making a tedious task much more stimulating.

Being prompt can be very stimulating if you make a game of it. You can play the Cutting It Close Game with your PO. To win, you must get to work (or school) exactly on time, not a minute sooner and not a minute later. To play, you and your PO have to construct routines that ensure perfect promptness.

In Jerry's case, to achieve perfect promptness he needed not only an evening routine that jumpstarts his morning, but also a morning routine that gets him to work exactly on time (occasional lateness owing to events beyond one's control is permitted). So with his PO Jerry took a close look at his morning routine and put together a plan to get to work right on the button.

"It took me eight days of tinkering with my routines to win at Cutting It Close. But I can't tell you how much more fun it is to make a game of getting to work right on time without a minute to spare. Yesterday, I beat my personal best and got to work early!" exclaims Jerry.

Rules of the Cutting It Close Game:

A. What time do you have to be at your desk or work station to be considered on time? For example, 9:00 a.m.
B. Now, thinking backwards, how long does it take you to park, hit the restroom, get a cup of coffee at the break room, and do all the things necessary for you to get seated at your work station? Subtract that amount of time from A. Let's say it's 12 minutes, so 9:00 a.m. minus 12 minutes = 8:48 a.m.
C. Picture yourself in the parking spot. Thinking backwards, how long did it take you to travel there, accounting for typical traffic and assuming you have gas in the car? Subtract that amount of time from B. Let's say it's 25 minutes. Subtract that from B and you get 8:23 a.m.

D. This is the tricky part. Be very realistic and calculate how long it takes you to leave the house after you've dressed and showered not counting breakfast. Let's say it's 30 minutes. Subtract that from C. That means you'd have to leave the house at 7:53 to be seated at your workstation at 9:00.

E. Because you're distractible, let's subtract another 10 minutes and make your departure time 7:43. Try it out and adjust accordingly.

F. See if you can get to work at exactly 9:00. When you do, give yourself a reward!

If you have the kind of job without a workstation or desk, you can still play the Cutting It Close Game. Maybe it's when you turn your laptop on, no matter where that is, or that first business call that begins your workday even if it's out in the field.

> ## Review
>
> - Seek constructive sources of stimulation.
> - Avoid counteracting boredom with risky or escapist behaviors.
> - Develop strategies to transition from hyperfocus.
> - Learn techniques to limit hyperfocus escapes.
> - Recognize how hyperfocus affects your time awareness.
> - Play the Cutting It Close Game.
> - Seek a career that feeds your stimulation hunger.
> - Put your hyperfocus to work *for* you.

Chapter 7

First Things First

Learning to Prioritize

"Anyone who looked at my life from the outside would think I have it pretty good," Jim remarked. "I've got a good job, a great family, and, thanks to my wife, our household runs pretty well." But suddenly, after a recent medical checkup, Jim was looking at the high price he'd silently paid to keep up his daily pace. "Keep going like this," his doctor had warned, "and you may be heading for an early heart attack."

Jim's childhood hyperactivity had transformed into mental hyperactivity as an adult. He is a great problem-solver and troubleshooter in his job, and juggled his demanding schedule by frequently staying up well beyond bedtime to catch up on bill paying, tax returns, or other work. Jim joked that it was a good thing he was hyperactive, because otherwise he'd never get everything done. Jim hit the ground running each morning. "I'm out the door early to beat the traffic. No matter what I'm doing all day, it feels as if I ought to be doing something else—when I'm in the car with the kids, I'm talking on my cell phone to my boss. If I'm out of town on a business trip, I feel bad that I'm missing the kids' soccer games."

The ability to prioritize competing goals and demands is a crucial executive functioning skill that requires a clear focus on what's most important in our lives as we deal with the barrage of daily life. Many adults with ADD let the world prioritize for them, staying in reactive mode, responding to requests from others all day long without stopping to think about their top priorities and how not to let them be sidelined by everyone else's priorities. And even when only focusing on their own priorities, many with ADD find it difficult to order them to align with core values and long-term goals. When everything seems important, then nothing is treated as truly important.

In Jim's case, as for many others like him, he raced through his days at top speed, responding to events as they occurred. Which meant that important, but not urgent, priorities in his life, such as exercise and healthy eating, were sorely missing from his busy life. His weight had been creeping up. "What exactly am I supposed to give up to fit in exercise?

And how am I supposed to find time to eat healthy meals when I can barely manage to grab a fast-food lunch during the day at work? And what about when I travel?"

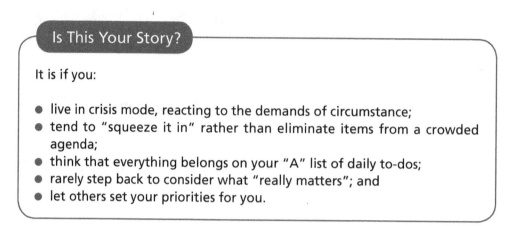

Is This Your Story?

It is if you:

- live in crisis mode, reacting to the demands of circumstance;
- tend to "squeeze it in" rather than eliminate items from a crowded agenda;
- think that everything belongs on your "A" list of daily to-dos;
- rarely step back to consider what "really matters"; and
- let others set your priorities for you.

Too Busy to Prioritize

Instead of planning and prioritizing, Jim had always coped with overload by working at warp speed, neglecting his personal health and giving up much-needed sleep whenever he was in a crunch. His doctor insisted that he make regular exercise and good nutrition a priority. "Prioritize?" Jim asked. "How do you do that? It's *all* important! I've got a job to do, kids to raise, a house to maintain, a wife, a family." Now, for the first time, his old ways of coping couldn't work. In fact, they were a big part of the problem. Instead of racing and juggling, he needed to learn to prioritize—not so easy, and even more of a struggle when you have ADD.

The Challenge of Prioritizing

It is only when we take stock that we can prioritize, asking ourselves, "Is this really necessary?" "If I'm going to take this on, what am I going to give up?" "Am I really living my life according to my deepest values, or just reacting to whatever pops up?"

Prioritizing is difficult for everyone, especially in the fast-paced life that so many adults lead today, bombarded with choices and burdened with high-pressure jobs in addition to the responsibilities of home and family. When ADD is added to the mix, prioritizing often goes out the window in favor of rapid reaction—reacting to demands as they hit you, without deciding whether they are your top priority. Rarely, in a jam-packed day, does an adult with ADD take time to realistically assess what can be accomplished and then prioritize, asking, "If I can only accomplish three tasks on my list, which three should I choose?" Often, top-priority items may be the least likely to be chosen, while many less important things are placed first.

Faulty prioritizing patterns

Instead of prioritizing "first things first," many people make choices according to other rules:

- **Whatever's on top.** Paper shuffling.
- **Whatever is the easiest.** Easy does it.
- **Knock-knock.** Responding to whomever asks me first.
- **False progress.** The more I can check off my list the more productive I feel.
- **Proximity.** Might as well do it while I'm passing by.
- ***You* decide.** I don't want the responsibility.
- **Conflict avoidance.** If you yell loudly about something, it'll go to the top of my list.
- **Whatever I'm in the mood for.** I'll do it if I feel like it.
- **Save the worst for last.** Anything but that!
- **Go with the flow.** Doing whatever the others do.
- **Habit.** Just doing the usual.

All of these ways of "prioritizing" aren't really prioritizing at all. In fact, they are ways to avoid prioritizing, letting habit, circumstance, or the priorities of others determine how you spend your time. Adults with ADD who "prioritize" according to these rules often find that they've never met many of their life's goals.

They're All on My A List!

Then there are those who put *everything* on their A list. Instead of passively letting people or circumstances decide their priorities for them, they frantically try to take charge of their lives.

Anne was an A-list prioritizer. She had so many top priorities that they all interfered with one another. Her aging mother had recently moved to the area to be near Anne. "I want to spend time with my mother. Who knows how many good years she has left?" Anne's son and daughter were both in high school. She tried hard to be at all of their sports events and to work with them nightly on homework. Exercise and nutrition were high on Anne's list. She had a running partner and worked hard to fit in a morning run on weekdays. Anne had a background as an urban planner, and currently was engaged in contract work with a local urban planning consultation group. The demands of her work varied, but could be quite intense at times. Anne's marriage was another top priority. The marriage had become increasingly strained as both she and her husband were overcommitted and chronically stressed. They had entered couples counseling to improve their communication patterns and to work on making their marriage a priority in their busy lives. Anne's efforts to reduce stress and to get in touch with what's really important in life had led her to join a women's spirituality group at her church—a group that met weekly.

The harder Anne tried to make everyone and everything in her life a top priority, the less she succeeded. Unable to set priorities and set limits, the end result was that everyone in her life felt short-changed while Anne raced in frantic circles, never sure what commitments should take precedence. The A-list approach to prioritizing leads to failure because, if *everything* is important, then nothing is treated with importance.

LEVEL ONE SOLUTIONS: WAYS TO HELP YOURSELF

Take Time for Daily Quiet Reflection and Prioritization

When the pressure is on, ADD impulsivity often leads people to dive in and work as fast as they can instead of stepping back to look at the big picture. Instead of prioritizing, you're just putting out fires. Instead of hitting the ground running, as Jim described his mornings, try a different approach. Get up 15 minutes early, make yourself a cup of coffee or tea, and go to a quiet place in your home to think and prioritize.

Think about your day not just in terms of the actions you must take immediately, but also in terms of your long-term goals. Set the day's priorities accordingly. And remember, reprioritize every day because priorities can turn on a dime when circumstances change.

Slow the Flood to a Trickle

Too often, today, we are bombarded from all sides—by choices, by opportunities, by responsibilities, and by information. Consciously choose to limit your exposure to this bombardment from advertisers, the Internet, radios, televisions, and social media. Mark out time on your calendar to do "nothing." The fewer the choices and the fewer the demands upon us, the easier it becomes to prioritize.

Rotate Your Priorities

Adults with ADD often have a broad range of interests, and often attempt to pack too many of those interests and activities into each day. Instead of giving up an interest, think instead of "rotating" them. For example, Joan developed better focus and balance in her life by rotating her activities according to the season. In winter months, Joan focused on indoor activities—reading, cooking, and playing the piano. She attended more cultural events during the cold months, enjoying season tickets at a local theater and attending movies or concerts. In the spring, she rotated her priorities to gardening and bike riding. In the heat of the summer months, she spent her leisure time traveling or relaxing on her deck. Then, as cooler weather came in the fall, she returned to more active pursuits. Her friends often asked her how she could "do it all"—cooking, reading, attending cultural events, gardening, playing the piano, riding her bike, and traveling to exotic destinations. Her secret? She didn't do it *all at once.*

Move from an Endless A List to a Top Five List

Warren Buffet is said to have advised a close friend to prioritize by carefully listing his top 25 most important tasks. He then asked him to circle the top five among those 25. Finally, he instructed his friend to completely write off the 20 tasks he didn't circle until he had *completed* his top five tasks. This approach keeps things simple and is the perfect antidote to the "everything is important" approach to not prioritizing.

Complete It or "Kill" It

Another prioritizing guru advised his clients to "Complete it or kill it." In other words, don't clutter your world with partially completed tasks. Give yourself permission to change your mind and move on if you haven't completed a particular task after a reasonable period of time. Set your time limit—a week, a month, a year—depending upon the importance of the task. Then, if it's not done, wipe it off your list and focus on what your top priorities are *now*. Don't keep dragging the past into the future.

Use the "Eisenhower Method"

President Dwight Eisenhower was known to use a very simple but effective way to prioritize his many tasks. He divided them into:

1. Important and urgent—do now.
2. Important and nonurgent—do later.
3. Unimportant, but urgent—delegate to others.
4. Unimportant and nonurgent—don't do at all!

This Eisenhower Method can be used in conjunction with Todoist (todoist.com), a free prioritizing program with an inexpensive upgrade that many recommend. In Todoist, as you create tasks, you place them in today's task list or schedule them for later. If you combine this process with the Eisenhower approach, you would place the "important/urgent" tasks on your today list and important nonurgent on later days, and would not put *anywhere* on your list tasks that you deem "unimportant."

Can't See the Forest for the Trees and Drowning in To-dos

Often it's not so easy to determine what's "important" and "not important." There are many shades of gray. The app Prioritize me! (available in the App Store) may be the answer to your prayers. Create a to-do list and then hit the "prioritize" button. The app will put you through a series of forced choices between two tasks on your list until you've compared every task to every other task on your list. In this way, you only have to answer the question "Which is more important?" between two tasks displayed on the screen. This simple selection process finally results in a list of most important to least important based on your series of comparisons.

Make Sure You're Not Using Your Packed Schedule to Self-Medicate

When we're always in a state of rushing, racing from one task to the next, feeling almost breathless, our adrenaline levels are high. Many people with ADD keep the demands at a high level to keep the adrenaline rush going. Without realizing it, they are self-medicating for ADD. Adrenaline is what's produced when we're in "fight or flight" mode. And adrenaline is a naturally occurring neurochemical that is produced to help us function better in a crisis. Ask yourself whether you're keeping yourself in a crisis state because you're afraid, if things slowed down, that you would lose motivation altogether. If all of your minutes are "the last minute," then you're treating your ADD by becoming an "adrenaline junky." Instead, consider talking to a professional about taking stimulant medication for ADD (or increasing your dose if you're still relying on adrenaline despite taking stimulants.) Staying in a state of high alert may feel exciting, but over the long term it's very destructive for your health.

The Neglected Four

Time management experts find that, of all high-priority activities, four are most neglected: socializing, doing paperwork, reading, and exercising. These activities are neglected because they place no clear, active demand on us for our attention and time. In a packed schedule, you are more likely to respond to things that *must* be done today, or things that call your attention: dinner must be served, children demand your attention. Meanwhile, your paperwork, book, and treadmill sit quietly by, and friends who don't keep calling you go neglected. Ultimately, you pay a high price for this neglect.

One: Socializing

You're more likely to stay in touch with friends if you can see them at regularly scheduled events that don't require planning and initiation on your part. It's the planning that's hard when you have ADD. If all you need to do is show up, you'll enjoy more contact with people. Clubs, book groups, support groups, and school activities all fit the bill. And don't get caught up in "shoulds" such as "I should entertain more." If cleaning your house and planning a meal feel overwhelming, don't let that stand in the way of spending time with friends. Think about building social contact into the events of your daily life. For example, see if a friend is going to soccer practice on the same day you are. That will give you time to catch up while you're watching your children on the field.

Two: Doing Paperwork

Financial and Personal Paperwork

Paperwork can get done more quickly and efficiently if you designate a particular time for paperwork each week and build it into your schedule. You'd be surprised how little time paperwork can take (filing important papers, paying bills, filling out forms) if you do it on a weekly basis. And you can reduce your paperwork enormously by going paperless. Most companies are happy to e-mail your bills and statements. That way you don't need to file them and can't lose them! And paying your bills online means that you don't have to find stamps, address envelopes, and remember to mail them. Balancing your checkbook online becomes a simple matter of checking your checkbook register against the digital bank register—the adding and subtracting is done for you. Go digital with your paperwork as much as possible and you'll find it's a much less onerous task!

> **Plan your paperwork slot for a time when you're not fatigued and you'll find it's much less onerous.**

School-related paperwork

Although some schools are getting on the digital bandwagon, many schools still send endless notices and forms home with children, meaning that there are endless possibilities for lost or misplaced papers.

- *Backpack Unpack*—Try building a habit with your child of unpacking the backpack together each evening before dinner. That way, you'll make sure there is no food spoiling in one of the pockets, and you'll be more likely to find all of the forms announcing school events and field trips. Then fill out forms or record the information on your calendar routinely on the day it arrives, before it gets a chance to get lost on the kitchen counter or dining room table.
- *Curating Your Child's Artwork*—Many mothers lament not knowing what to do with the river of artwork and desk work sheets arriving daily via their young children—each one of which is precious to their child. One way to manage the flood is to have a daily posting on a bulletin board of your child's terrific grade on the spelling test or his magnificent painting. In posting today's triumphs, you will automatically be removing yesterday's triumphs, to be stored in a large plastic container with a snap top. (Keep this container near the bulletin board for easy transfer each day.) This is a great teaching moment to model for children how normal it is to throw old things away to make way for new things. Every child is different, If you must, you can also discretely cull these papers periodically when your child is not around to protest.

Three: Reading

To read more, make it easier to read and more difficult to post on Facebook, answer e-mail, or whatever other activity interferes with reading. For example, remove the TV from your bedroom and never take your tablet to bed with you! You'll be more likely to read when you get into bed at night. Schedule regular times for reading professional journals, newsletters, and other materials necessary to keep you up-to-date for your job (and to control your stacks). Always keep reading material with you so that any waiting time can become reading time even if your primary way to read is digital.

Four: Exercising

We all need proper exercise to meet the demands of everyday life. It reduces stress, increases mental clarity, and generally keeps us fit. Regular exercise is a critical part of ADD management, helping to reduce stress and feelings of restlessness. Regular exercise is difficult to maintain—but it's more likely to happen if it is part of your daily pattern plan. Walking is the simplest form of exercise to build into your day. Bring your lunch and walk during lunch, eat outdoors, and walk back to work. Take the stairs. Get a dog, and you'll automatically need to walk twice a day! Some people report that getting a Fit Bit or Jawbone Up helps to keep them on track with their exercising goals. These wearable motion trackers can keep track of your steps during the day, encouraging more daily walking.

Combine your neglected four to maximize your use of time

- No time to socialize? No time to exercise? Think about inviting a friend to be your walking buddy or to sign up for a yoga or exercise class with you.
- No time to read? No time to exercise? You can combine reading and exercise by reading on your tablet or listening to a downloaded audio book on your smartphone while using an exercise bike or treadmill. And the exercise time will speed by quickly when you're engrossed in your favorite book.
- Want to combine reading, exercising, and socializing? Consider joining a book group, then read your book-group book while exercising!

Socializing, doing paperwork, reading, and exercising are appointments you make with yourself. And these activities can support one another. For example, exercise with a friend or join a book group to support regular reading. Paperwork is a different matter. It's hard to turn that into a social event, but it's easy to minimize it by going digital.

LEVEL TWO SOLUTIONS: HELP FROM FRIENDS AND FAMILY

Support Groups to Help You Set and Maintain Priorities

Anne was on the right track when she joined the women's support group at her church. On some level, despite her overcommitted schedule, she was aware that she needed to get back in touch with the things that matter most in life. A support group can provide you with *structure* through its regularity and with *support* from group members as you work to achieve more balance in your life.

Examine Your Priorities with a Trusted Friend or Family Member

When you feel stuck, unable to prioritize, conflicted by your commitments, you may gain a better perspective by talking things out with a trusted friend or family member. Karl had always made community involvement a high priority in his life, serving on the local PTO, coaching his children's sports teams, and serving on the board of his community organization. As his family grew, he and his wife decided to remodel and expand their home rather than move out of the community where they had developed such strong roots. As the remodeling plan got underway, however, Karl's stress levels rose and he felt that his priorities were increasingly conflicted.

After several conversations with his wife, his priorities became clearer. A larger, more comfortable home would significantly improve the quality of life that he and his family would enjoy. The children would have a recreation room of their own, a place where they could enjoy socializing with friends. He and his wife would have a quiet refuge in a new master bedroom suite. But, for the moment, his commitments to the community organization and the PTO would have to take a lower priority so that the remodeling project could move to the top.

Help with the Neglected Four

A Time Tutor can help you develop a daily plan that includes time for these neglected four. Instead of waiting to *find* time for them, you and your Time Tutor can *make* time for them by placing them in your week's schedule.

Your Time Tutor can help you identify patterns in your day that waste valuable time that would be much better spent on the neglected four.

LEVEL THREE SOLUTIONS: HELP FROM PROFESSIONALS

Get in Touch with Basic Values

If you're like Anne, daily moments for quiet reflection may not help you set priorities. You have too many A-list priorities to comfortably fit all of them into any single day. When this is the case, you may need to gain perspective by talking with a therapist, taking a look at unrealistic expectations of yourself (and others' expectations of you) and your inability to set priorities. Anne, like the "old woman who lived in a shoe," had so many priorities she didn't know what to do.

A therapist can help you better understand what drives you in your efforts to be all things to all people, or to be accomplished at all things. Setting priorities doesn't mean saying "yes" to everything. By its very nature, prioritizing is a process of deciding what is more important than other things in your life, a process of achieving balance in your life.

Prioritizing with a PO or ADD Coach

A PO, Organizer-Coach, or ADD coach can help you assess the practicalities of your priorities. By assisting you in making more realistic time assessments and creating workable plans for your day, your priorities will be more likely to fall into place. A coach or PO can help you stay in touch with doing "first things first," instead of simply reacting to whatever life throws at you during the day.

> ### Review
>
> - Don't let people and events prioritize for you.
> - Not everything can be on your A list. Cut things down to your top five.
> - Use the Eisenhower Method to eliminate, delegate, and focus.

- Take time for daily reflection.
- Learn to make time, don't wait to "find" time.
- Link neglected but important activities so that they support each other.
- Rotate your priorities.
- Gain perspective through explorations with others.
- Work with a therapist to examine basic values and unrealistic expectations.
- Work with a PO or ADD coach to stay focused on doing "first things first."

Chapter 8

Out of Sight, Out of Mind (OosOom)

Remembering to Remember

On Edgar's couch is perched a slightly precarious stack of empty picture frames. "I plan to go to the do-it-yourself frame store soon and spend the day framing my posters and photographs," Edgar explains. The chair near the front door holds several shipping boxes. "I need to return those items I ordered online," he comments with a sigh. Edgar's dining room table serves as his household finance center, complete with heaps of bills to pay, piles of investment material to review, and bunches of bank statements. Out in full view is a lamp to rewire, a chair to recane, and a weed whacker to unsnarl. A power tool sits at the end of the kitchen counter, and his large toolbox has been living in his bedroom for some time because he's been meaning to mount the shelves he ordered several months ago.

Out of Sight, Out of Mind—Creating Clutter with Visual Reminders

Like many adults with ADD, Edgar is an "OosOom"—out of sight, out of mind person. Edgar does what he can see, and does not do what he cannot see. So if Edgar wants to be certain that the books get returned to the library and that the greetings cards go out on time, he must have them out in front of him. He leaves the items he ordered online that he needs to return, the framing project, and even bill paying chores in full view as daily visual reminders of tasks to perform. Without his things as prompts and cues, Edgar would simply not remember to do what he needs to do.

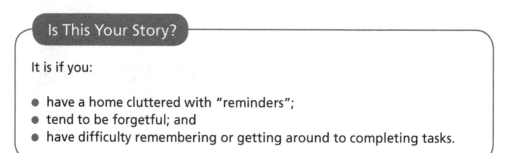

Is This Your Story?

It is if you:

- have a home cluttered with "reminders";
- tend to be forgetful; and
- have difficulty remembering or getting around to completing tasks.

Edgar does not prefer that his home look cluttered. He'd rather put the broken things out of sight and the papers in files so that he can entertain his friends in comfort and style. But he's afraid, and rightly so, that he'll simply forget to pay his bills or fix his lamp if the visual cues are gone. "The thought of putting things in the closet or storage shed fills me with fear," he admits. One problem is that Edgar's visual reminders lose their impact over time. The toolbox in his bedroom no longer serves as a reminder. It has become part of the landscape rather than a reminder to install the shelving he bought months ago.

Why Are So Many People with ADD OosOoms?

Many people with ADD have a problem with working memory, that is, keeping things in mind in order to complete a task. Working memory is another all-important executive function. One of the typical symptoms of ADD is forgetfulness, another term for poor working memory. You need good working memory to remember to drop off the dry cleaning and put gas in the car on your way to work. People with poor working memory may remind themselves of these tasks as they head out the door, but 20 minutes later they find that they have driven right past the dry cleaner's and the gas station without stopping because their minds are on something else. They are OosOoms (out of sight is out of mind) and without a reminder of what they need to do, they often forget.

Frequent Causes of Forgetting

- **Hyperfocus**—While hyperfocus can bring great energy to the task at hand, your working memory pays a price. Your attention is entirely focused on what you *are* doing, leaving no attention to remembering an intended future action—such as putting the laundry in the dryer.
- **Distractibility**—For others with ADD, distractibility, rather than hyperfocus, is the culprit. When you are bombarded by immediate distractions—a phone call, a shop window, a chance encounter with a friend—you may be prone to forget an intended task.
- **Tasks that are time-sensitive**—Those tasks that must be completed in a specific sequence (on your way home from work) or at a specific time (call home at 4 p.m.) are most vulnerable to being forgotten because the window of time during which we must remember them is very small. Other future tasks are more forgiving. If you forget to water your plants or to put the laundry in the dryer, you can do it later that day, even tomorrow, with little ill effect.

LEVEL ONE SOLUTIONS: WAYS TO HELP YOURSELF

Short-Term Clutter Is OK

Leaving things out as a visual reminder in a manner that creates hard-to-ignore clutter can be very effective, if you respond to the reminder right away: for example, putting a chair blocking the door from which you exit the house in the morning, and placing critical items you don't want to forget on that chair. Of course, return the chair to its normal place after picking up the critical items. Another short-term intentional clutter approach would be to place your laundry basket right in the middle of the hallway to remind yourself that you are in the midst of doing your laundry and need to move a load from the washer to the dryer.

Make Immediate Corrections

One key habit to getting your life in better order is to immediately self-correct when you realize you've forgotten a task. Instead of saying, "Oh no! I'll do it tomorrow," whenever possible immediately turn back and complete the undone task. Otherwise, you are inviting repeated forgetting. And once we've forgotten a task repeatedly, even the reminders tend to become part of the background and don't catch your attention.

Pull Yourself out of Hyperfocus

If you need to do a critical time-sensitive task, but you're starting a hyperfocus task, you'll need to arrange for an impossible-to-ignore reminder that will pull you out of hyperfocus. Some people with ADD are so prone to hyperfocus that they use an app to preprogram their computer to shut down at the predetermined time so that they will be sure to remember to move on. If you are not so deep in hyperfocus, you might also try scheduling an alarm on your smartphone to pull you out of hyperfocus or to remember to return to a time-sensitive task.

Contain Yourself! The Art of Orderly Clutter

Most adults with ADD need some type of "cue" to remember to perform the task, and a visual cue is a permanent cue that continues to remind you as long as it can be seen. Keeping everything in sight in stacks and piles is a form of visual cueing. The problem is that such visual cueing can lead to clutter and chaos.

Instead of cluttering your environment with visual cues, contain yourself. When you view your things, it directly "tickles" your memory to take action. The trick is to make things visible and visually appealing at the same time. Open baskets, clear shoeboxes, acrylic bins, see-through plastic drawers, even large plastic food storage bags are great in-sight in-mind tools. Put everything you possibly can in clear containers that reveal the contents but are attractive to look at.

Make a One-Cue Rule

The best visual cue in the world won't be of use if you keep looking at it and walking right past, telling yourself you'll do it later. Eventually, an ignored visual cue becomes part of the background and won't cue you at all. So be honest with yourself about your forgetfulness and develop the one-cue rule of doing a task the moment you are cued to do it, if at all possible.

Create a "Take-Me-with-You" Basket for Your House

Next to Edgar's daily exit door is placed a large, open, flat woven basket. It looks great. Inside are things that need to go to and from the house to the car and destinations beyond. Clothes to drop off at the cleaner's, store returns, and stuff to go to Edgar's office are in the basket. He just scoops the stuff up on his way out the door.

Create an Errand Box for Your Car

The clutter of things in your home often represents incomplete tasks and projects that you do not want to forget to complete. Much of this clutter is actually in transition to the car.

Your errand box is an open plastic crate on the *front* seat of your car that contains all of the visual reminders for the day's errands. Move your items from the take-me-with-you basket to your errand box as you move from house to car.

For instance, if you're an OosOom and you toss a book to return to the library in the back seat of your car, you can easily forget about it. But if you toss the library book in your errand box on the front seat, you'll have a clear visual reminder to go to the library. This errand box has the added advantage of having the books handy right in the car with you when your prospective memory kicks in and you suddenly remember to go to the library; obviously, you don't want the clutter of your house to simply migrate to your car. A full errand box is your cue to run errands.

Make Stubby To-Do Lists

A to-do list is another visual reminder. If you find that to-do lists haven't worked well for you in the past, try developing the daily habit of making a "stubby to-do list." A stubby to-do list is bold and big and hard to ignore. It is also very short, with no more than five items on it. Too often, people make long, unwieldy to-do lists in their planner, or worse yet on a slip of paper they stuff in their pocket or purse. On a long list, items become lost in the shuffle and lose their sense of priority.

How to Make a Stubby To-Do List

1. Purchase brightly colored sticky notes—that are lined and large enough to write five to-do items in large print using a felt-tip pen.
2. Write no more than five to-do items on the paper in lettering about a half inch high.

3. Write only to-do items that you intend to do *today.*
4. Choose a single place to keep this list—try sticking it to an item that you keep with you at all times—like your purse, briefcase, iPad, or smartphone.
5. Make a new stubby to-do list each evening. Keep the felt-tip pen and sticky note pad in a convenient place so that you can add items during the evening as you think of them.
6. Transfer any undone items from today's list onto tomorrow's, but keep it to a maximum of five items.
7. If you find that most days you transfer items over to tomorrow's list—that's a clear indication that your list is too long.
8. Set a goal of shortening your list until it's realistic to complete it on most days.

Edgar's stubby to-do list looks like this:

☐ *Buy* basket for front door
☐ *Return* library books
☐ *Pay* bills today!
☐ *Get* oil change
☐ *Send* birthday card to Mary

Your stubby to-do list will be most effective if you write your to-dos in order. For example, if Edgar plans to mail the card in the morning, that should be moved to the top of his list. If bill paying takes place at home in the evening, it should go last on the list.

> **Start each item on your to-do list with a verb—an *action* to get you going.**

Develop Habits

Habits, by definition, are a memory enhancement tool because when something is habitual it requires less of our memory. A habit is something we do almost without thought. A bus driver, for example, is extremely unlikely to drive past a bus stop, because he has a very ingrained habit of stopping there. You, on the other hand, forget to stop at the post office or library because it's not a daily habit.

You may protest, "I've never developed a habit in my life!" Whether you're aware of it or not, you have many daily habits—the habit of hitting your snooze alarm several times before getting up, for example, or the habit of tossing your coat on the chair instead of hanging it in the closet. You develop these habits because they're easy; they're compatible with immediate needs.

In developing new habits, try to use the same concept. Habits will develop more easily if they are designed to be compatible with your body clock and with your lifestyle. For example, if you are typically very tired in the evening, try to develop a bill paying habit that takes this into account. Pay your bills in the morning, on the first and third Saturdays of each month. (See Chapter 3 for more on ADD-friendly habit development.)

Daily, weekly, and monthly habits are useful and reduce the forgetful factor in life maintenance.

Daily habits might include:

- a morning routine;
- a routine for daily errands;
- a meal-preparation and cleanup routine;
- a routine to prepare for the following day;
- a bedtime routine;
- a routine to make a to-do list for the next day.

Weekly habits might include:

- a laundry routine;
- a routine for watering houseplants;
- a house-cleaning routine;
- a food-shopping routine;
- car maintenance;
- a routine to process paperwork;
- a routine to create a weekly task list.

Monthly habits might include:

- bill paying (monthly or bimonthly);
- changing the furnace filter;
- balancing the checkbook;
- making a monthly goal list.

Reduce the Stress Level in Your Life

Forgetfulness tends to increase in direct proportion to your stress level. In fact, some adults with ADD have learned to use their frequency of forgetting as a quick and easy sign of too much stress. Misplacing your keys, forgetting your doctor's appointment, rushing from here to there, forgetting to bring what you need—these patterns all intensify with stress. The good news is that lowering your stress level can reduce these same ADD patterns. Some stressors are outside your control, but often ADD stress is self-induced, the result of trying to cram too many commitments into too little time. Slow down the pace of your day, subtract commitments and complications, and you may be surprised at how much more you remember.

LEVEL TWO SOLUTIONS: HELP FROM FRIENDS AND FAMILY

ADD-Friendly Family Reminders

Families in which one or more members have ADD function best with family structure and support. Group activities are much easier to remember than solo activities. For example, if the whole family is working to develop a better morning or evening routine, then family members can remind one another to stay on track.

Likewise, weekly and monthly routines can become family routines. Bill paying may go more smoothly if you and your partner work on bill paying together at a designated time every two weeks. That same time can become an opportunity for routine discussions of budgets and spending priorities.

Develop the stubby to-do list habit as a family. For example, each family member could have a different brightly colored sticky note pad, all kept in the same place, somewhere very visible and hard to miss—a bulletin board on the front of the refrigerator or on the table next to the kitchen phone. That way, family members can also write on each other's

lists. For example, if your son needs you to purchase something for him the next day, he can write that on your list. A Web-based family calendar can also serve this purpose and has the added advantage of being accessible from any device at any time. Your Tech Tamer, a friend or family member good at technology, can be a big help here. Your Tech Tamer can help you research a Web-based calendar and, in one or two lessons, teach your whole family how to use it.

In recognition of ADD forgetfulness, create a family motto:

> **If you haven't written it down, you haven't told me!**

That trains all family members to operate in a more ADD-friendly way, a way that helps all of you to remember.

Create Task-Completion Occasions

Edgar's home is cluttered because he leaves reminders for himself all over the house. The broken lamp reminds him to make the repair. The picture frames remind him to do framing. And so on. But if Edgar had an *automatic* way to remember to take action, he would not need to clutter his environment with *things* to jog his memory. One way to automatically deal with your chores and tasks and actions is to create task-completion occasions.

When you create task-completion occasions, the occasion—and not the visible stack or pile or clutter—is the reminder. This method is simple, but since it involves marrying thing organizing to time organizing, you'd better use your Time Tutor to help you. Here's how task-completion occasions work:

1. Get your calendar or day planner. It doesn't matter whether your calendar is hardcopy or digital.
2. Now, walk around your house with your Time Tutor.
3. When you come upon a stack of clutter, open the calendar to the nearest holiday or other occasion, and assign a specific task to that day.

For example, Edgar and Jeff, his Time Tutor, came upon his dining room table heaped with tax-related papers. The next holiday or occasion on his calendar was Valentine's Day, so Valentine's Day was designated "tax day" on Edgar's calendar. They next came upon a huge stack of photographs. Edgar renamed President's Day "photo day" and assigned himself the organizing chore of going through his photographs. St. Patrick's Day was designated as "framing day"—the day on which Edgar would take the prints and photographs he'd collected and purchase frames for them.

Jeff was especially good at finding just the right occasion to convert into a task-completion occasion. "Father's Day is not a good time to organize tax papers, since the filing date for taxes will have passed. On Memorial Day all the stores are open, so it's a great day to bring things in for repair. On President's Day the stores are closed—a perfect time to go through photographs," Jeff explains.

Edgar comments, "I like task-completion occasions because I don't have to rely on my memory to remember what chore I am doing when. It's all written on the calendar. I put all my stuff away because I don't need it out anymore to remind me. I'm bound to forget on President's Day where I stowed my box of photographs to organize, so I also added that information to the calendar. What a relief to have it all out of sight—but in mind!"

LEVEL THREE SOLUTIONS: HELP FROM PROFESSIONALS

The Home-as-Memory Method

You may need to use a professional organizer to help you with this method because, though easy to implement, it involves physically moving your things around, out of their usual location, which you might find disorienting if you have ADD. And it requires someone with good thing- and time-management skills.

The idea is to turn your entire home into a big memory bank. When you use the home-as-memory method, time is associated with the physical proximity of space. The things you need to remember soonest in time are put in the rooms of the house closest to the front door. The things you need to remember in the long term are put in the rear of the house. As the date for doing something with your long-term things approaches, you move the things closer to the front of the house.

Let's say the room closest to your front door is the living room. All items that you need to take action on go in the take-me-with-you basket near the living room door. For *really* critical items, such as a birthday gift to be delivered tomorrow, place the gift in the errand box on the front seat of your vehicle.

A back room can serve as your long-term memory. If it is only May but you don't want to forget to mail Christmas cards, put them in the long-term memory room. Move them to the short-term memory room as Christmas nears. Projects that have no particular deadline, like picture framing, or the making of your scrapbook, are better dealt with by assigning them a "task-completion occasion." Start them out in your long-term memory room, moving them to your short-term memory room shortly before their assigned task-completion occasion date.

More Serious Memory Difficulties

The memory aids discussed in this chapter are appropriate for standard ADD-related forgetfulness. However, there are other factors that may contribute to memory problems. If you are a female in your forties or older who experiences an increase in memory difficulties, you may want to discuss with your doctor the possibility that lowered estrogen levels have added to memory difficulties. If memory difficulties suddenly increase, or become progressively worse at any age, it's important to discuss such changes with your physician.

Identify Ways to Reduce Stress and Decrease Forgetfulness

If you've tried to reduce stress on your own, with limited success, it may be time to work with a professional who can help you do a comprehensive analysis of the stressors in your life, and work with you to find creative strategies for stress reduction. Many adults with ADD become so accustomed to high stress that they are blind to the ADD patterns that contribute to daily stress.

> ### Review
>
> - Acknowledge your out of sight, out of mind (OosOom) tendency.
> - Learn techniques to pull yourself out of hyperfocus.
> - Develop a do-it-as-soon-as-you-think-of-it approach.
> - Make a take-me-with-you and an errand box.
> - Make a stubby to-do list.
> - Create task-completion occasions.
> - Develop habits so that tasks don't get put off.
> - Work with a Time Tutor to schedule tasks.
> - Try the home-as-memory method with a professional organizer.
> - Work with a therapist or coach to reduce stress.

Organizing Things

Getting over Clutter Overwhelm

Jane's house has a double personality. In the front rooms of the house, where guests and friends visit, it is neat and well organized. But the rear rooms of the house, which nobody sees, are cluttered with things—all kinds of things. "I love to entertain and have people stay over, but I abandoned that idea years ago when the guest bedroom became a catchall for the overflow from my own bedroom," said Jane. The dresser in the guest bedroom is covered with perfume bottles, unmatched earrings, pens, small batteries, little ceramic figurines, and the ubiquitous loose change. The night tables overflow with magazines, tissue boxes, tape dispensers, and more loose change. The bed itself, though made up, is strewn with clothes. Clumps of shoes and handbags sit on the floor, together with an array of shopping and gift bags, some containing items to return to the store. Pictures to be framed are crowded under the bed. The closets are crammed and the dresser drawers overstuffed.

More than once, Jane has come to the door of this guest bedroom and opened it widely with a determined gusto, intending to organize the room. She sucks in her breath, gathers her courage, and takes a step in. Feeling anxious, first in the stomach and then in the head, a small panic races across Jane's mind as she struggles to find a place to begin. "Where should I start?" she asks herself. For a few moments Jane does nothing at all. Finally, she picks up a handbag from the floor, and then, feeling overwhelmed and ineffectual, she doubts herself and thinks, "Maybe I should begin over there instead."

Jane walks toward her bed, the handbag still dangling from her hand. Halfway across the room, she spies a tennis racket propped against the wall. Abandoning the handbag, Jane lifts the tennis racket and gives it a good swing. Still holding the racket, she turns slightly and the closet catches her eye. Jane approaches the closet and peers inside. As quickly as she has approached, she walks away, deciding it is a lost cause. Jane looks at her watch. It has been almost half an hour and she's accomplished nothing. She stands and surveys the cluttered room, racket still in hand.

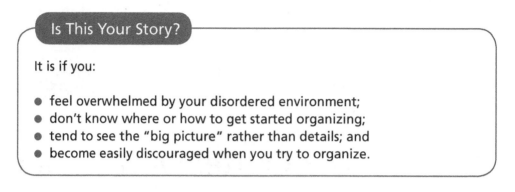

Is This Your Story?

It is if you:

- feel overwhelmed by your disordered environment;
- don't know where or how to get started organizing;
- tend to see the "big picture" rather than details; and
- become easily discouraged when you try to organize.

"I can't get started. The barrage of clutter is too much for me. No matter how hard I grit my teeth and say 'today is the day,' I move from one thing to another, accomplishing very little." Feeling dismayed and defeated, she closes the door in self-defense against too-much-stuff-all-at-once. Maybe tomorrow she'll get it organized. Jane is stuck in "clutter overwhelm."

Clutter Overwhelm and ADD

Jane's source of overwhelm is her cluttered environment. However, feeling overwhelmed can be triggered by other problems as well—for example, by having too many commitments and too little time to meet them; by a huge project with a looming deadline; or by having to juggle multiple tasks while being interrupted frequently. Adults with ADD often get stuck in "overwhelm" when the challenge facing them feels impossible to meet. This chapter will focus on dealing with overwhelming clutter, but many of the approaches that we suggest will also work for other kinds of overwhelm.

Clutter Results from Countless Incomplete Tasks

Clutter tends to accumulate, unnoticed, around an adult with ADD as he or she moves from one act to the next throughout the days—leaving the bedroom without hanging up clothing, leaving the kitchen without putting away the newspaper or placing breakfast dishes in the dishwasher, leaving papers on the desk rather than filing them. Clutter consists of the remains of incomplete tasks. One of the most common "incomplete tasks" in the lives of adults with ADD involves the acquisition of objects that are never given a "home" of their own. Individuals with ADD tend to bring things into their environment on a daily basis—mail, craft items, bargain and thrift store purchases—never taking the time to find an appropriate place to keep them, and rarely taking the time to discard those items that are "just passing through." Why do adults with ADD go through their lives leaving incomplete tasks in their wake?

Contributors to the Chaos

1. **Moving toward appealing activities while avoiding tedious tasks.** One woman with ADD described her clutter accumulation as the result of always rushing ahead to the next

interesting activity, unable to slow down to complete the "boring" tasks of hanging things up or putting them away. "There's always something much more interesting that's calling to me."

2. **Acquiring objects without thought for giving them a "home."** Just as adults with ADD often make time commitments without considering whether they have the time to do them, they also make acquisition commitments without thinking of "Where will this go? Do I have room? What will I get rid of to make room?" Often these are impulse acquisitions. One woman with ADD was making her best effort to off-load duplicate or unnecessary items. She took these items to the basement laundry room in her condo where everyone left unwanted items. Unfortunately, each time she went there to off-load a few things, she inevitably found other items irresistible and took them up to her apartment. Her off-loading could never keep up with her impulsive acquiring.

3. **Constant state of lateness.** For others with ADD, clutter is the result of always rushing. Remember the Mad Hatter in *Alice in Wonderland*? "I'm late, I'm late, for a very important date. No time to say hello-goodbye, I'm late, I'm late, I'm late!" Many with ADD rush out the door late in the morning, never leaving time to make beds, hang up clothes, wash breakfast dishes, or clear up clutter.

As clutter accumulates, overwhelm follows. And feelings of overwhelm often lead to avoidance. An adult with ADD may fall into a pattern of staying late at the office, sticking earbuds in their ears and watching videos, or endlessly engaging in online shopping in order to block out the growing sense of overwhelm. A vicious cycle is created in which overwhelming clutter leads to avoidance and neglect, which only increase feelings of overwhelm.

ADD Challenges That Get in the Way of Decluttering

We've talked about ADD traits that lead to the accumulation of clutter, but there are other traits that make it challenging to declutter, once the clutter has accumulated. One difficulty lies in staying focused on the organizing activity rather than reacting to more immediate, more engaging stimuli encountered during the decluttering process, like a letter or photograph, long forgotten, now rediscovered in the effort to organize a shelf or closet, or a text or call while sorting through heaps of papers. The ADD brain is wired to react—to impulses, moods, people, or events. To be able to remain focused on organizing, an adult with ADD needs to develop strategies to maintain their focus, such as "sprinting to the finish line," using a Body Double, or turning it into a challenging game (all ADD-friendly strategies introduced in Chapter 2). Another ADD challenge that makes it difficult to organize clutter is difficulty with decision-making. Should I keep it or pass it? If I keep it, where should I put it? (See Chapter 5 on decision dilemmas.)

Learn to Maintain the "Right" Level of Focus

It's important, but challenging, to maintain the "right" level of focus while engaged in an organizing task. Adults with ADD can tell many tales of taking the "ant's view" (micro-focus), concentrating on a single organizing or cleaning activity while the rest of their world is falling apart. Often this micro-focusing results from a need to reduce feelings of overwhelm. Jane can manage to focus on one particular item, but when she looks at the whole mess she feels overwhelmed.

One woman, whose initial goal was simply to box up the contents of her desk in preparation for relocation to another floor in the office building, found herself rereading each document in her To Shred box and feeding them one by one into the shredder. Meanwhile, the new occupant of her office had to wait hours to settle in. Needless to say, shredding wasn't the most productive use of her time, or the highest-priority item on her chore list.

Others with ADD are comfortable only with the big-picture approach to organizing— a macro-focus. Big-picture people with ADD might say, "It's obvious that we need to clean this place up, get rid of half the stuff in the house and clear out the garage." They can see the big picture, but when it's time to get started, when specific decisions must be made, they feel lost. "Where do I begin? How do I decide what to keep, what to throw away? Should I start in the garage or the kitchen?"

Different Levels of Focus Are Appropriate for Different Problems or Goals

Macro-focus

In macro-focus, a focus on the big picture, the greatest effect is achieved in the shortest time. A super macro-focus might mean simply stuffing misplaced items from each room into large garbage bags, labeling them "living room," "family room," or "kitchen," for later reference, and dragging these bags to the garage. If you've got company coming in an hour, you need a super macro-focus.

In a slightly more in-depth approach, but still focused on the big picture, you might go around the house gathering misplaced items in a laundry basket. Then, like a clerk reshelving items in a grocery store, you return those items to the room, shelf, or drawer in which they belong. You might choose to have a box in each room where you can place items that belong in that room but don't yet have a "home."

Detail Focus

In detail focus, you would work on a single room, or even a single area within a room. Detail focus involves placing every item within that area where it belongs, creating "homes" for items that don't yet have a designated place. Your goal, in detail focus, is "a place for everything, and everything in its place." This detail focus also involves gathering items in

separate containers for "reshelving" in other parts of the house, as well as for throw-away, give-away, and long-term storage. At the detail-focus level, sorting and organizing are happening. This level of focus is appropriate once you've gotten your home to a "livable" level in macro-focus. For these detail-focus activities, you are more likely to need the support of a Clutter Companion, a family member or friend who is good at dealing with "stuff."

Micro-focus

This kind of focus is super-detailed and rarely appropriate. An antique restorer works in micro-focus, carefully cleaning, repairing, and refinishing a valuable piece of furniture. An archivist works in micro-focus, reading each document in detail to determine its value and where it should be filed.

You need to take care that you don't leap into micro-focus as an escape from feelings of overwhelm in reaction to your cluttered environment. In micro-focus, you may escape into the Internet, browsing websites that advertise storage units, shelving, or varieties of file folders, telling yourself that you are being productive. Meanwhile, the items to store, file, or discard go untended. In micro-focus, you might start detailing your car when your task for the afternoon was to clear out the garage. In micro-focus, you might obsessively clean out the metal runner of a sliding glass door with a toothpick, while ignoring the mountain of dirty dishes in the sink.

Flexible Focus

The most useful mode is a flexible focus, where you can move from macro to detail focus, and back again, depending upon what is most appropriate.

LEVEL ONE SOLUTIONS: WAYS TO HELP YOURSELF

If you're like Jane, stuck in overwhelm, unable to get started on an organizing task, following are some ways that you can help yourself.

Think about the Level of Focus Appropriate for the Task

One of Jane's tasks is to organize the guest room closet. Unlike one of the common areas of the house, it's unlikely that there are items in the closet that belong in other rooms, so a macro-focus—gathering and "reshelving" items—won't help. Her task is a detail-focus task—sorting items into give-away, throw-away, stow-away and keep, making sure there's a "home" for each item that's "kept".

Develop the Habit of Breaking Things Down

Breaking things down means quite literally dicing up an organizing project into smaller parts. For example, instead of tackling an entire closet or room, divide it into parts, such as a dresser, a bed, one side of the room, or a closet shelf. Breaking a task down into parts adds *structure* to your task—one of those three ADD-friendly S's (*structure*, *support*, and *strategies*) that can help you to succeed.

Once the whole is broken up into smaller parts visually, it's easier to find a starting point physically. Concentrating on one part at a time and breaking things down counteracts the overwhelmed feelings experienced by so many people with ADD when they face a complex task. And it makes task initiation easier.

Breaking Things Down Exercise

Walk around your home. Open a closet. Notice the parts—shelves, a floor, and perhaps a rod for hanging clothes. You can organize a whole closet one shelf at a time, or do the things on the floor first and then the shelves. Now look at your desk—made up of a desktop and probably a few drawers. You can organize your desk by starting with only one part—the desktop, or even one drawer. Train yourself to see the parts that make up a whole.

Use a Spyglass

Jane first needed to see the parts of the whole in order to break things down. For that she used a "spyglass," a cardboard tube from a paper towel roll, to narrow her visual field. Jane put the spyglass to her eye and scanned the room. Using her spyglass, she could see only one segment of the room at a time, helping her break down her task into parts. She "spied" her dresser and decided to start there.

> **→ ADD-friendly strategy:**
> **Reduce distractions to maintain focus**

Sheet Sheathes

Then, Jane used another ADD-friendly technique—reducing visual distractions—in order to stay focused on her task. To eliminate distractions due to clutter in other areas of the room, Jane spread sheets over the bed and night tables, leaving only her dresser exposed. Focused only on the dresser, Jane set to work organizing it. Her efforts went well, but not perfectly. Two perfume bottles were discarded outright, but others were kept. Orphaned earrings had to be saved "just in case" the mate showed up, but most of the other jewelry was put back in the jewelry box. The loose change was rounded up and stashed in a nice pottery jar that remained on the dresser top. Pens, batteries, and other small objects were swooshed into the top drawer of the dresser. Once her dresser top was organized, Jane removed the sheets covering her night tables and focused on them.

"I suppose someone more organized would separate out the pens from the batteries and put each in a proper place," Jane remarked, "but this is the best I can do." The important thing is that Jane finished the task to her satisfaction, using ADD-friendly organizing approaches to help her succeed, breaking tasks down—in this case using the spyglass technique— and reducing visual distractions by using sheets to cover distracting clutter.

Get into an Organizing Mood

Jane was able to get in the mood to organize her dresser, but later her motivation waned. Jane, like other adults with ADD, has energy and motivation when she is "in the mood." When she's not in the mood, however, sorting and decluttering seem tedious and endless, and she is rarely successful in completing her task.

If you are like most adults with ADD, trying to force yourself to organize through guilt and self-criticism is rarely successful. Instead of barraging yourself with negative messages—

"I'm a slob . . . I should be ashamed of myself"—you'll be more successful if you try a more positive, ADD-friendly approach. What are some ways to get in the mood to organize?

Catch the Wave

Adults with ADD often get in the mood at unexpected times. You may find yourself sorting through stacks of loose CDs looking for the cover to a favorite CD, and suddenly you are going through your entire collection, putting CDs into cases, and cases back into the CD rack. Go with the flow, unless the consequences are negative—for example, don't let the impulse to order your CD collection make you late for an appointment or late to bed.

Get the Most Bang for Your Buck

Start with a task that will maximize your sense of progress. When your first impulse is to run and hide, instead choose an organizing task that will encourage you. Select the most noticeable area that will take the least time. You might even start with the macro-focus technique of sweeping clutter into garbage bags, just to get started. Then, with your main living areas less cluttered, you'll feel more encouraged to take on detail-focus tasks later.

Share the Pain

Members of one online ADD support group helped each other complete "odious tasks" by "meeting" online—declaring a goal—immediately tackling the "odious task," and then getting back online to joke, commiserate, and congratulate each other.

Make It More Fun

Play loud music that will energize you. Take "dance breaks" to keep your motivation up. Make it a group task. "I'll help you, if you'll help me." Group activities are usually more motivating than solitary ones.

Set up an Immediate Reward

Plan a fun activity that you'll do as soon as you finish your "odious task."

Be a "One-Minute Wonder"

Anyone can do most anything for one minute. When you find that you're feeling overwhelmed, dive in, literally, and see what you can accomplish in one minute. Perhaps you could take all the dirty dishes and cups to the sink from the family room. Or, you might gather magazines strewn across the coffee table and floor into one neat stack. Next time you walk into the room, do your "one minute wonder" routine again. Soon, you'll see the chaos receding. As you feel less overwhelmed, you may find that one minute can extend to five or ten before you get that "run and hide" feeling.

Getting Over Clutter Overwhelm

"Age" Your Clutter until It's "Ripe"

If reducing clutter is difficult because you're afraid to throw things away that you'll later regret, try "aging" your throw-aways. Sort your clutter into four categories:

1. give away (donate or gift);
2. throw away (recycle or trash);
3. stow away (age until ripe);
4. keep (in your prime real estate for regular use).

Recycle the obvious clutter. Donate or give away items that are useful, but that you clearly don't want. When you're not sure what to do, "age until ripe" by placing them in the stowaway container. It's a little like not tossing leftovers from your refrigerator until they're spoiled. Six months to one year later, during your next round of decluttering, return to the stowaway box or bag. It will probably be a much easier decision at that point to toss or donate items you haven't seen or used in months.

LEVEL TWO SOLUTIONS: HELP FROM FRIENDS AND FAMILY

Work with a Clutter Companion

After Jane organized her dresser, she arranged an organizing day with Peggy, her friend who lives next door. Jane often babysits for Peggy's two children. In return, Peggy periodically comes over to serve as Clutter Companion for Jane when she's feeling overwhelmed. Their decluttering routine has become a regular event, a couple of times a year, typically just before relatives are scheduled to visit.

How to Work with a Clutter Companion

A Clutter Companion is much more than just an extra pair of hands. A Clutter Companion provides structure that helps you maintain focus and support through companionship and encouragement. With a Clutter Companion by your side, taking a break won't stretch into procrastination and avoidance. However, unless your Clutter Companion is a fellow ADDer, it's important to explain your needs. Tell her, for example, "It's better if you don't interrupt me when I'm in the middle of a task." Or, "Remind me to take a break in half an hour. Usually, I just keep going until I'm exhausted, and end up leaving a huge pile in the middle of the floor." Or, "Don't let me hang on to everything. I really need to clear out the things I don't wear anymore."

Tackling the Job

Armed with empty trash bags, cold soda, and an oldies station on the radio, Jane and Peggy tackle organizing the rest of the guest room. Peggy is helpful, nonjudgmental, and doesn't try to force her own methods on Jane. She's an ideal Clutter Companion.

Keeping It Going

Jane gathered clean clothes strewn about the room and placed them on hangers in the closet, while Peggy plucked handbags, shoes, and other non-clothes, gathering them in a big stack. She waited for Jane to finish hanging up clothes so that she would not distract her. Then Peggy held up one shoe, handbag, or belt at a time and Jane announced, "Out," "Donate," or "Closet." When Peggy noticed that Jane was keeping most things in the "closet" pile, she reminded Jane of her packrat tendencies, asking, "Do you *really* need to hang on to this? I haven't seen you wear it in years!" Jane appreciated the reminder and humorously added a few more items to the "donate" pile.

Maintaining the Right Level of Focus

Working with Peggy helped Jane to maintain a flexible focus. Peggy asked questions such as, "Shouldn't you just get these piles off the floor [macro-focus] rather than cleaning out your old purses [micro-focus]?" Or, "Instead of rearranging the guest room furniture [macro-focus], didn't you want to get this closet organized [detail focus] first?"

Reaching the End

Peggy tossed the "outs" and "donates" into separate plastic bags and Jane put the closet articles away. If something belonged in another room, Jane threw it next to the guest room door for pick-up and delivery to other rooms. Jane did not stop to deliver the items right away. Her juices were really flowing and her energy practically wiped Peggy out. After clearing off the bed, they cleared the night tables, and then the floor, using the same process—dividing articles into "out," "donate," and "closet." Exhausted, but satisfied with what they'd accomplished, they toasted their success with cold sodas and called it a day.

"I knew that once I got started, I'd get a lot done!" Jane exclaimed.

LEVEL THREE SOLUTIONS: HELP FROM PROFESSIONALS

Working with a Professional Organizer

Getting over overwhelm is difficult. If you do not have a trusted friend as a Clutter Companion, organize with a professional organizer. A professional organizer knows that getting started is a big hurdle for people who feel overwhelmed. A professional organizer can recommend a place to get started, and their hands-on assistance can get you over the initial hump. Working with a professional organizer also mitigates your feeling overwhelmed by all the detail that is involved in getting organized. You'll take it one step at a time, at your own pace, until the job is done.

When Your Disorganization Goes beyond ADD

In addition to ADD, there are many other conditions that can cause difficulties in daily life management and organization. If you feel paralyzed and unable to act, even with assistance from coaches and organizers, this may be a symptom of chronic depression or anxiety that must be treated before you can take action. If your packrat tendencies are extreme, for example if you:

- find yourself irrationally attached to items, retrieving them from the trash after they've been discarded;
- tend to collect huge numbers of items that you can never realistically use;
- have accumulated piles of stuff to the point that it's difficult to walk through rooms;
- feel tremendous anxiety when you try to organize and declutter; or
- feel so demoralized that your clutter paralyzes you,

then issues other than ADD may be part of the picture, and may need psychological treatment before you can begin to organize your environment.

Review

- Use the level of focus (macro, detail, and micro) appropriate to the task.
- Break things down visually.
- Break things down physically.
- Reduce visual distractions.
- Get into an organizing mood:

    - catch the wave;
    - share the pain;
    - make it fun;
    - reward yourself;
    - be a one-minute wonder.

- Age your clutter in a stowaway container until it's "ripe."
- Work with a Clutter Companion.
- Work with a professional organizer.
- Consult a therapist when it's more than ADD.

Chapter 10

CHAOS

Can't Have Anyone Over Syndrome

In many chapters of this book, therapy or counseling is suggested only when other organizing approaches are not successful. In some cases, however, treatment for ADD needs to come first, before organizing approaches can be used constructively. This was true in Marge's case.

Marge laughingly describes herself as suffering from CHAOS (the Can't Have Anyone Over Syndrome). Jane's clutter, described in Chapter 9, was confined to the back rooms of her house, and could be described as "contained chaos"—pockets of chaos within a home that was otherwise in reasonable order. In Marge's case, there is nothing contained about her chaos. Every room is cluttered with shoes, articles of clothing, piles of newspapers and magazines, as well as plates and cups. Marge describes her second bedroom as a "private landfill." Her dining room table has not seen the light of day since the last time her parents visited from Florida some five years ago. Even then, her apartment was so chaotic that she "straightened up," with the help of her sister, by stuffing clutter into large garbage bags that were hauled to the bedroom at the last minute.

Routine cleaning in Marge's apartment is next to impossible because dusting and vacuuming require that the floor and other horizontal surfaces not be covered by clutter. Unopened mail is lost, resulting in unpaid bills, a poor credit rating, and late payment fees she can ill afford. At times, her phone or a utility is cut off, requiring her to take time from work to pay her overdue bill with a cashier's check so that service can be resumed.

Marge's chaos is too great to tackle alone, but before she can benefit from the services of a professional organizer, she needs to examine the pervasive patterns that create the chaos in her life. A friend suggested to Marge that she might have ADD. Although resistant to the idea at first, Marge read the book her friend loaned her and recognizes many ADD patterns in herself.

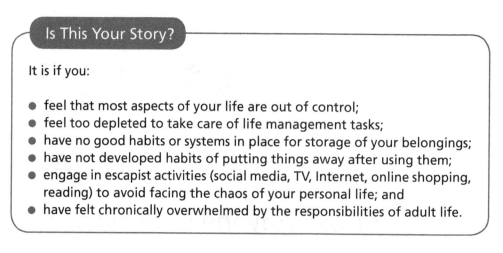

Is This Your Story?

It is if you:

- feel that most aspects of your life are out of control;
- feel too depleted to take care of life management tasks;
- have no good habits or systems in place for storage of your belongings;
- have not developed habits of putting things away after using them;
- engage in escapist activities (social media, TV, Internet, online shopping, reading) to avoid facing the chaos of your personal life; and
- have felt chronically overwhelmed by the responsibilities of adult life.

Marge scheduled a consultation with a psychologist who specializes in treating adults with ADD. After an extensive interview about her work history, school history, and family history, she was given a series of cognitive tests. As the psychologist reviewed her history and test results and explained that many patterns she demonstrates are typical for adults with ADD, Marge begins to understand the basis for some of her lifelong struggles. Forgetfulness, poor time management, disorganization, impulsive decision-making, poor sleep habits, and patterns of moodiness and anxiety have been present for years. Although very bright, Marge never earned grades in high school or college that were commensurate with her intelligence. Now, in her thirties, she has achieved some success in her career, but she has always had difficulties on the job—trouble with arriving on time in the morning, meeting deadlines, and keeping up with paperwork.

Marge began treatment for ADD—a combination of psychostimulant medication and regular weekly therapy sessions focused on helping her to understand and take charge of her ADD. She reviews patterns in her daily life with her therapist and discusses different strategies that might reduce or eliminate some of her daily struggles.

The Daily Cycle of ADD Disorganization

A chronic "night owl," Marge often stays up until 2 a.m. or later. In the morning, she hits the snooze button on her alarm repeatedly until she finally drags herself out of bed, arriving late every morning to work. Marge has fallen into a pattern of working late to compensate for her late arrival, not coming home until 8 p.m. or later. By that time, she is in no mood to wash dishes, answer e-mail, or pay bills. Ignoring the clutter, she falls onto the couch, microwaves a snack for dinner, and eats while playing Solitaire on the computer. Her evening progresses with phone calls, time spent on the Internet, and watching late-night TV. Finally Marge crawls into bed, reading until her eyelids begin to close in the early morning hours.

Because she rises late each morning and manages her time poorly, Marge always feels tired and in a rush. She rarely takes the time to workout anymore at the gym, or even wash the dishes. E-mail goes unopened for days, and though she'd love to watch videos of her little nieces on Facebook, she can't seem to find the time. Tasks are rushed and rarely completed, adding to the general disorder. The more chaotic her life becomes, the less she can deal with it. Her attitude becomes, "What's one more dirty dish or coffee cup? It will never be noticed in all the rest of the clutter."

Her therapist helps her prioritize the issues she needs to tackle. Once she knows where to begin, her feelings of being overwhelmed lessen. Marge begins to address these issues one at a time. Whenever the "overwhelm" returns, she and her therapist review her priority list. "First things first. One step at a time" becomes her mantra.

Increase Sleep to Reduce Chaos

Top priority is given to her chronic night-owl patterns that make it next to impossible for her to get up on time in the morning. Marge learns that ADD patterns become worse with sleep deprivation. Both ADD and sleep deprivation have a negative effect on the brain's frontal lobes, the part of the brain responsible for judgment, planning, and organization. When an individual with ADD has chronic sleep deprivation, life is almost guaranteed to spin out of control.

Though resistant at first, Marge begins to shift her sleep patterns, gradually working toward getting into bed by 11 p.m., then reading until she feels sleepy. Her therapist also recommended that she use a white noise machine from which she can select her favorite sound (rainfall, waves, etc.). She reports that falling asleep to white noise improves the quality of her sleep as she is more relaxed and not distracted by any other noises. As she falls asleep earlier, rising in the morning becomes easier. Her supervisor and coworkers are pleased and surprised as she begins to arrive at work on time, ready to begin the day.

Seasonal Affective Disorder

During the fall, as the days become shorter, Marge again begins to have more difficulty getting out of bed in the morning. Her therapist discusses the importance of light in regulating sleep patterns and mood. Many women with ADD also have another condition known as seasonal affective disorder (SAD) that causes them to have difficulty rising in the morning, to feel lethargic and depressed, and to overeat during the dark months of the year. SAD can often be treated very effectively by exposure to bright light in the morning. On her therapist's advice, Marge purchases an "artificial dawn" device that slowly brightens her bedroom every morning so that she wakes to a "sunny" day. To her surprise, she finds it much easier to get up in the morning, feeling more alert and energetic. In addition, the use of a high-intensity blue light as she gets ready for work also increases her energy and alertness.

Building Routines to Reduce Chaos

Once her sleep patterns are better regulated, Marge has more time and energy to devote to organizing other aspects of her life. She leaves work at 5:30 p.m., arriving home with the energy and motivation to prepare a simple, healthy evening meal. With her therapist's help, she develops routines for household maintenance and for essential tasks like checking e-mail. Even with nightly chores to complete, Marge finds she has time to check out Facebook, be in touch with friends, and still get to bed at a reasonable hour.

Can't Have Anyone Over Syndrome

Shifting Focus—from ADD Management to Organizing Strategies

Marge has been successful in developing daily routines that work, but her apartment is still cluttered, and her closets are precariously stuffed with belongings. She continues her last-minute cleanup routine of throwing everything into the bedroom and shutting the door when she has company.

With more control over her daily life, Marge feels ready to tackle the clutter. Marge's therapist suggests that she contact a professional organizer to help her rather than trying to take on this huge task alone. The professional organizer talks with Marge at length about common ADD patterns that lead to clutter and chaos such as keeping things in view as reminders, uncompleted tasks, and things not having a home which are covered in previous chapters. Marge's professional organizer is particularly helpful with developing home maintenance routines.

Marge's professional organizer has experience with adults with ADD. She knows that Marge can never declutter everything at one time. What Marge needs is a plan—for conquering the accumulated clutter, and for stopping clutter from this day forward. The latter part of the plan requires a few simple routines to curtail clutter creation at its source. Marge, now on medication and able to concentrate like never before, is a great student. With the PO's support and encouragement, Marge puts in place the routines for household cleaning, laundry, the dishes, and the mail that she and her therapist helped create.

Conquering the backlog requires that one take different approaches. The help of a professional organizer and an assistant—together with Marge's hard work—will be necessary. Marge, better rested and more able to take control of her time because of the support of therapy, is now eager to take on this hard work.

LEVEL ONE SOLUTIONS: WAYS TO HELP YOURSELF

In this section, we introduce routines that you can develop to reduce the chaos by managing the basics of household management, including laundry, routine cleaning, kitchen cleanup and regular decluttering. If you find that you are not able to implement these routines without more structure and support, try developing the routines with Level Two support from friends and family.

Routines for Laundry

There is a rhythm to laundry, and once you learn the rhythm it goes pretty quickly. Have two laundry baskets, a dark one for dark clothes and a white one for whites. Load the dark items first into the washer. Once the load begins (don't forget detergent!) you'll have 30 to 40 minutes before a second load goes into the washer and the first goes to the dryer. Set a timer with an alarm if the alarm on the washer is not loud enough to catch your attention. Set your alarm again when you put that load in the dryer, and place your "whites" in the washer. That way your clothes won't sit in the dryer and get wrinkled and require a lot of ironing—something you definitely want to avoid. You'll have about 30 to 40 minutes each time you load either the washer or the dryer. When the drying is finished, which usually takes another 30 to 40 minutes, fold the dark clothes and pop your whites into the dryer. You have a final 30 to 40 minutes to wait for the last load.

Altogether, on laundry day, you'll have three 30- to 40-minute segments available for other activities. Use them to conquer hand washing laundry or household chores that won't take you far afield. Don't run errands, visit with friends, or get into a computer project that requires deep concentration during the 30- to 40-minute slots. You'll never get back to the laundry. Instead, use your laundry minutes to do time-limited chores such as:

- hang up your clothes;
- put clothes away in the dresser;
- gather clothes together to go to the cleaner's;
- rinse out hand laundry;
- strip the beds;
- match socks and put the orphans aside until next laundry day, when their mates will magically appear; or
- organize the linen closet (but not the clothes closet—that's much too distracting and too big a job to do on laundry day).

Depending on your family size, your need to do laundry will vary. But count on roughly two hours once a week. If you're fortunate enough to be able to afford it, many housecleaning services will also do the laundry for just a few dollars more.

Routines for General Housecleaning

A great system (another word for "routine") for household cleaning for people with ADD (and those without) is the "Mount Vernon method," based on the way George Washington's estate in Mount Vernon is cleaned. For people like Marge, it is ideal because it follows a routine but has enough variety to keep you interested, and it doesn't take a huge amount of time or focus. It's found in detail in Sandra Felton's excellent book *The Messy Manual*.

The Mount Vernon Method

1. Start your cleaning at the front door.
2. Work your way around the house, room by room.
3. In each room, do simple dusting, once-over polishing, sweeping or vacuuming, wiping down all surfaces, putting things away, and making beds. A room is finished when its appearance is neat and its interior is clean.
4. When one room is done, proceed to the next.
5. Don't try to do the whole house in one day. Spread it out over two or three days once a month.

This system will not root out all the accumulated clutter, nor is it appropriate for heavy cleaning. But once the clutter is cleared out, the Mount Vernon method will keep clutter from ever accumulating again.

As a rule of thumb, if you are taking more than one hour per room and the rooms have been decluttered, you are probably cleaning too heavily, getting distracted, or going into micro-focus. The tendency for Marge and others with ADD is to overdo it, so pace yourself.

Three-Box Decluttering

1. Give-away box
2. Throw-away box
3. Transport box

Take three labeled boxes with you on your journey around the house: a give-away box, a throw-away box, and a transport box. The transport box is key. It is for stuff you find that does not belong in that room and needs to be transported to another room. Tossing it into the box keeps you from jumping up to take each misplaced item into another room, an act sure to break your concentration.

Routines for Dishwashing

Assuming you have an automatic dishwasher, the trick to managing dirty dishes lies in thinking of the sink as a rinsing station and your dishwasher as a holding station. Dirty dishes get rinsed in the sink and put in the dishwasher, held until you turn the dishwasher on. If you use the sink to hold your dirty dishes rather than your dishwasher, you're sunk! Naturally, there will be times when the dirty dishes come so fast and furious that you'll need to hold them in the sink for some period of time before they go in the dishwasher. But remember this: the longer they are unrinsed in the sink, the harder they are to clean in the dishwasher. Can't keep track of turning the dishwasher on? Tie it to a nighttime habit. Turn out the lights, turn on the security alarm, turn on the dishwasher.

The second roadblock in the dishwashing routine is a dishwasher full of clean dishes that hasn't been unloaded. Typically, dirty dishes begin to accumulate, once again in the sink. For your system to work, you need to have a set time for unloading clean dishes.

In a busy workday schedule, mornings are often too busy for unloading clean dishes. If so, a workable weekday system is to rinse breakfast dishes, leaving them in the sink. Then, unload clean dishes during preparation of the evening meal so that your dishwasher is empty, ready for breakfast and dinner dishes. Just turn on the dishwasher after the kitchen is clean and you've completed the day's cycle.

- a.m. —rinse dishes, leave in sink;
- p.m. —empty clean dishes from dishwasher before dinner;
- —load day's daily dishes after dinner;
- —turn on dishwasher.

Cut Down on the Mail That Comes into Your Home

1. Go as paperless as possible. Switch to communications by e-mail, texts, social media, and cloud-based communications.

2. Get off of mailing lists and reduce junk mail by signing up with the National Do Not Mail List Registry at DirectMail.com.

3. Register for online bill paying with your bank.

(If you don't have a good system established, with a definite place for bills, action items, and file folders for important documents, refer to Chapters 17, 18, and 19 for ADD-friendly paper management systems.)

LEVEL TWO SOLUTIONS: HELP FROM FRIENDS AND FAMILY

Conquering the Backlog of Clutter

Backlogged residential clutter is possible to organize and get rid of, but it takes hard work involving at least one other person. Use the three-box technique or the Mount Vernon method described above, and enlist your Clutter Companion as an assistant (remember, if you have no friend or family member to serve as a Clutter Companion, hire a professional organizer to help you).

This time, instead of starting at the front door and working your way around to each room as in the Mount Vernon method, pick the room that is most challenging to you. Getting that room behind you will make decluttering the rest of the house easier. With the help of your Clutter Companion, break the room down into smaller parts. A crammed closet, one side of a room, or a messy desk are good-size chunks of disorganized rooms to take on. Concentrating on perfecting each shelf of a closet or each drawer in the desk will be too "micro" to give yourself a sense of accomplishment, whereas trying to do the whole home office or the entire guest bedroom is clearly too "macro." You'll just get overwhelmed. *Do-ability* is the operative word here. Pick parts of the room that are do-able, that you will be able to organize with success. Your Clutter Companion can help you set do-able goals and provide support that keeps you going.

LEVEL THREE SOLUTIONS: HELP FROM PROFESSIONALS

Integrating Therapy and Organizing

Marge became increasingly aware of the interlocking influences of ADD and a disordered environment. The more she was able to take charge of ADD patterns—such as chronic sleep deprivation, poor time management, and lack of daily life management routines—the better prepared she was to reduce the chaos in her life. The more calm and ordered her environment became, the easier it got to control her ADD symptoms.

With the structure and support of a PO, she was able to implement strategies that her ADD patterns had undermined in the past. Through a combination of therapy and working with a professional organizer she made consistent progress in changing the daily living patterns that had so strongly interfered with her professional and personal life.

Review

- Know when ADD treatment must precede organizing efforts.
- End the daily cycle of ADD disorganization.
- Increase sleep to reduce chaos.
- Counteract seasonal affective disorder.
- Build routines to reduce chaos.
- Establish home maintenance routines.
- Go paperless as much as possible.
- Conquer the backlog of clutter.
- Integrate therapy and organizing strategies.

Packrat Syndrome

Lois is known for her big heart. She is a generous person, eager to share her possessions with anyone in need. Lois' friends and neighbors can count on her for tablecloths, wrapping paper, or screws and bolts of any shape and size. Her children have tons of arts and crafts materials. Lois can hardly contain herself whenever she takes one of her kids to the arts and crafts store. All the surfaces in Lois' home are covered with things someone might need someday. A true "people person," she saves every gift anyone has ever given her. That explains the exotic vinegars, herb pots, and multiple salt and peppershakers that crowd her kitchen counters. Totes, handbags, luggage, plastic rain caps, tiny sewing kits, and all sorts of travel supplies cram her closets, though Lois herself only travels once or twice a year. "You just never know when someone might need these things," Lois explains.

Lois is concerned about her clutter in every room and is also worried that she's setting a bad example for her kids. They don't have any habits of putting things where they belong, because items in Lois' world don't have a "home". Wherever they happen to land after they've been brought into the house or after they've been used is where they stay. When company comes, Lois makes a mad dash around the common areas of her house, tossing everything into large garbage bags that she then throws into one of the bedrooms. In fact, the bedrooms are now populated with trash bags that have not been unpacked since the last time Lois had company.

Lois had never heard of ADD until she had a discussion with her daughter's teacher. "Mary can't find her homework, her desk is the messiest in school, and she saves everything," her teacher said. Mary is in the second grade and already has saved all her schoolwork, drawings, and books from first grade. "Sounds like the poor thing is a packrat like her mother," Lois bemoans.

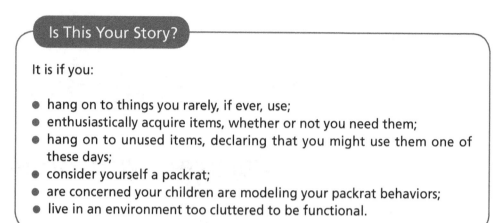

Is This Your Story?

It is if you:

- hang on to things you rarely, if ever, use;
- enthusiastically acquire items, whether or not you need them;
- hang on to unused items, declaring that you might use them one of these days;
- consider yourself a packrat;
- are concerned your children are modeling your packrat behaviors;
- live in an environment too cluttered to be functional.

John is another sort of packrat with ADD, a collector of items large and small. While Lois hangs on to a random assortment of things, John actively and frequently collects things—*large* things. John has not one canoe, but several. The scoutmaster of his son's troop was selling his canoe at a rock-bottom price and John couldn't resist. With two canoes in the family, now he and his son can go canoeing on weekends, he reasons. John can't pass a neighborhood yard sale without picking up a tool, a piece of hardware, or lumber that he knows will "come in handy." "And, for only two dollars, how can I pass it up?" he asks. Like many adults with ADD, John has many enthusiasms, and an unrealistic sense of the time available to actually use the items he frequently acquires. For years there has been no room for cars in his two-car garage. Now John is talking about building a huge storage shed in the backyard to house more of his overflowing collection of items.

A "packrat" is someone who collects things and can't bear to get rid of things, even things with little practical use or value. Certainly, not all packrats have ADD, but there are several common ADD patterns that can lead to being a packrat:

- **decision-making challenges**—what to discard, what to keep;
- **inertia**—not taking action until prompted by a "crisis";
- **oblivion**—not noticing the accumulated clutter;
- **adding without subtracting**—accumulating without any reasonable discarding;
- **procrastination**—leading to the clutter of incomplete projects; and
- **too many interests, too little time**—having an unrealistic sense of what you'll have time to actually use.

Indecision

Although Lois defends her clutter collecting on the grounds of thrift and charity, the real driving force behind this pattern may be a difficulty making decisions. Over the years, when faced with nagging complaints about her clutter, she defended herself, saying, "This will come in handy someday. Just wait and see." Then, feeling triumphant when she eventually finds a need for one saved item or another, her pattern is further reinforced. Lois has made a virtue of her vice. But Lois' tendency to hang on to things has become a real dilemma, undermining her quality of life. For years she has lived in a cluttered environment in which it is hard for her and her family to function. Her kids are following in her footsteps, living in chaos and having difficulty finding important belongings amidst the clutter.

> **If decision-making is not your strength, accumulating things will be your weakness.**

When Lois is not sure what to do with something, her "default decision" is to hang on to it.

Inertia

Struggling with inertia is a common ADD phenomenon. If nothing prompts an adult with ADD into action, he or she is unlikely to initiate an organizing project. For many with ADD, if it doesn't have to be done *now*, it doesn't have to be done. Individuals with ADD tend to react to external events rather than to internal initiative. The clutter that is always there becomes so familiar that they don't react to it at all. Then, some change or external event suddenly demands a reaction, drawing them out of inertia. One client with ADD required such an extreme event or "critical mass" that it took the threat of eviction by his landlord to throw him into organizing overdrive.

Hanging on to clutter to the point of critical mass may look like a *breakdown* of an organizing system, but in actuality it *is* a system, though not a very functional one. Lois says, "I don't pay much attention to the clutter. Then, something triggers me. It might be that I'm unable to find an important piece of paper, or that a huge pile of magazines has grown so tall that it collapses in the hall and I can't walk around it anymore."

Oblivion

Lois explains, "My piles have been there for so long that they are just part of the landscape, like tables and chairs. Then, when I'm about to have someone over to my house, I step back and see the clutter the way someone else would and I'm horrified."

John's oblivion was so great that his wife was driven to desperation. Her nagging and complaints had been completely ineffective in getting him to pick up after himself. John loves to tell the story about his wife's ultimate solution. "One day, when I arrived home from work, I sat down on the couch, as usual. I put my feet up on the coffee table, getting ready to watch the news. I tried to shove the accumulated clutter aside with my foot, but it wouldn't move. Leaning over to inspect, I saw that everything had been stapled to the coffee table, right where I'd left it the night before. As I stood up to walk across the room, I noticed that everything was stapled right where I'd left it—to the carpet, to the stairs, to the kitchen chairs. She'd finally found a way to get my attention!"

Adding without Subtracting

Not only was John oblivious to the clutter, but he also had the strong ADD tendency to *add* without *subtracting*. John, an enthusiastic accumulator, never stopped to consider whether he'd actually have time to use, or the space to keep, his latest acquisition. Acquisition (*adding*), for those with ADD, is often done on impulse. Discarding (*subtracting*), however, is a greater challenge because there's no impulse to discard, as there is to acquire. For example, John may pass by a neighborhood yard sale and spot a set of metal storage shelves for sale—a stimulus to impulsively acquire the shelves. "If I don't get it now, it will be gone," John reasons. The time-limited opportunity prompts his action. However, there is rarely a strong immediate stimulus to promptly discard. Many with ADD continue to add, while rarely subtracting.

Procrastination

Greg is an "armchair handyman" with ADD. He has lots of experience doing household repairs and home remodeling projects. With his busy schedule and poor time management, he often starts a project but then leaves it unfinished for a year or two while his wife fumes and complains. Each incomplete project is, of course, accompanied by accumulated clutter—paint cans, tools, lumber, electrical fixtures, hardware. Not only does Greg procrastinate in completing projects, but he also insists upon leaving the clutter of materials in sight as a reminder, telling his wife, "If I put everything away, I'll never get around to finishing the project."

Too Many Interests, Too Little Time

Many adults with ADD have wide-ranging interests, with their focus shifting rapidly from one to the next. Prompted by a friend, Anne registered for a quilting course, acquiring several books, magazines, a new sewing machine, and piles of fabric scraps for her quilting project. As winter turned to spring, Anne's interest shifted to gardening. Abandoning the quilt project, she began to purchase gardening supplies and materials. A time management class at work sparked her interest and she purchased not one but half a dozen books on time management, all of which remained on her bedside table, unread, as her focus of interest shifted yet again. Her multiple interests, and rapid shifts from one to the next, had led her environment to become chronically and increasingly cluttered. Magazines related to each of her interests continued to arrive in the mail, which she would set aside for future reading.

LEVEL ONE SOLUTIONS: WAYS TO HELP YOURSELF

Go for Quality over Quantity

If you are an excessive saver, and have trouble with decision-making, focus your attention on one decision only, the decision to save only the best. Quality over quantity works especially well with items you have in redundant supply. Twenty containers of oregano, nine spools of black thread, and several "spare" laptops are not uncommon among packrats.

The freshest oregano, the best spool of black thread, and the laptop that actually still works might be the quality thing to save. If items are nearly identical, save only one or two. How many three-ring binders do you really need? As an excessive saver, your new mottos for off-loading clutter are:

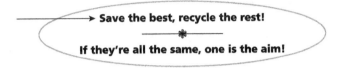

Save the best, recycle the rest!

If they're all the same, one is the aim!

Mottos like these provide you with structure, a guideline for rapid decision-making.

Create a "Crisis" to Stimulate Decluttering

Adults with ADD are more likely to act when there is an external stimulus. Create a strong signal that will tell you it's time to organize—this is an example of working *with* your ADD to get organized.

- Invite company over—creating a cleanup deadline.
- Join a block yard sale—creating a deadline for decluttering and tagging items for sale.
- Collect unread magazines in a small basket; when they spill over, that's your cue to sort and toss.
- Save unsorted mail in a wall pocket. When you can't stuff another thing in, it's time to go through it.

The Ripening Drawer Strategy

You probably have a ripening drawer or something like it right now. It's that place where you stuff things away that you are not quite ready to toss out. Things tossed in a ripening drawer are of low consequence. Not much will happen if the wrong decision is made, or even if no decision is made at all! It is a netherworld between trash and to-do. But the real magic of the ripening drawer is that when you look through it again a week from now or a month from now, it will suddenly become crystal clear whether an item is trash or a keeper. The ambiguity resolves itself.

Lois' ripening drawer contains pens that may or may not be working, almost working ear buds, questionable flash drives, small miscellaneous parts, batteries, loose change, and coupons. When she opens the drawer to add new items, she is able to quickly discard a few unwanted items to make room for the new ones. Items that Lois can't decide upon remain in the drawer. "I just can't deal with these right now," she says. No problem. That's what the ripening drawer is for. There are only two rules:

1. Do not put bills, anything to do with money, or anything with a deadline in the ripening drawer.
2. Never stuff the drawer so full that it's difficult to open.

Packrat Syndrome

Containing your small decisions in a small space gets them out of your way so they don't distract you from other things. Each time you toss something new into the ripening drawer, look for a couple of "ripe" items to toss out.

Adding and Subtracting

If you're prone to addition—constantly bringing new possessions into your life—add a new guideline to your life as well. Make a two-for-one rule: for every item you add, you'll subtract at least two. If you acquire a book or pair of shoes from a thrift store or yard sale, donate two books or two pairs of shoes before adding them to your collection. If you purchase new clothing, toss two items that you rarely wear. Items don't necessarily need to be the same category. Just stick to the rule:

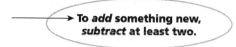

To **add** something new, **subtract** at least two.

When your addition is related to a serious collection—figurines, books, pottery, artwork—set a rule that you won't add a new item to your collection before you create an attractive, practical storage space in which to keep it. In other words, no more piling books on the floor beside the chock full bookcase. You'll need either to purchase a new bookcase or to discard books to make room for the new ones.

Make Room for the Future

Hanging on to the clutter of past projects is often related to feelings of shame and regret—shame that you didn't live up to your declarations ("This year, I'm going to get in shape"), regret that you didn't have the discipline to master a skill ("I'm going to learn to play that guitar"). As long as you hang on to the guitar or rowing machine, you tell yourself, you'll get around to it eventually. By giving them away, you feel you're admitting defeat.

One constructive way to deal with the clutter of abandoned interests is to embrace this aspect of yourself. Anticipate and accept your pattern of short-term interests. Look for less-expensive used equipment, then resell it for little or no loss and move on to your next interest without guilt or regret.

Another constructive way to rid yourself of clutter is to frame it in terms of making room for the future. Individuals with ADD tend to crave stimulation, a craving that may send you forward into new interests and adventures instead of sticking with previous interests. If you're an adult with ADD who belongs to the "School of What's Happening Now," you need to make room for what interests you *now* by clearing out relics from your past.

Set a Deadline for Project Completion

If some of your clutter is related to never-finished projects, set a deadline for project completion, with a promise to yourself (and the people that you live with) that you'll toss it if you haven't used it by the deadline. Make the deadline realistic, but soon enough to create a sense of urgency. For example: "I'll finish that sewing project by my niece's birthday and give it to her as a gift."

ADD-Friendly Habits to Combat the Collection of Clutter

1. *Reward yourself with experiences instead of things.* Many people with ADD reward themselves by purchasing clothing, books, CDs, or gadgets. If you're feeling down, instead of shopping, develop other ways to give your mood a boost—a massage, a hot bath, time with a friend, a movie.
2. *Guard the door!* Become super-vigilant about what comes in the door. If it doesn't enter your home, it can't become clutter. Magazines, newspapers, junk mail, and casual purchases have a way of permanently populating your tables and counters if you let them in the door.
3. *Make throw-away/give-away into a daily habit.* Keep a box or bag in a storage area to collect give-away items. As you notice an item that you don't want or use, immediately take it to the give-away bag or box. Don't let unwanted or unused items take up valuable space waiting for a periodic dig-out. Place small throw-away items in the trash, and larger ones in a storage area for trash pick-up day.

It's Never Too Late to Learn

Some of us, whether we have ADD or not, missed out on the often subtle life instructions about how to declutter. It's never too late to learn. While many books and seminars exist on the topic of decluttering and organizing, consider watching YouTube videos. Viewing videos is an ADD-friendly way to learn. Simply go to www.youtube.com and type in a topic in the search box such as "declutter a closet," "declutter a garage," or any other topic. You don't need an account and it's free!

LEVEL TWO SOLUTIONS: HELP FROM FRIENDS AND FAMILY

Set a Deadline with a Family Member

Projects that lie incomplete, cluttering areas of the home used by others, can lead to tension and annoyance. "Are you *ever* going to finish that?" Setting a deadline with consequences can be very effective for adults with ADD.

Sometimes adults with ADD begin to clutter the common areas of their home because their "own" space is too cluttered to use. This is the case for Art. He has an office upstairs so filled with clutter that he has developed the habit of doing paperwork on the dining room table. Soon, his clutter migrates to such an extent that the dining room table is no longer a clear, distraction-free area for him to work.

Art and his wife are both learning about ADD and how to find ADD-friendly strategies to reduce clutter. Art recognizes that he works better with deadlines, but rarely keeps deadlines that he sets for himself. Working with his wife, they both agree that he can *temporarily* continue to use the dining room—but only if he agrees to gather his papers into a basket at the end of each evening. They also agree upon a second deadline—that Art will declutter his office by month's end, so that the dining room table will no longer become his office annex. If the office remains cluttered at the end of the month, Art agrees to dedicate that weekend to an office dig-out, allowing his wife to be his Clutter Companion during the dig-out. Because Art never wants anyone else interfering with his "private space," the end-of-the-month deadline is one he takes seriously.

For Greg and Linda, incomplete home repair and remodeling projects were a chronic problem. They also agreed to deadlines with consequences. For each incomplete project Greg—who has ADD—sets a realistic completion deadline. He agrees that if the deadline passes without project completion, his wife can hire someone to finish the job. Soon, projects were being completed—some by Greg and others by professionals. Clutter began to vanish, to their joint satisfaction.

Decide When "Someday" Is

How often have you said, "I'll get around to cleaning this place out someday?" But you don't have to wait until someday comes. You have the power to decide when someday is. By making a commitment to a Clutter Companion, you'll have more structure and support, so that someday really arrives and your decluttering happens. Here is how it's done.

1. **Pick a date in the future.** Choose a date that works for both your schedule and that of your Clutter Companion—any date 30 to 90 days away. Any longer than that and you will be living in too much clutter; any shorter than that and you might feel like someday is closing in on you too fast.
2. **On your calendar write "Someday" on the date you have chosen.** Now you've actually designated when someday is.
3. **Choose a date one week before "Someday" and write, "Get supplies"** on that date on your calendar. That day, purchase the supplies that you'll need, including empty boxes, plastic bags, file folders, or other organizing supplies. You may want to discuss supplies with your Clutter Companion as he or she is usually experienced in planning a dig-out day.
4. **On the day before "Someday," write "Prepare" on your calendar.** Prepare by purchasing food and drinks that will be on hand for the big day. Go to bed early and get plenty of sleep. Plan to rise and eat breakfast well before the hour you've set to begin. Organizing can be hard work, physically and mentally.
5. **Spend "Someday" with your Clutter Companion, deciding what to give away and throw away.** Place items for charity pick-up in large plastic bags, labeled and placed out of the way. Throw-away items should leave the house that day—out to the trash cans, larger items taken to the dump. Give as many items as you can to friends, family, and neighbors, but don't let the give-away process prolong your dig-out process.
6. **You won't get it all done, so plan another "Someday" in two or three months.**

Declutter as a Family

Decluttering can be a lonely, tiresome task, but doing it as a family can be much easier, and even fun. Remember:

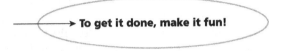

To get it done, make it fun!

Make decluttering a regular, monthly family event. Instead of nagging family members about their mess, and feeling guilty about your own, organize the "Clutter Olympics." Offer a prize to the family member who collects the most throw-away and give-away items in one hour. Give prizes for speed, endurance, and clutter poundage.

LEVEL THREE SOLUTIONS: HELP FROM PROFESSIONALS

Put a Professional Organizer on Your Organizing Team

When your decluttering strategies haven't been effective, and even after asking for help from a Clutter Companion your home is still in great disorder, then it's time to call in a professional organizer. A professional organizer makes a living getting others organized. When clutter causes chaos, a PO can inject order and systems. A PO will work with you on-site at your home, helping you decide what to keep and what to toss, and making sure you stay on task. You'll find that your morale will be higher and the work will go faster. POs will also have ideas for getting organized you probably never thought of and that will keep you stimulated.

Decide Who "Somebody" Is

One creative idea, developed by a PO, is to decide who "Somebody" is—that unnamed somebody that you're saving everything for, because "Somebody" might need it someday. Instead of saving for "Somebody," your PO can help you decide who "Somebody" actually is. This will target your saving for specific people rather than saving for an ambiguous recipient called "Somebody."

You will need a supply of removable small adhesive labels available from any stationery or office supply store. Don't buy an excessive amount. One package contains hundreds of labels and it will do you fine.

1. Walk through your home and think about exactly who should be the recipients of the items you are saving. Come up with the name of a real person. Use your professional organizer to help you think it through.
2. Write the person's name on a label and affix the label to an unobtrusive part of the item, like inside a shirt cuff or on the bottom of a lamp.
3. Have your PO make an extra label for every one you write and affix it to a sheet of recipients.

4. Try to assign every item you are saving to an actual person that lives nearby. If the item is a family heirloom, then you can consider going to the trouble and expense of shipping items to a far-away relative if they are unable to come to retrieve the item(s). If nobody's name comes to mind, write "needy person" on the label and affix it to the item.

5. Once you have listed items by recipient, e-mail each recipient and ask them if they would like to come get the items you'd like to give them. If they do not express an interest, then place those items in the give-to-charity pile.

6. Take out your calendar and plan "Someday" as described earlier. Let your intended recipients know that you'll be giving the items to charity on that date if they have not come for them.

7. Call a local charity, and arrange a pick-up at the end of "Someday" so that anything remaining, including articles labeled "needy person," can be donated.

8. Another very handy way to off-load unwanted items is to list them as "free" on your local Craigslist. Typically, free items are picked up within a few hours of listing them on Craigslist. Your community may have other give-away sites, such as Freecycle.com, that you can easily find online. Be sure to observe the safety precautions Craigslist and Freecycle.com recommend.

9. After "Someday" has come and gone, whenever you save something for "Somebody" be certain to label it and e-mail the recipient right away to make sure that they want to receive it. Remember, even though an item may be difficult for you to give away, it may not be an appealing addition to the growing collection of items in your friend's or relative's home.

> **To save work, look for charities that will do pick-up at your home.**

Play Friends, Acquaintances, and Strangers

Conventional methods for decluttering require you to divorce yourself emotionally from your possessions. But people who save excessively can sometimes benefit from just the oppo-

site, from exaggerating your attachment to your possessions. In the process of exaggerating your feelings for your things, it becomes clearer what you really care about and what you do not. This clarity enables you to discard with ease those things you no longer care much about without a lot of decision-making.

You'll find your Clutter Companion or PO helpful because they will assist you in making fast choices, and also because it's more fun with someone else!

1. Clear a table, counter, or other waist-high surface for sorting.

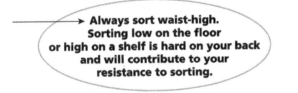

Always sort waist-high.
Sorting low on the floor
or high on a shelf is hard on your back
and will contribute to your
resistance to sorting.

2. Collect a bunch of items of a similar type that you want to sort—for instance, a bunch of books, a stack of clothes, or the entire contents of a kitchen cabinet.
3. Set them on the sorting table.
4. Select about a third of all the items as your "friends." Don't worry how to define "friend." Your friends could be your nicest clothes, or your favorite clothes, or the ones that look best on you, or any combination. Just go with your gut.
5. Keep your friends. Put them away right now.
6. Select about a third as "strangers." Again, how you define "stranger" is up to you. It could be clothes you know you will never wear, or the ones you don't even remember having, or the ones that don't fit, or any combination. Go with your gut.
7. Toss the strangers out! A large plastic bag right into the garbage is best, unless you care to donate them.
8. You are left with your "acquaintances." Acquaintances come into your life and usually pass through it, not staying too long. Acquaintances need to be donated. Put the acquaintances in a large plastic bag and put it in your car right now.

Use a PO and a Crew

If you have accumulated a large quantity of stuff that makes you feel overwhelmed just looking at it, you might need a crew to make a fast, long-lasting difference. A crew consists of you (the owner of the clutter), a PO supervisor, and at least one assistant. Your PO can locate an assistant. Together, they will presort your things according to your presort categories, such as:

- clothing;
- books;
- loose papers;
- gadgets and gizmos;
- photographs;
- stationery supplies; and
- recommended refuse (recommended by your PO).

You don't have to use these presort categories, but they are pretty common. Of all the presort categories, the most important is recommended refuse. Your PO and assistant are not allowed to throw any of your things away, even if they obviously look like trash. But they will put these things aside for you to review in a stack called "recommended refuse." It's your job to determine if these items should be trashed, donated, recycled, or kept.

Many people with ADD find the commotion of a crew a great relief. It creates an atmosphere of activity and productivity and capitalizes on your need for stimulation. However, there are also people with ADD who find commotion very distracting and unsettling. If you know yourself to be one of these people, a crew might not be your best option. You may be more comfortable working only with your PO.

Consider Psychological Help

Look out for warning signs of emotional or psychological obstacles to your organizing. These include:

- making a decision to throw something away and then retrieving the item from the garbage;
- an overwhelming feeling of grief or sadness when you throw something away;
- a total paralysis that prevents you from making any organizing decisions at all; or
- a declining level of sanitation or safety in your home.

If you experience any of these, speak with your therapist or doctor. If you do not have a therapist or doctor, call your local mental health association. These patterns signal a problem that might require counseling or medical attention.

Review

- Recognize that your packrat patterns may be due to ADD.
- Go for quality over quantity.
- Use organizing signals.
- Have a ripening drawer.
- Plan a reason to organize.
- Reward yourself with experiences rather than things.
- Guard the door! Don't let the clutter in.
- Watch decluttering and organizing YouTube videos.
- Make throw-away/give-away into a daily habit.
- Put a Clutter Companion on your organizing team.
- Decide when "Someday" is.
- Decide who "Somebody" is.
- Put a professional organizer on your organizing team.
- Play friends, acquaintances, and strangers.
- Use a crew.
- Consider psychological help.

Packrat Syndrome

David's Garage

Organizing Approaches for the Offbeat and Creative

David's garage is a nightmare. The cars are parked outside on the street because the tools, sporting equipment, old paint cans, and half-finished projects crowd the garage so much that the only item related to transportation that fits is a thin bicycle. When the garage door is lifted, something always shifts a little, threatening to tumble to the ground. If it were up to David, he might never change the way his garage is organized. "Messy as this garage is, believe it or not I know where everything is. I'd be afraid to move anything because once I did I'm sure I'd never be able to find it again."

According to David's wife, Rebecca, David is missing the whole point. "Sure, he can find anything when he wants to, but it takes him forever, and *I* can't find a thing!" she exclaims. "And I don't want to have to ask David to find things for me. A garage is supposed to be self-service. Last week I bought a new flashlight because I couldn't find one. Do you know we have four flashlights in that garage? If the garage were better organized, we'd know what we have and would be able to store more. Also, I hate the way it looks. David couldn't care less."

Dave's "organization" of the garage just evolved. He didn't plan it. Most of the paint cans are in one far corner of the garage, but the off-white semi-gloss is near the door. He stuck it there when he used it last. As he crawls around the chaos in the garage, he develops a visual image. "The bike pump is over there, near the rolled-up carpet remnant," he recalls. Although Dave claims he can find anything, it's really not as easy as he says. His wife has a point. If he knows where everything is, why does he own four flashlights?

Like many with ADD, Dave's memory system doesn't rely on organization and categories, such as large tools hanging on the wall, small tools in the toolbox. It relies on visual memory. "I know the monkey wrench is somewhere over there," David says to himself, "I can just 'see' it in my mind, somewhere on these shelves near the paint rags and sandpaper."

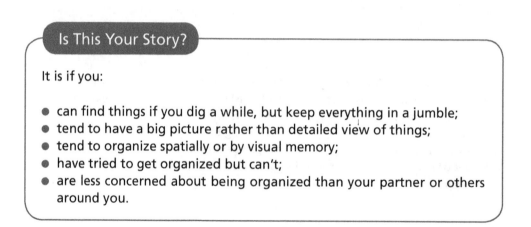

Is This Your Story?

It is if you:

- can find things if you dig a while, but keep everything in a jumble;
- tend to have a big picture rather than detailed view of things;
- tend to organize spatially or by visual memory;
- have tried to get organized but can't;
- are less concerned about being organized than your partner or others around you.

Part of the conflict between David and his wife may have as much to do with personality as with ADD. Not all people, with or without ADD, place neatness and order high on their value list (for example, the woman who humorously places a magnet on her refrigerator door that proclaims, "A well-kept home is the sign of a wasted life"). Not only does David have difficulty being orderly (an ADD-related trait), but also he doesn't feel that his disorder is a significant problem (a personality-related trait). David's primary motivation to organize is to please his wife. If his efforts are to succeed, his approach to organizing will need to be one that appeals to David's creative, offbeat personality. Otherwise, he'll feel that he's been placed in a straitjacket and will soon rebel.

In David's case, and for others like him, we don't suggest Level One Solutions (those he can implement himself) or Level Two Solutions (help from friends and family). In David's case, he is not personally motivated to change, but is only willing to try to make changes to please his wife. And Level Two Solutions, that might involve his wife, are not recommended because her values and approach are antithetical to those of David and might only lead to frustration and conflict. In the case of someone like Dave who has rejected all standard approaches to organizing, and only grudgingly agrees to attempt to become more organized to please his wife, we recommend that they start with Level Three Solutions from a professional organizer. Why? Because a professional organizer is trained to custom-tailor organizing approaches to best suit the individual. And in David's case, these organizing solutions will need to be offbeat and creative or they won't work at all.

LEVEL THREE SOLUTIONS: HELP FROM PROFESSIONALS

The same approaches can't work for everyone. For example, Marge, in Chapter 10, who suffered from the CHAOS, couldn't benefit from organizing assistance until she had received treatment for her ADD. In David's case, strategies to help himself, or to organize with the help of family and friends, are unlikely to work for several reasons. The organizing job he is confronted with is too big. David is resistant to organizing. *And* David has ADD.

David needs to start with professional organizing help. Without a professional organizer, he's unlikely to succeed. A professional organizer who is familiar with ADD can also assist his wife and other family members in better understanding ADD. If family members can learn ADD-friendly organizing strategies, they will be more successful in supporting David in the maintenance of organizing tasks after a professional organizer has helped him create order.

Use a Big-Picture Approach

Jane, in Chapter 9, found that breaking things down was helpful because she felt easily overwhelmed by surveying an entire room. David, however, does not feel overwhelmed by his clutter. In fact, he's rather comfortable with it. In addition, he's a big-picture person, more interested in themes and ideas than details.

Instead of breaking things down, as Jane did, David needs to do just the opposite. He needs to develop an organizing theme that encompasses his entire garage.

Dr. Lynn Weiss, in her book *A.D.D. and Success*, writes, of a client similar to David, that organizing takes place in the "creative mind," outside of consciousness, born whole. This creative organizing style is contrasted to the more linear style of planning and breaking a task down into steps to be accomplished one at a time. Weiss writes that neither organizing style is better; they're just different.

So David and his PO work together to develop a "big picture" approach to organizing his garage. What's the big picture? Since many of the items in the garage are like those found in a hardware store, they choose a hardware store theme for organizing his garage.

Use Creativity as a Motivator

The PO also tunes into another important aspect of David. Like all good POs, she is tuning in to what makes David tick instead of imposing her particular organizing approach on each client. In David's case, creativity and nonconformity are important aspects of David's personality. David's professional organizer understands ADD very well, and knows that if

Approaches for the Offbeat and Creative

it's going to work, it needs to be an approach that appeals to David and is not imposed upon him. The idea of organizing is very unappealing to David. Instead of associating organization with creativity, for him being orderly has connotations of tedium and rigidity. While we all prefer doing things we enjoy, when it comes to having ADD, enjoyment is a huge motivator, and engaging in a large task that is unappealing is almost sure to fail. So the PO enhances the attraction of the organizing task by appealing to his creativity. To David, developing a pretend hardware store in his garage, with departments just like a real hardware store, feels fun and creative rather than an undertaking just to please his wife.

Developing the Hardware Store Theme

A hardware store is organized into departments like the tool department, paint department, sporting goods, and so forth. With his organizer's help, David approached the task with a sense of fun—almost like a child developing a fantasy world. David gets to pretend that he has a hardware store. Family members can be his "customers."

David organized his tool department first. With his PO as supervisor, David and his kids pull tools from the clutter. They pick up tools from the floor, grab them from the shelves above, and gather them from every hiding place in the garage. David has a grand old time amassing all the tools together in a great big pile on the garage floor, tossing away broken ones as he goes.

David's 15-year-old son has been given the job of organizing the paint department. He is enthusiastic (he is being paid by the hour) in searching out paint cans, locating all the brushes, dragging over ladders, and gathering together turpentine cans, rags, and everything else to do with painting. Even David's 12-year-old daughter gets into the act. She is on a treasure hunt for sporting equipment. She finds all the old skis, baseballs, tennis rackets, and golf clubs and brings them together into a heap on the floor.

As paintbrushes, tennis rackets, and screwdrivers hurtle through the air to their appointed separate piles on the garage floor, David's wife Rebecca grows increasingly anxious. The garage is looking worse than ever. David doesn't seem to be fazed at all by the deconstruction of the garage.

Now that David (with his family) has deconstructed the garage and eliminated the broken and unusable stuff, he needs a model for organizing his hardware store, a visual model that he can use as a starting point. So David, his PO, and Rebecca head off to the local hardware store. Of course, the *real* hardware store has more inventory, space, and money to organize the store than David's family does, but David and Rebecca can see that inexpensive wall-mounted pegboards, simple prefabricated shelving, and large colorful plastic bins will be of great help. They take pictures on their mobile phone of the hardware store as a record of how its inventory is organized. David, in his typical ADD style, creates his hardware store, with his family's help, in several bursts of weekend energy.

David, unlike some people with ADD, is energized by the chaos that develops in the process of completing a creative task. He is able to tolerate chaos for long periods of time while the chaos undergoes a transformation to something new. David can organize if he experiences organizing as building something new instead of breaking something down. And if that creating something new causes more chaos in the process, so be it.

Drs. Ned Hallowell and John Ratey, in their book on attention deficit disorder *Driven to Distraction*, write (p. 177):

In order to arrange life, in order to create, one must get comfortable with disarrangement for a while. One must be able to live with the unfamiliar. . . In bearing with the tension of the unknown or the unfamiliar, one can enable something new to come into existence.

David is not only able to live with the unfamiliar, he thrives on it. Working with the structure and support of a professional organizer who developed strategies that worked *with* David's ADD and creative bent, David was able to enthusiastically engage in the organizing project and follow it through to completion.

If the creative, big-picture "theme" organizing approach appeals to you, there are other themes that work for different areas of your home:

Other Organizing Themes You Can Use

Organizing Project	Possible Themes
Home office	The war room Communications center
Kid's room	A board game Mini-apartment
Kitchen	A restaurant or inn The command center
Garage	A hardware store Mini "home" depot
The den	Alpine lodge Entertainment center

If you are someone that feels constrained by "typical" organizing approaches and needs something more creative and unusual, you'll need to find an organizer that really understands where you're coming from. To look for professional organizers that understand ADD, contact the Institute for Challenging Disorganization (ICD) or the National Association of Professional Organizers (NAPO). And take the time to interview a variety of POs until you find one that you connect with. If you're like David, the last thing you need is a PO that tries to impose his own organizing style on you.

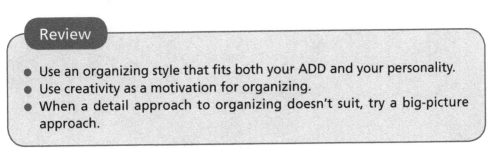

Review

- Use an organizing style that fits both your ADD and your personality.
- Use creativity as a motivation for organizing.
- When a detail approach to organizing doesn't suit, try a big-picture approach.

Approaches for the Offbeat and Creative

- Choose an organizing theme to add both structure and creative appeal to your organizing task.
- Look for an organizer that understands that organizing can actually be fun!

Organizing Time

Time Out

Tracking, Estimating, and Scheduling Time

Phyllis and her daughter, Kelly, both have ADD. Temporarily between jobs, Phyllis would like to use this time to get better organized. "I finally have time to organize the house and finish my overdue taxes. Two or three months at home will be heaven." Phyllis has a list of about 50 to-do items, a day planner, and a commitment to put the most important things first in her life: her daughter, her health, and spending time with friends, followed by organizing the house and attending to the taxes. All the elements of a well-organized person seem to be in place, and yet. . .

Today Phyllis is at her kitchen table, where she starts her day with a cup of coffee in front of her laptop. She checks her e-mail and Facebook account. An hour or so later, after responding to some e-mails and watching a video of her niece ballet dancing, a stack of unopened mail catches her eye. At the same time, she gets a text. It's a neighbor inviting her for a walk. "Perfect," Phyllis thinks. "I can kill two birds with one stone, exercise and socializing with my friend." Forty-five minutes later, she returns from her walk, hungry, when she receives another text. The mother of one of Kelly's soccer teammates needs to arrange the transportation schedule for the week. They text back and forth and finish off the discussion with a phone call. While on the phone, Phyllis takes the opportunity to discuss her concern about a school policy. They hang up 20 minutes later.

Realizing she has a dentist appointment in 45 minutes, Phyllis rushes to take a shower, quickly dresses, and grabs a pastry at the coffee shop on the way. In her haste, she has forgotten to bring her Kindle with her so she must settle for reading old magazines in the waiting room. A follow-up appointment will be necessary, but because her calendar is not on her phone and her day planner is at home, Phyllis must take the dentist's card and remember to call to make another appointment. It's almost noon. She dashes to the music store to pick up a flute rental for Kelly's band class and grabs a quick lunch at a nearby café.

Kelly will be home from school in two hours, and Phyllis wants to be there for her. Driving home, she spots a dress sale and decides to look inside. "This will only take a minute," she remembers saying to herself. It doesn't seem as if she's been shopping long, but a glance at her watch throws Phyllis into a panic. She quickly pays for her purchase and rushes to the grocery store to pick up milk. She is sure other groceries are needed, but without her list she can't recall what, and besides she's out of time. It's 3:15 p.m. and Kelly has just gotten home from school, enthusiastic about trying her new flute. A few minutes into her practice, Kelly announces that she needs extra school supplies for tomorrow. "I just got back from the store!" Phyllis exclaims with annoyance in her voice. "Well, I'm sorry, Mom. I just remembered now," Kelly pleads. So with snack in hand, they get back into the car and head for the office supply store.

Is This Your Story?

It is if you:

- tend to lose track of time;
- are poor at estimating how long a task will take;
- have difficulty scheduling your time; and
- feel you have little control over your use of time.

Returning home, it's now time to make dinner. Phyllis reflects on her annoyance with Kelly and wonders how she can become so frustrated with Kelly's forgetfulness when she herself forgets things all the time. As the evening passes, Phyllis realizes that, once again, another day has gone by without making any progress on her main goals: organizing her house and finishing her taxes. "I'm always frustrated. I'm busy all day, but I never seem to accomplish everything that I should."

ADD and Time Awareness

Several ADD tendencies complicate the time management picture so profoundly that most conventional time management advice simply does not apply to adults with ADD. Take Phyllis, for example. She tends to overestimate the time she has available to her, a typical time management mistake. Many of us do this because we fail to account for "unplanned" events like interruptions, traffic, and other things beyond our control.

But Phyllis's unrealistic sense of time is also affected by poor awareness of time itself—a trait very common to those with ADD. To Phyllis, time does not occur in neat little experiential bundles of minutes and hours. Drs. John Ratey and Ned Hallowell note that, "instead of being able to carve out discrete activities that would create a sensation of separate moments, for the ADD person everything runs together, unbraked, uninhibited." Because Phyllis experiences time as a constant, unpredictable flow, it is extremely difficult for her to accurately gauge the passage of time.

Distractions

Distractibility, a hallmark trait of ADD, also plays a role in Phyllis's poor time awareness. Distractibility is the tendency to become easily sidetracked, to lose focus because your attention is pulled away from the activity in which you are engaged. Phyllis is unable to block out distractions and also has difficulty remembering to return to her task after a distraction has occurred. Even though Phyllis sets out to open the mail, her attention bounces between e-mail, phone calls, texts, random thoughts, and back again to the mail (if she's lucky!) Bouncing somewhat randomly from one focus to the next, her sense of the passage of time is easily thrown off.

Internal Distractions

Many people with ADD have minds that are running constantly, filled with multiple thoughts and associations. As a result, even when the external world is not distracting them, they become distracted by internal distractions, including thoughts, ideas, worries, and mental to-do lists. For example, Phyllis may be reading a blog about hand-painted ceramics. This makes her think of her friend who creates hand-painted ceramics, and suddenly Phyllis remembers that she's forgotten to call this friend about the upcoming craft fair. Jumping up to make the phone call before she forgets again, she becomes engaged in a lengthy, rambling discussion with her friend. In this sequence, Phyllis is distracting herself, jumping from one related thought or activity to the next, with no planning and little awareness of the passage of time.

Time as a Series of "Nows"

For many adults with ADD, life is experienced as a series of "nows." Phyllis has difficulty keeping a focus on her long-term priorities because she is continuously caught up in the "now" of her immediate experience. For a priority to receive her attention, it must become part of her immediate experience. If a priority has been planned and recorded on a to-do list either digitally or on paper, it commands little or no attention in contrast to the "now" of the ringing phone, the ping of a text, or the stimulation of a live, real-time interaction with her daughter. As we've written about earlier, Phyllis and many others with ADD live in reactive mode, reacting to the stimuli that impinge upon them internally and externally rather than in the proactive mode of planning, prioritizing, and staying on plan.

LEVEL ONE SOLUTIONS: WAYS TO HELP YOURSELF

Pattern Planning

Pattern planning, a time management system recommended by Drs. John Ratey and Ned Hallowell, two well-known authorities on ADD, is an excellent way to manage your time better, instead of staying caught up in "nows." Pattern planning is a way to build structure into the course of your day, as well as a way to keep the relentless "nows" from stealing time from your priorities. Pattern planning begins with a daily pattern; then your weekly pattern is added; finally, monthly or irregular commitments are added.

Daily Patterns

Your daily pattern should include not only the usual daily events, but also regularly scheduled times to attend to your priorities. For example, if regular exercise is a priority for Phyllis, she should develop a pattern for each day, selecting an exercise time that fits into her other activities. Organizing her home and completing her taxes have also been declared top priorities, and Phyllis needs to assign regular times during each day to work on them.

Phyllis's daily pattern might look something like this:

7:00 a.m.	Get up
7:15–8:00 a.m.	Breakfast, read the paper
8:00 a.m.	Exercise: 45 minutes
8:45 a.m.	Shower and dress
9:00 a.m.	Breakfast dishes, general straightening of the house
9:30 a.m.	Household organizing (top priority): 1 hour
10:30 a.m.–noon	—
Noon	Lunch hour
1:00–3:00 p.m.	Errands
3:00 p.m.	Home to meet Kelly
3:00–4:00 p.m.	Time with Kelly (top priority)
4:00-5:00 p.m.	—
5:00 p.m.	Begin dinner preparations
6:00–7:00 p.m.	Dinner with the family (top priority)
7:30–8:30 p.m.	Work on taxes (top priority)
8:30–10:00 p.m.	—
10:00 p.m.	Get in bed to read
11:00 p.m.	Lights out

Weekly Patterns

In addition to a daily pattern, Phyllis also has regular weekly commitments. The flow of each day will vary depending upon these weekly events. Weekly events might include:

- a regularly scheduled class;
- meetings;
- chores;
- appointments;
- rehearsals.

After filling out her daily pattern, Phyllis can readily see that she has four flexible hours in each day, from 10:30 a.m. to noon, from 4:00 to 5:00 p.m. from 8:30 to 10:00 p.m. To maintain her daily pattern, these are the best time slots to schedule weekly or irregular events. Of course, life never happens so neatly. When Phyllis can choose, she should make appointments for mid- to late morning. A class, a choir practice, or some other activity may require flexibility in her schedule on those days. For example, she may decide that on choir practice night she will not prepare dinner, but will plan for carryout food, allowing her time to work on her taxes in the late afternoon, since she won't be able to work on her taxes in the usually scheduled slot that evening.

Irregular Commitments

Then, irregular commitments, such as doctor or dental appointments, or social events, need to be entered into the daily pattern. Often, these irregularly scheduled events must take precedence over the standard daily pattern. To implement pattern planning, you should:

- make a list of regular daily events;
- make a list of your fixed tasks, obligations, and appointments;
- use a week-at-a-glance calendar or appointment book and plug in your fixed tasks, obligations, and appointments; and
- make an appointment with yourself weekly to create your patterned schedule.

Soon you'll find that these fixed tasks will take on the character of regular appointments and will take root in your subconscious. The more you enter fixed tasks into your schedule, the less you'll need to rely on your memory, mood, or complicated planning. Also, by regularly building in blocks of time for your top-priority activities, you are more likely to move toward your goals.

Block out Unrealistic Thinking

Blocking is a visual aid that helps you *see* how much time your commitments actually take. Instead of simply writing an appointment into your calendar, write the span of time it will take and draw a bold line down from the start time to the finish time.

Instead of This	Do This
Sept. 2nd —Noon—Doctor	Sept. 2nd 11:30 | Doctor 1:00

Time Out

Blocking can be very helpful in dealing with unrealistic thinking. Phyllis thinks that because she is free from the demands of a full-time job right now, her entire day is open to use as she wishes. In her mind she sees vistas of ten-hour days one after the other like the open plains of Kansas. With her time commitments blocked in, Phyllis can see graphically how her time is already committed and what time is actually available to her.

Work on Big Tasks in Short Spurts

Phyllis, like many people with ADD, has just the right kind of energy for accomplishing things in short spurts of time. If you work best in short spurts but have a big project to accomplish, don't unrealistically set aside a huge block of time for the task. Many people with ADD who face a large, difficult task—such as Phyllis's goal of completing past-due taxes—feel they must set aside a huge block of time because the task seems so huge. They may set aside an entire week-end, only to find that they've actually spent little time on their taxes during that block of time.

Let Your Attention Span Be Your Guide

If your maximum length of effective concentration on a detailed or demanding task is 30 minutes, then set your goal at 30 minutes. You'll get much more done if you work on the "big" task for half an hour every single day than you will by trying to chain yourself to your desk all day on Saturday. Set a timer for 30 minutes as you sit down to begin your task. When the timer sounds, you've accomplished your goal for that day. If you're still focused and feel that you can keep going, reset the timer for another 30 minutes.

Use the Pomodoro Method

This easy productivity method works on the principle of a series of focused work periods with breaks. The process is simple:

Work for 25 minutes.
Take a five-minute break.
Work for 25 minutes.
Take a five-minute break.
After four segments of 25 minute work sessions, take a 15 to 20 minute break.
Repeat.

Use Other Tasks as Your "Break" from a Task

The Pomodoro method above is recommended when you have to work for long stretches on the same task. If you have tasks that can be done in brief chunks, you may find that your productivity increases if you shift from task to task using the alternate task as a "break" from the original task. This approach can be very effective if the tasks are of a very different nature. For example, use a half-hour of exercise or a half-hour of kitchen cleanup as a break from working on your taxes, or from filing paperwork. A complete change of pace can be more effective than a "break" in which you do nothing productive, and can keep you on track to complete your tasks for the day.

Should You Use a Tangible or a Digital Planner?

Choosing a paper versus a digital planner, or vice versa, is a personal decision. If you've used tangible time management tools (calendars, day planners, to-do lists, etc.) for years, it might be too much distance outside your comfort zone to change. Or the learning curve might be too daunting to you. Research shows that, for people with executive function challenges, a tangible system might be just fine. Handwriting activates cognition, memory, and information storage aspects of the brain in ways that typing and tapping screens does not. So the manual movement of hand to paper might actually help embed an appointment or task into your brain and memory better than digital word processing.

Using "Productivity" Apps

Productivity apps are generally defined as apps that permit you to integrate your higher-level goals and top priorities with your on the ground to-do list/task lists. Then those tasks and to-dos are associated with time using a calendar or schedule. Some productivity apps are stronger on list making, others are powerful prioritizers, and some have all kinds of special features like reminders and alarms. All of them are customizable, easy to enter and change data, and because they are mobile, they are "on the go" with you on any device you use. You'll have to experiment with productivity apps to find the one right for you. But here's the thing. You'll know almost instantly if it works for you. The look and feel will either resonate with you or not. One person with ADD conducted an "App and Tap" Night at her ADD Meetup

group. They met at a local brewery and spent the evening trying out various productivity apps. Based on ease of use, visual appeal, effectiveness, and *fun*, their recommendations, plus those of leading ADD magazines, are: Zenday, Epic Win, To-Do Tattoo, 30/30, Remember the Milk, ToodleDo, and Wunderlist. You can find a YouTube video on each of them. If accessing and comparing productivity apps is too difficult for you, ask a Tech Tamer to help. A Tech Tamer is a family member or friend comfortable researching and using apps.

Pick up Where You Left Off

Many people with ADD object to working in short spurts, saying that it takes them too long to figure out "where they were" each time they return to the task. Recent research on "recovery time" supports this. It can take between five and 20 minutes to pick up where you left off, depending on the nature of the interruption. There are several solutions to this problem:

- **Write on a tangible sticky note** where you left off.
- **Use digital sticky notes available at** www.zhornsoftware.co.uk/stickies/ to record where you left off.
- **Make a quick recorded message.** Instacorder is an iPhone app that allows you to push the record button and record a voice memo. When you release the button, the message is sent to you via e-mail.
- **Snap a fast photo** with your smartphone showing you where you left off.
- **Leave a message** to yourself on your voicemail.

Scheduling According to Mood

Some people with ADD have a strong aversion to living a highly scheduled life. If this is true of you, it's important that you make life choices that allow for maximum flexibility, for example choosing work that you can do at home at any hour. Of course, there are inflexible to-dos in any life, but thoughtful lifestyle decisions can reduce the number of inflexible to-dos in your life.

Mood scheduling is more spontaneous than standard scheduling, because it involves choosing your *preferred* time for a given activity whenever possible. In this way, your to-dos are more often "want-to-dos" and less often "have-to-dos." If you have a strong preference for doing tasks according to mood, build a flexible schedule for yourself that includes:

- regular high-priority activities such as work, family time, life-maintenance activities, exercise, and reading;
- your stubby to-do list for the day—a short list of errands or tasks that are outside your everyday routine (see Chapter 8 for more on stubby to-do lists); and
- a schedule of inflexible to-dos—those activities that *must* be done at a particular time, regardless of your mood or preference, such as a scheduled appointment or scheduled activities of family members.

Within that day's framework, you can feel free to operate according to mood. Rather do your paperwork first thing and get it over with? Go right ahead! More in the mood to do your exercise now and run errands later? No problem. A mood-driven schedule allows flexibility within the framework of the day. Do things in the order that feels best to you on that particular day, as long as you accomplish your goals by day's end.

Strengthen Your Time Sense by Staying on Task

If you rarely get to experience accomplishing something from beginning to end, you have very little to go on to figure out how long something takes to do. No wonder scheduling is such a challenge! To optimize your chances of completing a task from beginning to end, coping with distractions is key. You can accomplish this by making your intentions stronger and your distractions weaker.

Enhance Your Focus with an ADD-Friendly Environment

Set yourself up to stay focused until you reach your goal. Make what you intend to do noticeable, appealing, and compelling, and what you don't intend to do difficult and less convenient. For example, make your workspace appealing, well lit, and uncluttered—a place you *want* to be. Don't try to work in a dark, cluttered, unappealing back bedroom or basement.

Use Self-Talk to Get Back on Task

Self-talk is an excellent way to manage distractions. Whenever you have a random thought or idea that will take you off the task at hand, ask yourself out loud, "Where was I?" If an external distraction takes you from one task to another to another, stop and say out loud, "What do I need to be doing right now?" The key is to say these words out loud so that your intentions are in the foreground and distractions fade to the background.

Use Intention Markers

An intention marker lets you know exactly where you left off when you became distracted. Because Phyllis cannot resist picking up a ringing phone or responding to a text, she has a small, red sticky note pad stuck right to her cell phone case. (Just remove the paper backing on the sticky note pad and stick it to the phone.) Whenever the phone rings, she jots a one-word note on the sticky note and sticks it to her hand. It might say "dishes," for instance, reminding her to go back to putting the dishes away after the call or text.

Take Green Breaks to Increase Task Completion

Good time management involves not only focusing on tasks, but also scheduling breaks. Lack of task completion is a chronic problem for many adults with ADD. Typically, they work full steam ahead until they can work no longer. If the task is not yet completed, they may become distracted and have difficulty coming back to the task. Taking breaks to refresh your energy and concentration is an effective way to increase your chances of completing your task.

However, your "15-minute break" may stretch far beyond its allotted time, and you may become distracted by another activity, never returning to your original task. "I'll sit down to balance my checkbook, need a break, stand up, walk inside, and next thing I know, I'm on Facebook!" says Phyllis.

Try taking green breaks instead. A green break is a brief but effective way of refreshing the brain. It can be done as often as needed but won't take you far from your task. To take a green break:

1. Stand up facing something green. (A tree, a lawn, a leafy plant on a deck, or even a poster of a green pasture will do.)
2. Focus on the greenery.
3. Breathe in slowly. Feel your chest rise.
4. Exhale slowly. Let the air escape fully.
5. Breathe in again, this time bringing your arms up over your head, then lower them as you breathe out.
6. Now, drink a glass of water.
7. Finally, rock slowly from side to side.
8. Begin working again.

The color green, especially in nature, is calming. Rocking and raising your arms is relaxing, the water replenishes you, and the increased oxygen from deep breathing will make you more alert. A green break is ADD-friendly because it refreshes you, allowing you to benefit from a break without allowing you to become distracted by other things.

Time Out

Reducing Distractions to Increase Task Completion

Distractions often interfere with concentration for adults with ADD. When surrounded by distractions, you have to expend more effort to concentrate and are more likely to get off task or to tire before you've completed your task. To weaken external distractions, try some of the following tips.

Reducing Auditory Distractions

- When possible, turn off the distracting sound, such as the television or the ping of the text or other digital alerts.
- When nearby conversation is distracting, use "white noise." If you work in a small cubicle surrounded by talkative people, a small white noise machine can create a sound cocoon that can block out distracting sounds and conversations. You can buy a sound or white noise machine at Wal-Mart's or Target's or go to Amazon.com and search "white noise machines."
- Use low volume music to block out other auditory distractions.

Reducing Visual Distractions

- Turn off the TV if you find that you frequently glance at it when working.
- Close the window shades if outside activity captures your attention.
- Clear off your workspace. By eliminating the visual distractions of clutter, you will function more easily and efficiently.
- Turn off your computer, tablet, Gameboy, and anything with a screen. The light of the screen is distracting, as is the temptation to jump online instead of attending to the task at hand.
- When you cannot block out a visual distraction, use verbalization to override the distraction. For example, if you are sorting through papers, looking for a specific item, and find yourself distracted by other papers, talk to yourself to keep on track. Say, "I'm looking for that letter I wrote to the insurance company last week." When you find something really intriguing, use self-talk—"I'll put this aside to look at later. Right now, I'm looking for that letter."
- Sit facing away from distractions such as people passing by your doorway.

Reducing Tempting Distractions

- Tablets can be particularly distracting with the instantaneous access to videos, movies, and games. If you have serious work to do, consider using a laptop.
- Turn off the phone if you can't let it ring without answering it.
- Work on a laptop not connected to the Internet if you can't resist surfing the Web.
- Put up a "Do not disturb" sign to eliminate interruptions if you have difficulty resisting conversation with coworkers.
- Put temptations that pull you away from your task, such as food, out of sight and out of reach.

Reducing Internal Distractions

- "Capture" random ideas on tangible or digital sticky notes so that you can return to your task without fear of forgetting the fleeting thought.
- Read aloud if you find that internal thoughts distract you from reading material that is important but uninteresting or difficult to read.

Worry Outlets

A worry outlet is a place to put things that cause you to worry when worries are getting in the way of your accomplishing your tasks. For instance, Phyllis used to worry about her credit card debt every time she opened the mail because it would always be full of credit card offers that reminded her of her own debt. She has created a worry outlet labeled "Talk to financial planner" on her desk. This is a vertical file folder in which she stores credit card offers, articles on tax advice, and information on insurance and other financial matters. On her schedule, she has a standing quarterly appointment with her financial planner. Now instead of worrying unproductively about these matters, she has a worry outlet, a planned meeting with her financial planner. When she goes, she grabs her file folder and talks these things over with her financial planner.

Phyllis has created a set of "worry outlets"—vertical files on her desk—that allow her to stay focused on her immediate tasks because she has a system for taking care of her worries. Her files are labeled:

- Talk to spouse
- Discuss with teacher
- Ask lawyer
- Tell the doctor
- Ask PO
- Talk to financial planner

Of course, your worry outlet folders don't have to be tangible; they can be digital.

Setting up a place to file away your concerns or worries, and setting up a regular time to deal with each category, can help you stay focused on the activity of the moment without being frequently distracted by free-floating worries. Making an appointment with your "worry contact"—your spouse, your child's teacher, or whomever—can reduce anxiety in the present.

Time Out

LEVEL TWO SOLUTIONS: HELP FROM FRIENDS AND FAMILY

Use a Time Log to Increase Your Time Awareness

With the help of a Time Tutor, Phyllis developed a time log. A time log is a chart that measures how long it *really* takes you to finish a task. To use your time log, write a list of errands and tasks that routinely occur in your week. Write your estimate of how long you *think* each activity takes. Then, for a week, keep your log with you to record the start and finish time for each task. How long is your commute? How long does it take to drop off your child for soccer practice? How long does it take you to run errands on the way home from work? How long does meal preparation and cleanup take? Over the course of a week, a pattern will emerge showing you how long, on average, these activities really take you to do. With this information in hand, you can more realistically plan your schedule to accommodate the different tasks you have to do and how long it actually takes you to do them. Now Then is a terrific time tracker app with a graphical interface that shows you in color just how long you spend on various activities. The mobile version allows you to easily track time spent on activities on the go.

Get support in completing your time log. Let family members know about your project so that they can help remind you. Your child might enjoy being your official timekeeper. Ask your Time Tutor to call or email you daily to remind you to complete your time log. Even if it's not kept perfectly, you'll get a much more accurate idea of your *real* time expenditure. We've included a blank form you can duplicate.

> Sample Time Log

Task	Start Time	Finish Time	Total Time to Complete	Comments
Drive to Music Class	3:20 p.m.	3:55 p.m.	35 minutes	Allow 15 minutes more drive time!

Task	Start Time	Finish Time	Total Time to Complete	Comments

LEVEL THREE SOLUTIONS: HELP FROM PROFESSIONALS

Scheduling

A schedule is what helps your to-do list become a "done" list. A schedule is a when-to-do list that packages your tasks into small bundles of time, assigning a specific time for their completion. Scheduling your time does not mean you've abandoned all spontaneity. But scheduling is very helpful for those time periods when you need to function efficiently, because you have multiple tasks to accomplish. A schedule combines three elements:

- your repeating daily time commitments;
- less-frequent scheduled occasions and events; and
- additional tasks that must be fit in around these existing commitments.

You'll need your PO or ADD coach or Time Tutor to help you set up a schedule. A one-hour time management session can help you prepare a schedule for up to three months, so it is a great investment. To make the best of your time management appointment, follow these steps:

1. Gather together all your calendars, appointment books, day planners, time logs, invitations, flyers, notices, sticky notes, handwritten notes, refrigerator messages, and anything with a deadline or a due date on it. Be sure to include text messages that contain anything time-sensitive and print out any e-mail with time-sensitive information as well.
2. Inform your PO, coach, or Time Tutor about your staying power and your need for breaks.
3. Select only one calendar, day planner, or appointment book to use. It is a highly personal preference but you can talk it through with your PO, coach, or Time Tutor.

Basic Scheduling

Basic scheduling includes accounting for your standing appointments; tasks that are time sensitive (that must be accomplished *by* a certain date, or must be accomplished *on* a certain date); and tasks that tend to recur daily, weekly, or monthly. That is what your PO, coach, or Time Tutor is looking for when she goes through your sticky notes, calendars, appointment books, to-do lists, scribbles on napkins, and so forth.

Standing appointments are blocked into your schedule first, and then time to prepare for them is planned (scheduled). This is critical for people with ADD. If you have a dentist appointment, not much preparation is needed. But if you have a speaking engagement, part of scheduling includes blocking out time to prepare the speech.

With your standing appointments and your preparation for them blocked in, you can turn to that massive list of one-time to-do items and tasks big and small. First, prioritize them. "First things first" is a great motto. A simple system of A, B, and C for prioritizing will work fine: A for top priority, B for next in priority, and Cs last. Block your As into your schedule, then your Bs and Cs. Your PO or Time Tutor will also help you break down big tasks into smaller ones so that large tasks can be accomplished as a series of smaller ones.

It all sounds very neat and easy, but it's not always that way. With the help of a PO, coach, or Time Tutor, though, your scheduling skills will improve.

Eating Your Schedule

If scheduling in this basic, traditional way does not suit you, try "eating" your schedule, a more creative approach to scheduling. Eating your schedule involves dividing your tasks into "bites," "gobblers," or "munchers."

Bites

Bites are simple, single-step to-dos like an errand or a phone call that you can eat in one bite. Picking up Kelly's rented flute is an example.

Gobblers

Gobblers are to-dos that require concentration and gobble up more time than a bite. Usually a bite takes only minutes, while a gobbler, though it is a single task, can take hours. Paying bills and balancing the checkbook are examples of gobblers.

Munchers

Munchers are multistep, complex to-dos or mini-projects. A muncher is too big to gobble down at once, and is accomplished over a period of days or weeks. Reorganizing or remodeling your home are examples of munchers.

Your PO, ADD coach, or Time Tutor can help you sort your to-dos into bites, gobblers, and munchers. Here are the steps to take:

- Fold a single piece of paper into thirds.
- Title the left panel "Bites," the middle one "Gobblers," and the third panel "Munchers."
- List your bites (simple, single-step to-dos) on the bite panel.
- List gobblers (tasks that require more concentration and that will take hours rather than minutes) on the gobbler panel.
- List munchers (complex, multistep projects) on the muncher panel.

1. Now, place a star next to the most important bites, gobblers, and munchers—prioritizing them. If prioritizing is difficult for you (see Chapter 7), your PO, ADD coach, or Time Tutor can help.
2. Enter the starred bites, gobblers, and munchers into your schedule, assigning them to unscheduled times that fit around your existing time commitments and standing occasions.
3. After you've scheduled your starred bites, gobblers, and munchers, go back and schedule the unstarred ones. That way, you've made sure that you have time for your top-priority tasks before scheduling lower-priority ones.

Time Out

4. Scheduling munchers is more complicated than scheduling bites and gobblers. You'll need to work with your PO, ADD coach, or Time Tutor to break munchers down into do-able steps. Essentially, a muncher is a series of bites and gobblers. Sometimes they must be done in a certain sequence; for example, if you're remodeling your kitchen, certain tasks must be scheduled before others. For example, you have to install new cabinets before you lay the new flooring. You have to do the flooring before you do the painting. For other munchers, the sequence is more flexible; for example, if the task is to reorganize your home, you can choose to begin in any room.

5. Consider using a simple, graphic project management app like Trello.com. It's a digital card system. You can put the tasks on the cards and shuffle them in any sequence or order you need to break a muncher into smaller parts.

Review

- ADD can affect your awareness of time.
- Use pattern planning.
- Block out unrealistic thinking.
- Don't bite off more than you can chew.
- Improve time sense by staying on task.
- Put a Time Tutor on your organizing team.
- Take green breaks.
- Reduce distractions to increase task completion.
- Develop worry outlets.
- Use a time log.
- Eat your schedule.
- Schedule your day according to mood.
- Work with a professional organizer, ADD coach, or Time Tutor to learn how to schedule.
- To break down large projects try an app like Trello.com.

Time Out

Chapter 14

Overcoming Overcommitment

Ted is a highly educated, intelligent person who also happens to have attention deficit disorder. Despite his ADD, he has managed to earn his Ph.D., although his dissertation took him several years longer than planned. He has been married for over 20 years and has two daughters, both now in college. As Marian, his wife, has turned her attention away from their girls, she finds herself increasingly dissatisfied with her marriage. "I guess that I was so busy with our girls when they were growing up that my life was more separate from Ted's." Now, as she finally has time to spend with Ted, she frequently finds herself angry as he repeatedly arrives home later than planned. Not infrequently, he calls with an apology, saying that he won't be home until quite late due to some impending deadline.

Ted works for an educational think tank, participating in research projects, writing grant proposals, and developing educational policy. He finds the work fascinating and enjoys his interaction with other creative "idea people." The only problem is that his chronic overcommitment at work leads to greater and greater conflict at home. When he's up against a deadline at work, his immediate response is to cancel some commitment he'd made to his wife, assuring her that he'll make it up later. Because he tends to remain caught up in his work, he has little idea of how often he has let her down. In his mind it is "every once in a while, and only for a good reason." In her mind it is "most of the time; I can never count on him." Chronic overcommitment is beginning to seriously erode Ted's marriage. Marian's loud complaints are wake-up calls through which he is snoozing.

Karen's overcommitment has different sources. Karen heads up the Human Resources department at a local company. Like many executives, Karen can receive as many as 100 e-mails a day. She is never far from her cell phone. Karen finds herself compelled to attend every meeting and be active on committees. But regardless of the chronic stress at work, Karen is committed to creating a sane, healthy family life at home. Her ADD makes this juggling act even harder because she has difficulty developing organized, streamlined routines for herself and her family. The organizing challenges that so often accompany ADD lead her to forget to plan ahead. So, on top of an overly busy schedule, she's frequently pinch-hitting. Dinner plans go awry because she forgot to text her daughter to take the meat out to thaw, or because she forgot that she had a dental appointment that afternoon.

To make matters more complicated, Karen is a single parent of two daughters, one in middle school and one in high school. After several very rough years following her separation and divorce, Karen and her daughters have pulled together, supporting each other as best they can, but Karen often feels that she has placed too many responsibilities on her girls because of the demands of her job.

Avoiding chronic overcommitment depends upon a number of executive functioning skills that are often underdeveloped in those with ADD: planning, prioritization, time estimation, and time tracking. In Ted's case, he also may struggle with hyperfocus and needs to learn ways to signal to himself to pull out of hyperfocus and head for home to honor the priority he gives to his marriage. Karen's overcommitment is more a matter of circumstance. A single parent that works full time is, by definition, overcommitted. Karen will need to work extra hard to keep her priorities straight and to find ways to streamline tasks so that she can fit them all into her packed daily schedule.

Is This Your Story?

It is if you:

- don't carefully consider your commitments before saying "yes";
- have a hard time setting limits on your time; and
- feel chronically overcommitted, but can't seem to find a way out.

Overcommitment and People-Pleasing

Karen learned to be a people-pleaser long ago as a way of compensating for her ADD foibles. She agrees to work late whenever her boss asks, and she agrees to take her daughters shopping in the evening, even if she's exhausted. Of course, the more she overcommits, the more forgetful, disorganized, and exhausted she becomes, triggering another round of compensating through overcommitment. And the person she commits attention to the least is herself!

Overcommitment and Impulsivity

Overcommitment is a problem for many adults with ADD, especially those who tend toward the hyperactive end of the continuum. For some, it's as if life is a smorgasbord and their eyes are always bigger than their stomachs. Impulsivity leads them to dive in without carefully considering other commitments. Typically, they've crammed one more thing into their lives so many times that it's become their *modus operandi*.

High Cost of Overcommitment

If overcommitment is typical for you, you may even feel a sense of pride, at times, about the number of things you're involved in. As you rush from one activity to the next, you may not be aware of the cost, to yourself and to the people around you, of overcommitment. When you're up against the wall, struggling to meet a deadline, you quickly look for that individual that it is least costly to disappoint. Ted has fallen into a pattern of robbing his personal life to compensate for professional overcommitment.

For others, more often women with ADD, overcommitment results from approval seeking and difficulty in setting limits on the demands made by others. Karen lives with a frantic seesaw of imbalance—trying to measure on a daily basis whether she should shortchange her job to meet her daughters' needs, or whether she should disappoint her daughters to keep the boss happy.

You pay a high cost for overcommitment on a daily basis. You pay with a high stress level because you're habitually late. You pay with chronic fatigue because your overcommitment doesn't leave time for eight hours of restful sleep. Many people with ADD become almost proud of their ability to meet the crisis (often a crisis of their own creation) and prove the critics wrong: "I told you I'd get it done!" Sometimes adults with ADD become hooked on the excitement of crisis management as a lifestyle. For others, their overcommitment only leads to chronic anxiety because their life feels out of control and they can't find a way to keep a balance.

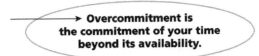

Overcommitment is the commitment of your time beyond its availability.

The Out-of-Balance Life

When Ted runs out of time at work, he steals it from his relationship with Marian, from his family life, from his sleep, and from all of the other activities that are part of a healthy, balanced life. Sometimes an adult with ADD doesn't recognize the emotional cost of overcommitment until his family relationships are damaged beyond repair. For Karen, the greatest damage is done to herself. No matter what she chooses, she feels she's let someone down. Most often, she shortchanges herself, going without enough sleep, without time to relax or enjoy herself, as she tries to juggle the demands of work and home.

People with ADD tend to add complications and commitments to their life without subtracting old commitments to make room for the new ones. Reactively responding to the requests of others, or to your own impulse of the moment, typically leads to overcommitment. To lead a more balanced life, you must step back to take stock of the big picture and then carefully decide what to add and what to subtract from your overcommitted schedule. Adults with ADD who remain in the reactive mode subtract things by default. When you try to keep too many balls in the air, you'll inevitably drop some. Instead of a planned decision, you drop a ball by accident—and often it's a high-priority commitment that is accidentally dropped.

Both Ted and Karen are guilty of "ADD math"—addition without subtraction. Ted continues to add commitments at work, stealing time from his personal life. Karen keeps trying to "do it all," unable to accept the limits of her time and energy and the fact that she can't be the kind of mother and homemaker she'd like to be if she had a spouse to share parenting and home management tasks with.

LEVEL ONE SOLUTIONS: WAYS TO HELP YOURSELF

Understand What Drives Your Overcommitment

Overcommitment has many sources. Sometimes the problem is related to poor time management skills, but often there are other psychological factors at work. You're not likely to learn to reduce your overcommitment until you understand all of the factors that influence you. Some common patterns are described below. Do any of the following sound familiar? Do you:

- crave challenges and love finding a way to do the impossible?
- need high stimulation and like the thrill of fast-paced activities?
- like to be the hero who saves the day?
- find that you're unable to turn down an opportunity?
- get caught up in the enthusiasm of the moment?
- compulsively take care of everyone but you?
- take pride in getting more done than anyone else?
- tend to be a people pleaser who hates to disappoint?
- place unrealistic expectations on yourself to meet high standards "no matter what"?

If one or more of these patterns describes you, you'll need to find ways to meet your psychological needs that aren't so costly to yourself and to the people who are important in your life. Recognizing what's driving you is the first step toward changing your chronic overcommitment.

Executive Functions and Overcommitment

For some adults with ADD, the primary factor leading to overcommitment may be the executive function difficulties associated with ADD that lead to poor self-monitoring and time management. Just as children need to learn to stop, look, and listen before running into the street after a ball, adults with ADD need to learn to stop, consider, and estimate time before chasing down a new task or project. You may need to work on your "stop, consider, and estimate time" skills if you:

- realize you're in a time crunch only *after* you've made commitments;
- frequently rob yourself of sleep to meet your commitments;
- habitually underestimate how long a task will take;
- impulsively say "yes" before you've taken time to really consider the consequence;
- find that you're often pulled away from your task by a new interest or idea.

Habits to Counteract Overcommitment

Here are important habits you can learn to slow down your overcommitment merry-go-round.

Stop Being a Sleep Thief

The idea of "enabling" developed in the addiction community. An "enabler" is someone who makes it easy for an individual to continue his destructive habit. You may be enabling your overcommitment if you're a chronic sleep thief. Karen fell into this pattern repeatedly. By trying to keep her boss happy and to meet her daughters' needs, she cheated herself, night after night. By robbing herself of sleep, she made it easier to continue her pattern of overcommitment. Finally, she learned to set a strict bedtime that allowed her to get seven to eight hours of sleep each night. Setting strict limits around the hours that she spent meeting her commitments helped her to become more realistic about what she could reasonably accomplish.

Become a Better Time Estimator

Each day, as you list your to-dos, write down your estimate of how long each will take. Then keep track of how accurate your estimates are. Chances are great that you always underestimate. Keep working at your estimations each day until you're accurate in your estimates. Of course things will happen that are beyond your control. But becoming an accurate estimator of tasks within your control will greatly decrease overcommitment patterns.

Put a Stop Sign in Front of New Ideas and Requests

Develop the habit of an automatic "stop" before taking on a new project. Estimate how long you think the new project will take. Then look at your calendar and look for time blocks for your new project. Chances are you'll need to remove already existing commitments in order to take on your new idea. Looking at your calendar during your "stop" will help you realize that time is not infinitely flexible. If you can't find the time on your calendar, you probably need to put your idea in the "cooler" (see below) for a while until other projects are completed.

Put Ideas in a Cooler Instead of on Your Plate

ADDers are notorious idea-generators. Often the generation and creation of ideas can lead to more and more work. It was Ted's idea to write a grant proposal for a manual on evaluating voucher programs. It was Ted's idea to join the State Office of Education's Committee for Non-violent Schools. It was Ted's idea to award business people for their school mentorship programs. And aspects of all of these projects have landed on Ted's plate. Marian wonders how Ted got himself so involved in all of these projects. "Other people have ideas, but they don't all seem to be as overcommitted as Ted is," she observes. To Ted's way of thinking, if you have an idea and you don't act on it, it will vanish. He has no place to put them other than on his plate. "If I don't run with an idea, I forget it," Ted says.

But there are other places to put ideas than on your plate. One place is the "cooler," a place where ideas are stored. The cooler can be a drawer or a tangible file folder. Or your cooler can be an electronic file. One adult with an ADD sense of humor actually tosses her ideas into an actual cooler!

- Take a minute right now to identify a cooler for your ideas. Put a sign on the drawer, or folder, or set up an electronic document called "Idea Cooler."
- As they occur to you, write your ideas on anything handy—slips of paper, sticky notes, or even napkins if your cooler is tangible. It really doesn't matter. If it's a digital cooler, use a document or digital sticky notes.
- Now get your calendar. On the thirtieth of every month write "Review Ideas." Review them more frequently if you need to, but always make an appointment with yourself; otherwise, you'll forget to review your ideas.
- Schedule times to act on an idea as your time becomes available through completion of earlier projects.

"Just having someplace to put my ideas has been a real plus. It helps me minimize my knee-jerk reaction to start working on every idea at once for fear I will forget the idea. Now the ideas never get lost," reports Ted. You'll also notice that some ideas are not as good as they originally seemed and you'll change your mind about acting on them.

LEVEL TWO SOLUTIONS: HELP FROM FRIENDS AND FAMILY

Help from friends and family is in order when you've tried to make changes on your own but have been unsuccessful. When, try as you may, you fall into your old patterns repeatedly, it may be helpful to ask for help in setting limits and changing patterns.

Who Are You Kidding?

Do you continue to tell yourself the same old things? "This crunch is only temporary." "Next month, things will be back to normal." "This project was too exciting to pass up, but it will only last for a few months." And do you believe yourself, despite so much evidence to the contrary?

When you receive messages from everyone close to you that keep you in a state of overcommitment, you may need to assign someone as your Time Tutor to help you assess every new commitment—before you take it on. Your Time Tutor can help you keep your addition and subtraction in balance.

Saying "Yes" without Overcommitting

For many adults with ADD, saying "yes" leads to trouble. There's already too much on their plate, and each "yes" only makes their overcommitment worse. But with the help of a Time Tutor you can learn to say "yes" in ways that don't make your commitments careen out of control.

1. Learn to Say a Qualified "Yes"

Saying "yes" without thinking through the time implications is a classic way of becoming overcommitted. But you need not avoid saying "yes." You just need to use qualified ones. A qualified "yes" is enthusiastic and cooperative, but will not lead to overcommitment: "Yes, I'd love to, if I can turn over responsibility for my current project to someone else." "Yes, I'm very interested, and as soon as my current commitments have ended, we can begin." "Yes, I'd be happy to become involved, but only on a consulting basis until I can clear out my calendar."

If you have trouble qualifying your "yes," work with your Time Tutor, even doing some role-playing, to develop the habit of the qualified yes.

2. The 1:2 Ratio Technique

For every new commitment you say "yes" to, say "no" to two old ones. Let's say Ted's colleagues want him to head up the annual awards dinner. Ted is a great choice. He's gregarious, enthusiastic, and knows all the people in the company. But Ted already has several committee involvements on his plate. He might say, "I'm interested, but I need a little time to think about it." Rule number one for keeping your enthusiasm from running amok is taking time to consider the consequences.

Then Ted, in consultation with his Time Tutor, chooses two existing commitments that can be retired in order to take on the new commitment. Ted is able to report back to his colleagues the next day. "If someone else takes over the education voucher programs, and the bulletins from the Office on Educational Reform, I'll head up the annual awards dinner."

Ted has proposed that he subtract two existing commitments (researching voucher programs and reading bulletins) in order to add one new commitment. Always retire *two* old commitments for every one new commitment you take on, because new commitments can swell to be larger than you anticipated and you don't want to find yourself overcommitted.

3. The Phase-in Technique

Another way to handle overcommitment is to phase commitments in over time. Karen might say to her boss, "I'm interested, but I need a little time to think it over." (Rule one: take time to consider.) Then, after consultation with her Time Tutor, she reports, "My plate is too full now. But in two months, when the performance reviews are completed, I can join the committee."

Both of these "yes" techniques—the 1:2 ratio and the phase-in— buy you a little breathing room. When you are asked to make a commitment, *always say*, "I'll need a little time to think about that." Then confer with your Time Tutor, ADD coach, or PO. Are there current commitments you can retire to bring the new one on? Can you phase in this new commitment? When you've established this with the help of your Time Tutor, you can report a "yes" back to the person asking you for a commitment. But it will be a new kind of "yes," a qualified "yes," the kind that does not lead to overcommitment.

Overcoming Overcommitment

LEVEL THREE SOLUTIONS: HELP FROM PROFESSIONALS

The Negotiation

When you negotiate, you buy yourself valuable time to complete your work. You need not call it a "negotiation," but whenever you set up a compromise, you're negotiating. Your PO, therapist, or ADD coach is an excellent person to practice negotiations with. All of them know how to role-play, have experience with negotiations, and will help you experience the negotiating process in a way that is as stress free as possible.

Here is Karen's negotiating situation: Karen's boss asks her to finish a report by Tuesday morning, but to do so she would have to work overtime (again).

First Karen plays the boss and the PO plays Karen. Then they reverse roles. This way Karen sees what it is like on both sides of the table.

Boss: Karen, I need the report on my desk by Tuesday morning.
Karen: Tuesday would be difficult, but I can guarantee it by Thursday morning.
Boss: Thursday is too late.
Karen: Okay, I can have it for Wednesday by 5.
Boss: I'll need it earlier on Wednesday.
Karen: I can have it on your desk Wednesday morning, but that will delay the project I'm working on now.
Boss: That's all right. This report is top priority.

In the negotiating process, Karen's boss started out with Tuesday morning as the deadline—his inside position. Karen started out with Thursday morning—her outside position. But they ended up with Wednesday morning, a position somewhere in between. Karen also negotiated letting another deadline slide, a critical technique in avoiding overload.

Negotiation Principles

- Always begin with a position that you expect to compromise.
- Never start where you hope to end—then there's no room for negotiation.
- Make the assumption that the other party expects to compromise too.
- Expect to meet somewhere between your starting point and theirs, although not always in the middle.
- Look for ways to meet their needs without overly compromising yours.
- Try to avoid expressing anger or antagonizing the other party.
- Let them know that you appreciate their situation, and communicate your position in a way that will elicit understanding.
- Look for ways to reframe the situation from win–lose to win–win.

Naturally, negotiations depend on the power and authority hierarchy of your business. In some cases, you won't be able to negotiate with your boss.

When Counseling or Psychotherapy Is in Order

When your overcommitment is long-standing, often there is more involved than the need for better time management skills. If you've tried to implement several of the techniques suggested in this chapter and find that, even with the help of a Time Tutor or coach, your patterns of overcommitment continue, it's time to explore the psychological factors involved.

Some people with ADD can become addicted to overcommitment—the challenge and excitement of rushing to meet deadlines, of pulling off the impossible. Certain professions or jobs are magnets for individuals with high stimulation hunger. Jobs in the media, entertainment, and politics, or high-profile positions with attractive perks, can become addictive and difficult to give up. ADDers with cutting-edge technical skills may be attracted to start-up companies where they work long hours for low pay with the dream of a big payoff just around the corner. Consciously or unconsciously, you may continue your overcommitment patterns because your behavior makes you feel important, needed, successful, appreciated, or stimulated.

When you're not able to modify your overcommitment patterns on your own, or when overcommitment is paired with other addictive patterns, psychotherapy can be very useful in helping you understand and change these patterns while still finding ways to satisfy your hunger for stimulation.

Overcommitment for many women with ADD is the result of a lifetime of trying to compensate for ADD traits, or trying to please others so that they can avoid negative reactions to ADD-related glitches. "So my boss won't be angry that I get to work late, I'll volunteer to work late when the office is in a crunch." A skilled therapist can help women work through self-esteem issues and help them establish a more ADD-friendly lifestyle that can reduce the tendency toward overcommitment.

Review

- Understand your psychological need to overcommit.
- Problems with executive functioning can lead to overcommitment.
- Say, "Let me think about it."
- Stop being a sleep thief.
- Become a better time estimator.
- Put a stop sign in front of new ideas and requests.
- Put ideas in a cooler instead of on your plate.
- Who are you kidding? Be careful of wishful thinking.
- Learn to say a qualified "yes."
- Practice the 1:2 ratio.
- Use the phase-in technique.
- Learn to negotiate.
- Sometimes psychotherapy or counseling is in order.

Chapter 15

Plenty-of-Time Thinking

Dealing with Procrastination

Steffie is a corporate trainer preparing to facilitate a training session. Since she has given this training several times before, Steffie believes it will only take a couple of hours to prepare. She'll need to go through a few files, revise some of the handouts, and print out copies. Unfortunately, her week turns out to be extraordinarily busy and overcommitted. Day after day, those two hours she needs never seem to be available. Now it is the day before the training session. With a full day of work ahead of her, Steffie's only chance to prepare is in the evening, but she has an early evening appointment she cannot change. "I'll just return to the office at 8:30 she thinks, pleased that her plan will still allow her a good night's sleep.

At 8:30, Steffie is exhausted. The effects of her stimulant medication have worn off. She cannot think clearly, so she drinks a cup of coffee. It takes her much longer than she anticipated to revise her handouts. Then, to her dismay, she finds that the printer keeps jamming. She arrives home at 1 a.m. feeling too wired to fall asleep easily and rises at 7:30 a.m. Her training session begins at 9 a.m., and she's already tired.

Is This Your Story?

It is if you:

- always think you "have plenty of time";
- can't estimate how long things will take to do;
- fail to schedule specific times to complete specific tasks; and
- don't give yourself a cushion of time for the unexpected.

Fuzzy Time Budgets

If you tell yourself you have plenty of time, there's no need to be specific about how much time you really have. You're using a fuzzy time budget. You feel no need to decide which particular time you'll spend completing your task. There's so much time stretching ahead of you that you can afford to keep your schedule fuzzy.

It's like people who think they've got plenty of money in their checking account, only to find that they've run out of cash and have gone into overdraft. When you don't keep track of how you spend your time, however, there's no overdraft protection. Instead, to pay the bill, you must steal time from something else. In Steffie's case, she robbed herself of sleep. But even stealing time has its limits, and then the penalties start rolling in.

If Not Now, When?

Plenty-of-time thinking is related to the ADD tendency to live in the "now." Many adults with ADD tell themselves, "If it doesn't have to be done *now*, then I don't need to think about it *now*. I've got plenty of time."

Although there may be a great deal of time between *now* and your deadline, chances are that time is already committed to other things.

Deduct Committed Time So It's Not Spent on Other Things

Just as it may seem that you've got "plenty of money" in the bank because you're not taking into account all of your usual expenses during the month, it may seem that you've got "plenty of time" in the bank when you've already committed most of that time to other activities. If you don't block out specific hours from the "plenty of time" that seems to stretch endlessly into the future, it won't be there when you need it.

Evaluate the Time Needed for the Task Before You Earmark a Block of Time

To earmark time for your task, you first need to evaluate how much time you'll need. If Steffie's handouts had not needed to be revised and printed out, she might indeed have had plenty of time to prepare for the training. However, Steffie didn't evaluate the situation in advance, to make sure that her materials were ready. Only at the last minute did she realize how much work needed to be done.

Operating at Warp Speed

The ADD tendency to rush through things at the last minute may contribute to your inaccurate estimates of how long things really take. Often, when you're under the gun, you can get things done in a hurry by operating at warp speed. Thus, you tend to underestimate the amount of time a task reasonably takes under normal conditions. You use warp speed as your measure. Unfortunately, as you can see from Steffie's story, you are not always in top form. If you have ADD, your ability to function efficiently can vary widely. And even if you could, operating at warp speed causes high stress that contributes to a "crash and burn" pattern common among adults with ADD in which they push themselves so hard at the last minute that they collapse, unable to keep up with daily responsibilities.

This Won't Take Long (I Wish)

Another factor in poor time estimating is wishful thinking. Many people with ADD don't like to admit the daily time cost of undesirable activities. You may not *like* that major portions of your day must be spent commuting, copying, fixing machines, answering e-mails, and so on. In your wishful thinking, you tell yourself that you can get to work in only 25 minutes (true, if there's no traffic), even though such thinking often makes you late to work. You tell yourself that you can get those handouts prepared in an hour or two (true, if you already have the handouts revised and the printer is in good repair). Life often seems too tedious to those with ADD. So you plan your days as if you can use your magic tele-transporter to fly above the rush hour and pretend that you can get all the boring stuff done "in a jiff."

LEVEL ONE SOLUTIONS: WAYS TO HELP YOURSELF

Cushions

From a time management point of view, plenty-of-time thinking can undermine even the best-planned day or week. So many things can happen that are unplanned—traffic, distractions, broken machines, lack of help, and the effects of medication, to name just a few that stymied Steffie. Even a well-organized person can get planning wrong when there is no cushion to allow for these unplanned circumstances. So the answer to the question of how long a task takes is: longer than you think.

Add a cushion to your thinking about how long things will take to account for the unplanned. People with ADD can underestimate the time required for tasks by as much as 50 percent. Here's the formula:

> **Your estimate of how long it will take**
> **+ 50 percent more time**
> **= *a better estimate***

The worst thing that can happen is you'll finish early and have more time to relax.

Watch Out

Analog watches and clocks, the kind that have actual faces and hands, can help you avoid plenty-of-time thinking better than your cell phone clock or a digital watch because you can graphically see the "distance" between one point of time and another. Steffie, when asked how long it will take to revise her handouts, might have said, "Not long, maybe 20 minutes." But if she were to look at an analog watch, she could see that 20 minutes actually takes up a pretty short distance from beginning to end and she might see that she needs more "distance" (that is, time).

Accurate awareness of time can also be promoted with the use of a special product called a Time Timer®. As you set the timer, the length of time you've set is shown in red as a "slice" of the "pie" on the white clock face. The passage of time is clear at a glance because the red portion becomes increasingly small as the time goes by, becoming a sliver, and finally disappearing as the timer sounds. You can find a time timer at timetimer.com

Make Appointments with Yourself

A crucial step in time management that many people forget to take is to move items from a to-do list to the get-it-done phase by assigning a specific time on a specific day for performing each task.

Instead of thinking, "I need to work on that report this week," say to yourself, "I need to schedule three two-hour blocks of time this week to work on that report." Then go to your day planner and look for available time blocks. If they are not available, and if this report is a high priority, you may need to change other commitments. Once you've made an appointment with yourself to work on the report between 2 and 4 p.m. on Tuesday, you'll be more likely to protect this time from casual encroachments.

Balance Your Time-Bank Account

You've got "outstanding checks" in your time-bank account that you've probably never subtracted from your balance. When you "balance" your account—subtracting time for all your standard commitments and extra commitments—your plenty-of-time thinking will rapidly become more realistic. (See the section on pattern planning in Chapter 13 for details about scheduling commitments to clearly see how much time is actually available.)

Anticipating Hyperfocus

When adults with ADD hyperfocus, they often lose all track of time, never coming up for air to check the time. When you don't have a clear sense of the passage of time, it can easily seem as if you have plenty of time to get other tasks completed. When you can anticipate your hyperfocus activities, then you can take precautions, such as completing other tasks first, so that hyperfocusing doesn't eat up all the time available. Or you can set an alarm to pull you out of hyperfocus so that you can move on to the next task. There is nobody better at alarms than the ADD community. You can find ones that shriek, vibrate, boom, or otherwise make a noise capable of snapping you out of hyperfocus. Google 'ADD and alarms' for plenty of choices.

LEVEL TWO SOLUTIONS: HELP FROM FRIENDS AND FAMILY

Play the Time Guestimate Game

 Use your Time Tutor to help you play a time game with yourself. With the help of your Time Tutor, write out the tasks that you must complete for the following day, with a time estimate beside them. Your Time Tutor may want to venture a time "guestimate" alongside yours so that you can see who is more accurate. Your list might look like this:

Drive to work	35 minutes
Download and respond to e-mails	30 minutes
Write letter regarding . . .	30 minutes
Team meeting	60 minutes
Lunch	60 minutes
Respond to voicemail messages	45 minutes
Work on quarterly report	90 minutes
Consult with George on project	30 minutes
Pick up dry cleaning	15 minutes
Groceries	25 minutes
Pick up kids at day care	15 minutes
Drive home	15 minutes

Then, the next day, write down the actual time that you spent engaged in these tasks. You'll find that unexpected things happened—more traffic than usual in the morning, more e-mails to respond to, a need to consult with someone before submitting a proposal, or your meeting with George dragged on for nearly an hour.

See how accurate or inaccurate you were. Was your Time Tutor more accurate? Now, play the game the next day. Do you find that you're leaving more time for the unexpected? That you build in more time for the usual?

Keep playing this game on a daily basis, with the help of your Time Tutor, until you find that you're pretty accurate in your estimates. You can consider that you've had a great day if most of your estimates are correct, even if a traffic tie-up in the evening extends your commute by 20 minutes. You can't control everything. But when you find that you're full of excuses about why things took longer, you need to face facts and allow for contingencies.

LEVEL THREE SOLUTIONS: HELP FROM PROFESSIONALS

If plenty-of-time thinking is chronic and causing you constant, stressful lateness and you can't turn it around with the methods discussed in this chapter, consider discussing it with your ADD therapist or coach. You may need to develop strategies, specific to your own situation, to combat these patterns. An ADD therapist, coach, or Organizer-Coach can help you pinpoint the particular patterns that lead to your last-minute rushes and can help you problem-solve to correct these recurring patterns. The added structure and support of a coach or therapist will make your time management strategies more likely to succeed.

Review

- Beware of fuzzy time budgets.
- You can't always operate at warp speed.
- Be careful of thinking "This won't take long" or "I've got plenty of time."
- Build in time cushions.
- Use analog clocks and watches.
- Use a time timer.
- Make appointments with yourself.
- Balance your time-bank account.
- Anticipate hyperfocus.
- Play the time guestimate game with your Time Tutor.
- Work with your therapist to pinpoint problems and develop strategies.

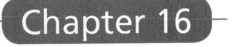

Chapter 16

The State of Rushness

Alisa lives in the state of rushness. She's always rushing from one event to the next, and is often late no matter how much she rushes. Her children have become so resigned to her pattern of lateness that they are accustomed to her screaming demands to "Get in the car!" followed by the breakneck drive to school, school supplies left behind, rapid good-bye kisses among flying lunch boxes and book bags.

Alisa knows that she needs gas in the car. Throughout the day, she mentally reminds herself to get gas so she won't have to stop in the morning and add precious moments onto what will no doubt be another rushed morning. But she never remembers at a time that's convenient. As so often happens, she forgets and finds herself pumping gas in the cold morning, kicking herself for not finding time the day before.

When she's in the state of rushness, nothing can happen fast enough for Alisa. Even an average traffic light causes her to drum her fingers impatiently on the driving wheel, and curse under her breath. Slow drivers frustrate her. Whizzing past them has resulted in several speeding tickets. Every unpredictable small event that slows her progress makes her nearly explode.

Having ADD often leads to living in a state of rushness because the executive functioning skills of planning, time management, and emotional regulation may not be well developed yet. In this chapter, we'll give you quite a few suggestions for strengthening these skills so that your daily life can feel calmer and in more control.

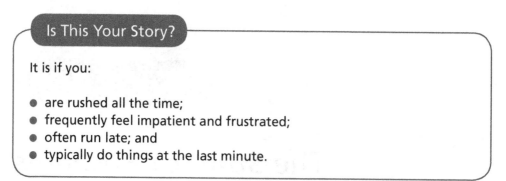

Is This Your Story?

It is if you:

- are rushed all the time;
- frequently feel impatient and frustrated;
- often run late; and
- typically do things at the last minute.

As she arrives at work, she dashes into the building late (again), pushing the elevator button repeatedly, though she knows full well this does not speed up the elevator. "I've just got to get my act together," Alisa declares to herself, shaking her head in frustration over the stress she feels as she begins her workday.

Alisa's rushness doesn't end when she gets to the office. In fact, most of her weekdays are spent in a continual state of rushness. She enters her office late and then makes a frantic effort to complete the memo that must be e-mailed before the ten o'clock staff meeting. As usual, it's done at the last minute and Alisa will have to apologize again for not getting it into her staff's hands sooner.

Low Frustration Tolerance

Many adults with ADD have low frustration tolerance. It is part of the general emotional reactivity that is common among those at the hyperactive/impulsive end of the ADD continuum. Frustration may also be a reflection of high stress levels and anxiety. A domino effect can occur in adults with ADD: poor planning, forgetfulness, tension, anxiety, and low frustration tolerance cause an emotional tinder box in which the next thing—it could be almost anything—can trigger an emotional explosion. Everyone has such an experience occasionally, when, after repeated frustrations, a "last straw" causes overreaction. Some adults with ADD, especially those who live in a state of rushness, are operating in emotional overload much of the time. For Alisa, chronic anxiety plus poor time management lead to lateness and a sense of urgency that escalates her frustration level every morning.

Some adults with ADD have a generally low tolerance for frustration. The brain's emotional center, the limbic system, is hyperaroused much of the time, with the chronic stress of ADD contributing to that arousal. As a result, minor frustrations can seem intolerable.

LEVEL ONE SOLUTIONS: WAYS TO HELP YOURSELF

If your days resemble Alisa's, it is critical that you find ways to reduce the levels of stress and frustration in your daily life.

Transition Time

Unforeseen circumstances are a source of frustration for many people—those small events, out of our control, that seem to plague us just when we most need to be on time or to arrive prepared. The best way to reduce the frustration of unforeseen circumstances is to anticipate them and make time for them. Some disasters are beyond prediction or control. If you must make a trip to the emergency room with a family member who is critically ill, or if you are involved in an automobile accident on your way, no one will fault you for lateness. However, when you are repeatedly late because of predictable "unforeseen" events—those that should be expected because they're so frequent—you need to adjust your timing.

To allow for these very regular unforeseen events, it's important to build transition time into your schedule. Alisa schedules no transition time. She butts one activity right up against the next and runs her appointments back-to-back. Even a tiny bit of running behind on one activity compounds the problem. Ten minutes late leaving the house becomes 15 minutes due to slow drivers and then becomes 25 minutes when she stops for gas.

Alisa cannot predict which unforeseen circumstances will arise, but many small events are "predictably unpredictable" such as:

- adverse traffic conditions;
- the needs of a hungry child or one who has to go to the bathroom;
- putting gas in the car;
- last-minute texts that have to be made before you get behind the wheel; or
- a forgotten item that delays your departure while you retrieve it.

Allowing time for unforeseen events can lower your frustration level considerably.

Does "One-More-Thing-itis" Contribute to Your Rushness?

Alisa has a bad case of one-more-thing-itis—the sudden impulse to do one more thing before she walks out the door. Sometimes her cell phone rings and she cannot resist answering it. At other times, she does one more thing because a task has not occurred to her until she is preparing to leave. Only then does she think to check whether there is enough water in the dog's bowl or whether she set her GPS to direct her to her next destination.

The best solution is a "departure checklist." Just as a pilot has a checklist that he carefully goes through before takeoff, so Alisa needs a departure checklist outlining the steps she needs to take before leaving the house.

Departure Checklist

Make your departure checklist bold and bright. Hang it in a conspicuous spot that you'll pass on your way out of the house. Or keep it on your cell phone for easy reference.

- Find keys, cell phone, day planner, and eyeglasses—put them in pocket or purse.
- Pack briefcase with files or paperwork.
- Check calendar and to-do list.

- Gather all items needed for appointments and errands (address to put into GPS, receipts, items to return, etc.).
- Gather together your coat, umbrella, gloves.
- Turn off lights, printer, TV, etc.
- Lock doors, turn on alarm.
- Stop, think. Say OUTLOUD "Did I forget anything?" Outloud self-talk can help you get focused.
- Suddenly remember something? Jot it down in the Notes app on your phone, on a digital sticky note, or on a tangible sticky note so it doesn't slow you down or distract you.

Develop the habit of gathering all listed items ahead of time (the night before) and placing them on your "launching pad" (see Chapter 4 for more on launching pads).

Plan to Arrive Early

Plan to arrive at your destination 15 minutes *early*. If you are usually late, this goal may seem impossible, but it's not. Your habitual lateness usually results from cutting it close, and allowing no time for departure preparation. When you leave no room for error, and combine this with forgetfulness, not to mention traffic tie-ups, you're sure to run late and to spend your day feeling stressed.

Two key steps to arrive early:

1. Build in 15 extra minutes for departure preparation. This is the time to go through your departure checklist, *not* a time to engage in one-more-thing-itis.
2. Plan to *leave* 15 minutes early.

In combination, this means a half-hour shift in your departure preparations. The rewards are *immediate*: you won't leave feeling stressed; you won't drive frantically or yell at the traffic in frustration. And, if all goes smoothly, you'll have time to decompress at the other end before launching into the next activity of your day.

Don't Drive Yourself Crazy

An important part of developing an ADD-friendly approach to life is the acceptance that sometimes your ADD will get the best of your well-laid plans. There will occasionally be times when you're running late. The trick is not to compound your troubles by becoming frustrated.

The number-one traffic violation is speeding. The number-one reason for speeding, according to police statistics, is "I'm late." Instead of risking life and limb, develop strategies to lower your stress level. Being late isn't the end of the world, but having an accident because you're speeding could be. Practice deep breathing to calm yourself when you're running late. Play soothing music on the radio. Do not text or check e-mail while driving. Instead of berating yourself, give yourself a break, and then do some constructive thinking about ways to avoid the problem next time.

Smooth Departures

Alisa began to realize that one of the sources of her lateness came from a lack of departure preparation. She made a list of events that had made her late in recent weeks, and developed a plan of action:

- Set the morning departure time 15 minutes earlier.
- Check the gas level on the way home each evening and stop to fill up the tank.
- Develop a schedule for routine car maintenance so that breakdowns are unlikely.
- Stock the car with an extra key and money for tolls.

Alisa's 16-year-old daughter, Tina, is learning to drive. Alisa has brought her into the departure preparations. It is Tina's responsibility to make sure that no car is blocking her mother's car in the driveway each morning. On cold mornings, Tina goes outside early, starts the car to warm it, and scrapes any ice off the windows in preparation for departure. In exchange, Tina is allowed to drive the car in the morning, dropping her brother off at middle school, then heading to her high school, where her mother takes the wheel, driving herself to work.

Avoid Procrastination Propulsion

Many ADDers increase their motivation for unappealing tasks by putting them off until they become urgent—using procrastination propulsion to get going. Although this may work, it is a high-stress way to live, leading to anxiety, loss of sleep, and disorganization in other areas as you have to "drop everything" to respond to the self-created "emergency." Alisa's procrastination is a major factor in the rushness of her workday. She always puts off completing her time and expense reports and other paperwork until the last minute, and sometimes not even then. Her dynamic energy and marketing skills lead her boss to overlook much of her lateness, but the chronic stress takes a huge toll on Alisa and certainly impacts her relationships with the family when she arrives home feeling tired and irritated.

Now that Alisa has developed strategies for a smoother morning departure, she's turning her attention to the causes of rushness throughout her day. Alisa doesn't have a perfect record yet, but she's focused on leaving fewer things to the last minute.

Constructive Waiting

Waiting, even for half a minute, used to raise Alisa's blood pressure. In her state of rushness she was always stressed, pressured by the next activity for which she was typically late. Now, Alisa has learned to wait constructively. To her surprise, she even looks forward to a few unexpected minutes when someone keeps her waiting. She gets many things accomplished while she waits, checking e-mails, sending a few texts, or looking up something on the Internet. In good weather, she takes advantage of waiting times by getting in a brief walk—clearing her mind and getting exercise at the same time.

Relaxation Techniques to Reduce the Effects of Stress

Numerous strategies have been listed above to reduce the number of frustrations in your daily life that lead to chronic stress. Some stress is inevitable, and some frustrations are beyond your control. When you're in a frustrating situation, it's critical that you learn ways to lower your stress response. In fact, recent studies have demonstrated that chronic stress can have corrosive effects on mental and physical health, such as raising blood pressure, increasing your heart rate, and shutting down your memory.

Deep Breathing

Breathing in a very deep, slow, controlled manner—inhaling through your mouth and exhaling through your nose—is an activity that you can engage in unobtrusively, and can be done in your car if traffic is your source of frustration.

Muscle Relaxation

These techniques are easily done in many situations and can go a long way toward counteracting the effects of stress. Stress leads to muscle tension, especially in the neck and shoulder areas. Tensing and releasing these muscle groups rhythmically can help reduce muscle tension. Another good muscle relaxation exercise is shrugging. Bring your shoulders up toward your ears; hold them as high as you can for 30 seconds, then release. Repeat several times to reduce stress in the neck and shoulders.

LEVEL TWO SOLUTIONS: HELP FROM FRIENDS AND FAMILY

Good Timing Gets Things Done

One of the reasons that Alisa has lived in a state of rushness is that she leaves tasks undone, which repeatedly results in mini-crises because she must rush to complete them at the last minute. In talking with her Time Tutor, Alisa has begun to analyze her procrastination patterns. One of the common reasons that she avoids certain tasks is that she tries to fit them into the times of day when she's most tired. For example, she tries to wrap up her paperwork at the end of each day. Alisa greatly dislikes paperwork and resents the fact that so much detailed record keeping is required by her company. By 4:30 in the afternoon, she's tired and eager to leave the office, so she tends to rush through paperwork, rarely completing it. The same pattern is true for doing errands on the way home. When Alisa is on her commute home, she'll only stop for absolute necessities, such as purchasing groceries for dinner. Otherwise, she'd rather not stop, so she passes by the ATM machine and the gas station, telling herself, "I'll do it tomorrow."

Strategic Scheduling

At the suggestion of her Time Tutor, she now rarely schedules paperwork at the end of the day. Instead, she starts her day with paperwork. A fresh cup of coffee and a high energy level can propel her quickly through these frustrating details, freeing her to concentrate on the more important tasks of the day. She carefully plans her errands on the way home, trying to have no more than one errand per day and coordinating with her husband if there are more errands that need to be done on a particular day. Other errands are scheduled for Saturdays and Sundays, when she is less rushed. And she focuses on eliminating as many errands as possible by purchasing online and even ordering grocery delivery online. She recognizes that many of her frantic "crunch" days are the result of procrastination and not planning ahead. She and her Time Tutor are working on improving in these areas.

Problem-Solve with Your Time Tutor

Make a short list of three main items that represent your "Why I Have to Rush" list. Go over it with your Time Tutor (or PO) and devise an anti-rush strategy for every item on your list. Here are some suggestions:

- The kids never wake on time.
- The kids are never ready to go when I am.
- I'm always hunting for something I need at the last minute.
- I need to stop for cash or gas.
- I'm not prepared for a meeting or appointment and have to rush at the last minute to gather materials I need.
- I never leave enough time to get from point A to point B.
- I usually underestimate how long things will take.

Develop Time Management Strategies

Alisa, with Marsha, her Time Tutor, went over her list. "Marsha is a great time manager. We went over my list of what makes me late and worked out a little preparedness plan for each problem area." Time management problems are often intertwined with a state of rushness.

Alisa has listed many factors that contribute to her state of rushness: lack of planning, disorganization, procrastination, and inaccurate time estimation. If you're like Alisa, and find yourself frequently living in a state of rushness, there are suggestions in other chapters of this book that may be directly useful. First, with your Time Tutor, you need to analyze the source of the problem. For example, if you're rushed in the morning because of frantic searches for misplaced items, creating a family "launching pad" will greatly decrease your morning rushness (see Chapter 4). If poor time estimation is a major factor, try to improve your sense of time by keeping a time log (see Chapter 13).

Prepare the Kids for Departure

In Alisa's case, as is true for many people with ADD, a big part of the morning rush is related to the children not having a good morning routine. Below are some suggestions of ways to help your children develop a smoother morning routine.

If the kids are not prepared to leave the house when Alisa is ready to go, the stage is set for confrontation and frustration. Just as Alisa and her Time Tutor analyzed the sources of her rushness, they also analyzed what leads to morning chaos and confusion for her children. With her Time Tutor's help, the family devised the following changes:

- *Earlier bedtime.* Alisa's kids are tired and hard to rouse in the morning. Her Time Tutor strongly suggested an earlier bedtime for everyone in the family. Rested kids wake up more readily.
- *Two alarm clocks.* To wake her kids, Alisa uses two alarm clocks *and no snooze alarm.* She sets the first alarm to go off near the child, and sets the second clock to go off three minutes later across the room so the child has to get out of bed to turn it off. That wakes them and keeps them awake. Alisa does not allow the kids to wake to a cell phone alarm. It's too tempting for them to start the day on social media than on breakfast.
- *Rewards for being ready on time.* Until Alisa's children develop new habits, they need a big motivation to change. Alisa came up with the idea of breakfast treats. Any child who's at the breakfast table by 7 a.m., having completed *all* of their get-ready-in-the-morning tasks, gets a special breakfast treat, while dawdlers get a grab-and-go breakfast to eat in the car. Frozen grapes, low-cal chocolate peanut butter cups, and yogurt sticks are great breakfast snacks.

(For more suggestions on streamlining your children's morning routines, see Chapter 4.)

Attention-Grabbers for Kids

ADD kids wait until the last minute just like adults do. Decals, stickers, and signs are attention-grabbing to kids and make them attend to things sooner rather than later. Alisa's kids always wait until she is practically in the car to feed the cat. She made a trail of contact-paper footprint decals on the floor. The first footprint decal the kids step on when they get out of bed says, "Brush your teeth, sleepy head." On the kids' bathroom floor another decal reads "Did you wash your hands?" Another one, leading to the kitchen, reads "The cat is hungry." Try not to make decals that give orders, like "Feed the cat," "Wash your hands," and so on. Just try to be encouraging so they attend to things in a timely manner.

LEVEL THREE SOLUTIONS: HELP FROM PROFESSIONALS

ADD Coaching to Reduce Rushness

Alisa has done a great deal of problem-solving with her Time Tutor. She was fortunate to have a friend like Marsha on her team. If working with your Time Tutor isn't effective, or if you feel you need more structure and support to change your rushness habits, try working with an ADD coach. Reducing rushness requires changing many different habits—which is never easy. A coach can help you problem-solve and prioritize so that you can be successful in changing habits. One of the big mistakes that many adults with ADD make is to try to change too much at once. Then when they're unsuccessful, they become discouraged and quickly return to their old habits of rushness.

With a coach, you can build habits gradually, so that each habit lends support to the next. Regular phone contact or texting with your coach can keep you on track and can help you problem-solve when snags arise.

When Your Anger Is More Than a Sign of Stress

Alisa was very concerned about how short-tempered she had become with her children, particularly in the morning when they were running late. She had scared herself more than once as she took chances in traffic trying to make up for lost time. As she gained better control of her time and her schedule, Alisa's frustration level decreased, her driving habits improved, and family relationships became calmer.

For Alisa, stress was the culprit that led to her angry explosions. Other factors, however, are often the source of anger. If you find that practicing better time management and stress management doesn't solve the problem, it's a good idea to consult a therapist. Anger and irritability are often signs of unrecognized depression that may need to be treated with psychotherapy and/or medication.

Ask for a "Reasonable Accommodation" at Work

You have the right, under the Americans with Disabilities Act, to request reasonable accommodations at work. It's important to understand, however, that asking for accommodations, without showing your employer a positive attitude and a strong work ethic, is not likely to meet with success.

Alisa's boss is aware of her ADD. They are exploring a more flexible schedule that would permit Alisa to work on a flextime schedule, perhaps 9:30 to 6:30 on Tuesdays and Wednesdays instead of 8:00 to 5:00. In this way, when Alisa's best efforts to leave the house on time fail, her stress level doesn't have to go into the stratosphere. So long as she works 40 hours each week, her boss is satisfied.

If you need advice on what your accommodation rights are and how to invoke them, contact www.ada.gov and speak in private with the human resources director of your company. Also talk to your therapist. Disclosing your ADD is not always the best course of action. You'll need to carefully weigh the benefits and costs of doing so.

Participate in "Time-Out" Activities

The demands of highly structured work schedules are difficult for everyone, and especially difficult for those with ADD, who must expend much greater effort to keep track of time. To relieve the stress of being "on time all the time," time-out activities can be highly therapeutic for adults with ADD. Time-out activities are those in which you can engage fully, feeling "outside of time," temporarily suspending the relentless pressure to keep track of time. Drs. John Ratey and Ned Hallowell write (p. 283):

> We also see people with ADD hyperfocusing on an activity, like rock-climbing . . . probably because it allows them to forget about the expectations associated with "time." Our patients frequently report that they are most calm when completely caught up in the thrill of it all, whatever that "all" may be. It could be fun, a catastrophe, or a life-or-death crisis. These situations allow the ADD person not only to get into forward motion, but also to forget, to disregard that they need brakes in the first place. In an emergency, it's full speed ahead. What a relief.

Your ADD coach or therapist can help you decide which time-out activities to engage in. Real-time live activities, as opposed to virtual and screen-based ones, are best. Vacations, including vacations from devices, are great. Thrilling (but not dangerous) physical activity, such as hiking up a mountain trail, or doing something new and exciting (and safe) can inject stimulation into your regular life and provide an out-of-timeness that nourishes your ADD soul. For others, the greatest relief comes from truly having a day off, a day in which they can wander from one activity to another without any pressure to attend to the needs of others, or to be in a certain place at a specific time. Being off the clock is a wonderful time-out activity,

Seek Careers That Are More Time Flexible

Many adults with ADD choose to work for themselves so that they can set their own highly flexible time patterns, limiting the number of weekly events that must occur at specific times. Others seek jobs that accommodate their night-owl tendencies, eliminating the ADD struggle with early-morning rising to prepare for the day. Speak with your ADD coach or therapist for more ideas about choosing a career that is a better match for your struggles with time.

Anxiety

Anxiety is a very common coexisting condition for many adults with ADD, and especially for women with ADD. Your "state of rushness" not only adds to anxiety, but can also be the result of chronic anxiety and stress. You may need to consult a therapist and consider medication for anxiety as well if anxiety plays a strong role in chronic stress and "rushness."

Review

- Chronic stress and low frustration tolerance are results of being rushed all the time.
- Schedule transition time between activities to allow for the unforeseen.

- Try not to succumb to one-more-thing-itis.
- Make a departure checklist.
- Plan to leave early.
- Don't drive yourself crazy.
- Prepare for departure.
- Procrastination propulsion is not a good long-term solution to lateness.
- Wait constructively.
- Use relaxation techniques to reduce the effects of stress.
- Good timing gets things done.
- Problem-solve with your Time Tutor.
- Reduce the rushness for kids.
- ADD coaching can reduce rushness.
- Consider therapy: anger and high anxiety can be a sign of more than stress.

Organizing Information

Hung up on Hard Copy

"I just can't explain it," Zoey says. "No one I know in business has a desk like mine. Most days I can't even see the top of my desk. If I don't keep the papers out in front of me, I forget what I'm supposed to do with them." Zoey is a successful life coach operating her business out of her home. "The paper clutter is really affecting my business. I can't bring clients to my home office anymore and stuff is falling through the cracks. I kinda, sorta, know where everything is, but it takes me longer and longer to find what I'm looking for. I feel like if I can't touch my information, I don't know where it is or what to do with it", Zoey explains. "And I'm afraid my clients would lose confidence in me if they saw my office. It projects disorganization. As a life coach that's deadly," Zoey observes.

Out of Sight, Out of Mind

Zoey, like Edgar in Chapter 8, is an OosOom, a person for whom out of sight is out of mind. Edgar's OosOom is stuff and Zoey's is information. Like all Gen Xs, Zoey's world is largely digital—electronic documents, e-mails, and apps—and she's a whiz on the Web. Zoey saves her documents to her hard drive, but not in any logical manner. She prints out just about everything so there is a hard copy twin set of everything she has on her computer. "I'd like to be better organized digitally speaking, but I can't without help."

Zoey's struggles are a reflection of her poor organizational skills. As we've written about throughout this book, planning and organization are key executive functioning skills. Zoey relies on a very faulty "see it—do it" that is failing her more and more often. Leaving a stamped addressed envelope on the table by the door is an excellent visual cue to put it in the mailbox. Nothing wrong with that. But when you leave *all* of your papers out hoping that they will cue you to take action, you've got no reminder system at all. Many people

173

start out with this type of visual cuing system when they are young and have very little to take care of. It becomes more and more critical to develop executive functioning skills as our lives grow more complex and demanding.

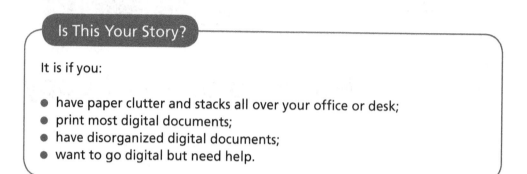

Is This Your Story?

It is if you:

- have paper clutter and stacks all over your office or desk;
- print most digital documents;
- have disorganized digital documents;
- want to go digital but need help.

LEVEL ONE SOLUTIONS: WAYS TO HELP YOURSELF

Keeping Papers in View

Zoey has the right idea. She functions best when she can *see* what she needs to do. But her way of keeping things in view, by piling things all over her desktop and office, is a very inefficient method. So let's deal with her tangible papers first and then discuss how to improve her digital documents.

A stack of papers is a visual cue, but the more stacks you have and the higher they are, the more time it will take you to find what you're looking for. Eventually, you will also run out of space.

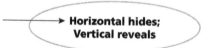

**Horizontal hides;
Vertical reveals**

"Horizontal hides and vertical reveals" is a helpful motto to keep in mind. Just rearranging her horizontal stacks vertically would make a world of difference in Zoey's ability to see what is where. A vertical system includes:

- vertical file holders;
- vertical desktop filers.

Chapter Seventeen

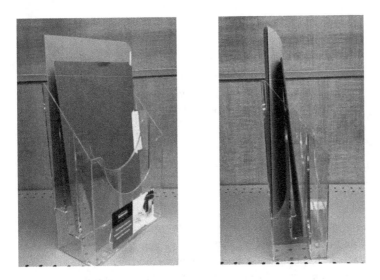

Unlike stacks, which can tend to homogenize your papers into one disorganized mass, papers held vertically can be separated, identified, and labeled by using file folders in a step-up holder. The file-folder tabs are clearly revealed, showing a subject, title, or other identifier.

Use Color

Use colored file folders instead of manila file folders. Colored file folders are very visually appealing and engender action-oriented responses in us. Use traffic light colors as cues. For Zoey, green files are client files that are already billed (green also represents money) and ready to go on the next appointment; yellow files warn Zoey of tasks and documents that are incomplete; red files might require urgent action. A fourth color is fine, but often more than four colors can start to become too complicated.

X-ray Vision

It would be wonderful to have X-ray vision and be able to see through file folders and be visually cued to the contents inside. The closest thing to having X-ray vision is to use transparent file folders. They are made of plastic and come in a wide range of see-through colors. Use removable adhesive labels on them so you can label and relabel the file folders as needed.

The Hot Spot

The hot spot is a place on your desk that contains a red, see-through plastic folio or red transparent file folder. It must be red because red is identified with urgency. The hot spot contains a maximum of six pieces of paper representing action that must be taken before the day is out. Too many items and your hot spot becomes just a pile of papers to process, corrupting the integrity of the hot spot. Your hot spot might include printed out e-mails to respond to, a project to bring forward, a document to sign, or even a few notes about key phone calls to make. A hot spot works like a stubby to-do list (see Chapter 8). Just as your stubby to-do list should contain only a few items, those that *must* be done today, your hot spot folder is for today only.

"Verb" Your Papers

Verbs are action-oriented and when used on files and papers they suggest what *to do* with your papers rather than what they are called. Verbs identify actions to take. Nouns, such as titles, subjects, and categories, identify what the papers are, but not what to do with them. "Verbing" your papers prepares you to take action on them. Many people with ADD are kinesthetic and relate well to words that describe movement or action.

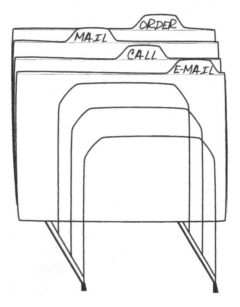

Set up a series of file folders vertically on your desk with verbs on their labels. Common verbs to use are: "Order," "Copy," "Email," "Call," "Pay," and "Blog About." Now, go through your paper stacks and file them according to these verbs or any other verbs you prefer. Verbing encourages action and groups your papers together by like-action. Grouping papers by like-action is very efficient. Instead of jumping from a call to copying to e-mailing, you are more apt to do a clump of calls in one sitting, a bunch of copying at one time, and several emails in a row, which is a way better use of your time. And the more actions you complete, the fewer papers you have.

> **When you're verbing your papers, be sure to put urgent papers in the hot spot.**

LEVEL TWO SOLUTIONS: HELP FROM FRIENDS AND FAMILY

Put a Paper Partner on Your Organizing Team

A Paper Partner is a friend or family member who is good at organizing hard-copy documents, files, and papers. Use your Paper Partner to help you put the following solutions in place.

Get Rid of Your Filing Cabinets!

"I call my filing cabinets 'the black hole.' Once I put something in them, I can never find it again." Instead, Zoey and her Paper Partner moved the active projects, client files, and other in-progress files from her filing cabinet into plastic crates on casters. With this new filing system, each folder is easy to see and retrieve. There is also an added benefit: the crates are mobile. Zoey can scoot a crate over to the desk, roll it near the conference table, or even roll it out of view into a closet.

Filing Cabinets Have Their Place

Filing cabinets can still be very useful for organizing and storing:

- inactive materials you need to keep for some reason;
- materials you save for very occasional reference;
- archival materials like back taxes that have to be kept for a long period of time; and
- confidential documents that need to be locked up.

So that you don't forget what you've filed away in your filing cabinets, create an index of their contents on your computer. Print a hard copy and tape the content list to the outside of the drawer for easy reference. As your files change, you can easily add or delete items on your computerized list and reprint it to keep it up-to-date. Another approach, if your file tabs are printed clearly, is to take a picture of the contents of your filing cabinet drawers or your crate files with your smartphone, print out the picture, and tape it to the front of the drawer or crate for a visual index.

"Mutter" Your Papers

The "muttering" filing system promotes organizing your papers emotionally, instead of categorically. It works by tapping into your emotional response to your papers. For instance, have you ever picked up a piece of paper and said, "I better hold on to that. It might come back to haunt me"? The muttering filing system would have you file that paper in a folder called "This will come back to haunt me." Another example: There's a stack of business cards on your desk, gathered at a networking event. You mutter to yourself, "I can't believe I haven't followed up with these people yet." Put them in a file called "Follow up with these people NOW" and also schedule time to do this task. Your Paper Partner can help you set up a muttering filing system.

Setting up a muttering filing system:

1. Supply your Paper Partner with straight-cut tab folders (the kind with the tab that runs the entire length of the file folder instead of one-third cut) and a thin black marker.
2. Walk through your office and pick up one loose piece of paper at a time.
3. Mutter out loud the first thing that comes to your mind.
4. Have your Paper Partner write that "mutter" on the file folder and place the paper inside.
5. Do this with all your loose papers.
6. Arrange the folders vertically on your desk.

Muttering System

Courtesy of Squall Press.

Popular mutterings include:

- "This may come back to haunt me"
- "If I win the lottery"
- "Good ideas"
- "These prove my point"
- "Treasures"
- "This is funny stuff"
- "For Uncle Sam"
- "Why can't I find this when I need it"
- "Did I get paid for this yet?"
- "I have got to call/write/e-mail these people!"

LEVEL THREE SOLUTIONS: HELP FROM PROFESSIONALS

Going Digital

Going forward, Zoey really wants to reap the benefits of digital organizing, but she can't make the leap from hard copy to digital without professional help. We advise her to put a Tech Tamer on her support team. A Tech Tamer could be a family member or a friend, but we're assuming she does not have this resource in her personal network and needs to use a professional. A Tech Tamer can help Zoey set up a simple, digital filing system.

Microsoft Office and other software programs that come with your computer automatically have a system for organizing files. In Microsoft Office, it's called Libraries. Just about everyone can use the default Libraries called My Documents, My Pictures, My Music, and My Videos. Zoey can use her Tech Tamer to figure out what other Libraries she might need and how to create sub-folders for each Library. For instance, as a life coach, other Libraries Zoey might add are My Clients. Under My Clients her sub-files might include Client Notes and Client Agreements. Sub-files to My Documents might include Marketing, Account Management, and Personal.

There is no end to the way you can organize your files and your documents within your files. A Tech Tamer with a head for organizing information can create a simple system that matches the way Zoey thinks about organizing information.

There are also several ways to retrieve files and documents. One of them is by keyword, which is sure to put Zoey at ease because she'll never have to remember hierarchically where something is filed. Again, a Tech Tamer can show you these tips.

Digital Notebooks

A simple, easy way to reduce paper going forward is to set up digital notebooks using Evernote.com or Amazon Drive. Your Tech Tamer can show you how. Digital notebooks can be set up on any topics you like. You can save digital documents, e-mails, attachments, photos, audio files, and just about anything you like to the notebooks, just like you would if you use a set of three-ring binders. But here's the beautiful thing; you don't have to

Hung up on Hard copy

remember what you filed where! Why? Because you assign keywords, called "tags," to your stuff. Think of any of the keywords and Evernote can find your stuff. The digital notebooks live on the Web and not on your computer hard drive, so you can access them from any device. Check out the Evernote tutorial on YouTube.com for a good overview.

Where to Find a Tech Tamer

Professional organizers who specialize in information organizing make great Tech Tamers. Like any other service provider who assists you, you may have to teach them a thing or two about your ADD symptoms like how often you might need to take breaks, or your hyperfocus traps. Search for one at www.napo.net by checking "Information Organizing, Paper and Electronic."

Zoey is a member of two networking groups. Networking groups are an excellent source of tech-savvy professionals who might be able to serve as Tech Tamers. Just be sure to ask around for someone you can trust to keep your service needs confidential.

A third source is an ADD coaching group. Ask for a tech-savvy coach to help you transition from hard copy to digital.

Review

- Work in conjunction with your out of sight, out of mind (OosOom) nature.
- Remember that vertical = visible and horizontal = hidden.
- Use color-coding for easy retrieval.
- Use transparent containers for visibility.
- Create a hot spot on your desk.
- "Verb" your papers.
- Use a Paper Partner.
- Use filing cabinets with an index.
- Use the "muttering" filing system.
- Use a Tech Tamer.
- Set up a digital filing system.
- Use digital notebooks.

Backlog Blues

Elliot is a landscaper with ADD. He is a recently divorced dad with two boys in middle school. Elliot has a wide range of interests, including camping with the kids, personal investing, and ("so the kids don't starve to death") cooking, as well as building birdhouses, running, and several other hobbies. And then there is his landscape business. "I have to stay up on design, sales ideas, how to go 'green', all sorts of stuff." Each project, hobby, and interest has its own paper trail, both digital and tangible. In Elliot's case, it's mainly tangible. Information, papers, and projects are on every surface of his home—the dining room table, every chair, countertop, shelf, and windowsill; wherever something can land, it does, including magazines, clippings, catalogs, maps, manuals, and newsletters. The guest bedroom, long abandoned, now serves as a storage room for boxes of old taxes, the kids' schoolwork from elementary school, medical records, and loose papers of unknown origin. "I'd like to set a better example for the kids before it is too late and they pick up my bad habits," Elliot says.

Is This Your Story?

It is if you:

- have a disorganized backlog of accumulated papers;
- collect materials related to a wide range of interests;
- tend to keep a lot of hard-copy reading and reference materials; and
- want to be a better role model.

Gather–Keep–Discard

Based on our interests, we gather information, keep it while it remains interesting or useful to us, and then, when our interests change, most of us shed the information we have accumulated because it is no longer interesting or is less useful. As we move from job to job, home to home, and interest to interest, our information follows a process of gather–keep–discard, gather–keep–discard. This keeps us from becoming backlogged with a glut of unnecessary information and paper.

> **The ideal paper flow should be a continual process of Gather–Keep–Discard**

Without a doubt, the Internet has decreased the amount of tangible information and paper in our lives, but certain ADD patterns can distort or interrupt the discard portion of the gather–keep–discard process. These include:

- difficulty with decision-making;
- a pattern of ignoring routine life-maintenance activities;
- a wide range of interests pursued with enthusiasm, but rapidly dropped;
- a difficulty with project completion;
- a dependence upon paper as a visual reminder; and
- an unrealistic sense of what you'll actually have time to read.

These patterns have been discussed earlier in relation to "thing" organization and clutter. This chapter will address how these ADD patterns contribute to information backlog. Elliot's wide range of interests brings tons of information, paper, and projects into his home. Discarding them requires a decision. Typically, the ADD default decision is "I'd better keep it, I might need it." The Internet has nearly unlimited capacity to store digital information, but one's home is another story.

An unrealistic sense of time leads you to delude yourself that "someday" you'll read all those magazines and catalogs. To compound the paper problem, a tendency to leave projects incomplete leads you to save all the tangible stuff that relates to each project. To throw the papers away is to admit you'll never finish the project. And, finally, you may hang on to paper as a memory aid.

LEVEL ONE SOLUTIONS: WAYS TO HELP YOURSELF

Gathering Guidelines

Use the following guidelines to reduce the amount of information you gather. They work for both tangible papers and digital documents. If you find them helpful, you may want to laminate a printed list of guidelines and post it next to where you use your laptop, by your desk, or in other places where you tend to gather information.

Chapter Eighteen

Gathering Guideline Questions

1. *Am I still interested in knowing/doing/having this?* Elliot was once keenly interested in investing in start-ups, but since the divorce his priorities have changed.
2. *Do I know/understand this already?* Elliot is now a veteran landscaper. He no longer needs to read topics meant for someone less experienced.
3. *Is a better/fresher version of this likely to come into my life soon?* Elliot is tempted to keep an article on hot mutual funds, but did you know that financial information becomes obsolete eight minutes after it comes off the press?!
4. *If I will use/read/do/share this, will I do it before it goes out of date?* Elliot plans to buy an SUV in a year or two, but the information he is accumulating now will be out of date by then. It will make more sense for him to gather SUV information when he's closer to his purchase date.
5. *Can I deal with any regret I might have if I throw it away?* Elliot knows that even if he makes a mistake and throws something away that he should not have discarded, he can likely get it again on the Internet and he will get over his regret.

Read Your Reading Materials

The best solution for handling a backlog of reading materials is to read them! This may seem obvious, but unless you read your material it has nowhere to go and stays in the "gather" phase. Once read, it can move to "learned" in your brain, "keep" in your digital or hard copy filing system, or "discard" as in delete or the wastebasket, depending on what it is. Left in the "gather" mode, reading materials can only accumulate. Gone are the days when we read during "downtime." There barely is any downtime anymore. So finding the time to read, especially professional reading, needs to move into the mainstream of your schedule (see Chapter 7 on prioritizing.)

- Read whatever you can, whenever you can. (See Chapter 16 on constructive waiting.) Keep reading materials in the car, your briefcase, the office, house, bathroom, at your bedside, and other convenient places.
- In addition to reading "whatever you can, whenever you can," set up regular reading times for professional reading. Fifteen minutes a day, an hour a week, or five hours a month are roughly equivalent. Choose the regularity that suits your needs and pattern plan your reading time. (see Chapter 13 on pattern planning.)
- Protect your reading time, giving it the same high priority that you would give a meeting with your boss.
- Learn how to skim (see below).
- Be very selective about what you decide to read. Make sure it is not below your knowledge level.
- Use Kindle or another e-book reader in addition to hard copy reading.

Learn How to Skim

Elliot's brand of ADD makes it difficult for him to read and retain what he's read. Unless he's reading something that really interests him, like science fiction, he finds that his mind wanders and he gets to the end of a page realizing that he needs to reread it because he doesn't remember a thing. Skimming is a great skill for ADDers to develop. Skimming involves a level of effort somewhere between the brief glances that allow you to decide whether to read it at all, and the detailed, word-for-word reading that should be reserved for only the most important material.

1. Read the entire first paragraph.
2. Read the opening sentence of each succeeding paragraph, choosing to read the entire paragraph if the opening sentence is eye-catching.
3. Highlight as you go.
4. Read the entire last paragraph.

Get Your Information in Digital Formats

Information comes in all kinds of formats now, and most of it is free. For ADDers this is a really wonderful development. Some ADDers are strong in absorbing information through

their ears in audio formats such as podcasts or MP3s. Others really love videos that can hold your attention like mini-movies. You can attend webinars in the comfort of your own home and teleclasses that transmit over your phone, or listen to Internet-based television programming and radio stations.

Ask your Tech Tamer to help you access your information in digital formats.

Use a Speed Reading App

There are a large number of speed reading apps available for iOS and Android devices. Many are highly rated and some guarantee that the user will be reading two to three times as fast as normal with improved retention after a short period of time. Be sure to read the fine print about what can be read using which speed reading app. Velocity, Quickreader, and Acceleread are three highly rated apps for iOS, but do your own research as more are coming onto the market all the time. A Faster Reader, Speed Read Inspired by Spritz, and Speed Reader are available for Android devices.

Kurzweil Reader

The Kurzweil Reader is a very sophisticated program that provides text to speech and so much more, including the ability to highlight text and create study outlines from highlighted text. It offers a number of voices to listen to and the chunks of written material shown on the screen at one time can be customized so that the Kurzweil can be used by anyone from a six-year-old to a graduate or professional student. If you have ADD and difficulty retaining information when you study, the Kurzweil, although expensive, may be an excellent investment in your college or graduate level education. Any printed text can be scanned and then read by Kurzweil, if you need to read text that isn't digitized. Unlike the speed reading apps, the Kurzweil increases attention and retention through allowing the reader to access the information visually and auditorily at the same time.

Are You an Information Junkie?

Adults with ADD tend to find many ways to escape from the tedium of daily life management tasks. While you may not feel you can justify spending large amounts of time on activities that are clearly recreational, you may fiercely defend going out on the Web or checking LinkedIn every hour as "valuable" activities.

Being an informed person is essential in a democratic society, but those with ADD may expand this civic duty until it has qualities of escapism, even addiction. If you find that you spend hours on end on the Internet to the neglect of other activities, it's important to ask yourself whether this has become a task-avoidance technique. Instead of mowing the lawn, doing the laundry or dishes, or running errands, you're spending time that you can ill afford "informing" yourself.

LEVEL TWO SOLUTIONS: HELP FROM FRIENDS AND FAMILY

Set up Google Alerts

Information comes in from many sources: e-mails, links, Facebook messages, tweets, texts, and on and on. For people with ADD, it is very common to feel overwhelmed. Rather than react to all the information Elliot is bombarded with, his nephew helped him set up Google Alerts. Google Alerts now "push" information to Elliot on the exact topics he is interested in.

- Go to www.google.com/alerts.
- Type in your topic.
- Enter an e-mail address. Use a secondary e-mail address that can be exclusively dedicated just to your Google Alerts.
- Google will send you e-mails with links to websites, articles, blogs, audio files, or videos on the topics of your choice. You can designate the sources you want and the frequency.
- When you no longer need the information, cancel the alert so it doesn't clog up your e-mail inbox.

Focus Your Interests

Focus your attention on what's most important to you, clearing out old interests to make room for the new. To get focused and make room for the future, try this exercise with a friend or family member.

How Wide *Are* Your Interests?

1. Grab a stack of miscellaneous papers.
2. Stand in the middle of the room, leaving plenty of floor space around you.
3. Imagine three concentric rings around your feet: One ring near your feet, the next ring about two feet farther out, and a third ring four or five feet away.
4. Place a large trash container next to you.

5. Look at the first paper in your hand. If it concerns a highly valued interest of yours, put it down on the floor in the inner circle. If it is of less interest to you, put it in the second ring. If you want to save it but it really only interests you slightly, put it in the third ring.

6. Toss all the papers, one at a time, into one of the rings. Just make quick, intuitive decisions about the papers. The longer you ponder, the harder it will be. If a piece of paper no longer interests you, throw it away in the trash container.

7. If you come across a paper related to financial, medical, business, or professional matters, set it aside to sort according to the methods described in Chapter 17.

How wide are your interests?

When you are finished, your papers arranged according to your level of interest will surround you. Save the papers in the innermost ring in your reminder filing system. Commit to saving the best articles, the most informative columns, and the latest information only on these topics.

Second-ring papers are the ones most apt to grow, so be very choosy about these broader interests. Make sure you are not just saving them out of habit. Then file these in your reminder filing system.

Consider letting go of your third-ring interests altogether.

Rotate Your Interests

The sorting system described above may be difficult for some adults with ADD, especially for those who have difficulty prioritizing. In the exercise above, if you find that you're putting most papers in your innermost ring and almost nothing in your outermost ring, you're having difficulty prioritizing. Everything seems important to you, and you're resisting giving anything up.

If this is your experience, then try rotating your interests instead. Sorting by rotation may help you set some of your interests aside for now, so that you can focus on a few interests. By rotating your interests, you keep them all, but rotate them in and out of action.

Use the Ring Method

To rotate your interests, use the same ring method, but label the rings "now," "later," and "next year."

Set a strict limit on the number of interests that can be placed in the "now" ring, as well as in the "later" ring. If you have difficulty setting limits, get help from your Time Tutor.

Once your papers have been sorted into "now," "later," and "next year," place the "next year" papers in storage boxes, loosely grouped by category. File the other papers in two rolling crates labeled "now" and "later." Then create an index for each crate, just like the index described in the preceding exercise.

During the year, you are free to move any interest you choose from your "later" file to your "now" file, so long as you move an equal number of interests from "now" to "later." You are also free to add an interest to your "now" file that hasn't been there before. The only rule you should follow is to keep a limit on the number of interests in your "now" file, moving the rest to "later."

Once a year, bring out your "next year" storage boxes. Decide whether you want to rotate any of those interests into your "now" or "later" files. Remember, as you rotate an interest in, you must rotate another interest out into the "next year" file boxes.

LEVEL THREE SOLUTIONS: HELP FROM PROFESSIONALS

The Body Double

For many with ADD, dealing with paper piles can trigger such feelings of overwhelm, even anxiety, that they cannot stick with it long enough to create order. If this is true for you, a Body Double may be your answer. A Body Double is a passive partner who sits quietly by your side while you sort through your papers, handing you papers one at a time. Although your Body Double does not organize or even offer you advice, his/her role is very important.

A Body Double creates an atmosphere in which organizing can take place. With a Body Double present, you are able to remain focused on organizing and not be distracted by other things. In this way, the Body Double acts as a kind of anchor, anchoring you to your organizing activity.

Working with a Body Double

- The ideal Body Double is quiet and unobtrusive. You may have a friend or family member who can fill this role, but often a PO is best.
- Put two chairs side-by-side at a desk or table.
- Pull a trash container nearby.
- Put a stack of papers on your Body Double's lap.
- Have your Body Double hand you papers one at a time.
- Toss papers that are no longer needed in the trash.
- "Verb" all papers that require action (see Chapter 17) and place them in the appropriate action files on your desk.
- Continue until all the papers on your Body Double's lap have been processed.
- Take a break.
- Then do another stack if you (and your Body Double) have the time and energy.

The Crew

The crew is another option for organizing a large quantity of accumulated, mainly inactive papers. You are a member of the crew, along with one or two assistants, supervised by a professional organizer. Together, you and your PO assemble the crew. Assistants can be friends, family members, or someone you pay to assist you. The crew presorts large quantities of papers according to categories established by you and your PO. After all papers have been presorted, you and your PO sort through each category of papers, eliminating, filing, or setting them aside for action, as appropriate. Using a crew:

- reduces overwhelm;
- makes a large job go faster;
- keeps up morale;
- keeps you focused; and
- gives you a sense of progress as space is rapidly cleared out.

If you are dealing with paperwork at home, your crew can consist of yourself and at least one family member, plus your PO. If your paperwork overwhelm is at work, you'll need to enlist a coworker or consider paying a teenager (your own or a friend's) to work on your crew at the office to conduct the Big Dig-Out.

Paper Tiger Software

The Paper Tiger software enables you to file and retrieve computer files, hard-copy documents, books, CDs, anything that you collect by using keywords. It operates much like a search engine and indexes all your stuff by using keywords and locations. Then, whenever you need to find that file again, you type in any of its keywords, and in five seconds Paper Tiger tells you where to find the file. You can print out indexes of all your documents and can cross-reference files. Check out www.papertiger.com for more information.

Ask your Tech Tamer to give you a hand installing either the computer-based or the Web-based version.

Head for the Cloud

Elliot says he would print out less of his information and store more of it in the cloud if he was certain he could find it easily. A cloud solution like Dropbox.com is just the ticket. Whatever is currently on his computer, Elliot can send to the cloud using Dropbox.com and easily access it again. The advantages are many. If his computer goes down, he still has his documents. If his house burns down, he still has his documents. The amount of paper in his home will recede. He'll be able to share any of his digital information with anybody from any device. Take a look at *Everything you need to know about Dropbox*, a video available on YouTube.com, for a simple tour of Dropbox's power. It's easy to set up with the help of a tech-savvy friend or your Tech Tamer.

Scanning

Elliot can also scan his tangible documents and turn them from paper into digital documents. From there, he can save them to his computer or send them to the cloud. The benefits of scanning are many, including:

- It saves space by reducing the need for filing cabinets.
- Digital documents are easy to share with anybody who has a computer.
- In the event of a natural disaster, digitized documents are safe from loss or damage.
- Digital documents are searchable by keywords and can be easily retrieved without even knowing the exact file name.

The price of scanners has come down, their speed has become faster and faster, reducing the risk of boredom, and they are simpler than ever to use. Scanning is a great solution for financial, legal, or medical records, but anything is fair game, even photographs! Read an article such as PCmagazine.com/scanners to learn which type is best for your needs.

Create!

If you are an adult with ADD and even a bit creative, consider organizing your papers by creating something with them. Maybe the materials you are gathering are the makings of a book, a photo album, a presentation, or a class. Creating a product from the information you are gathering is one way to organize it. It packages the information and leaves you free to move on to other projects. If you undertake a creative project, an ADD coach or an Organizer-Coach is a good choice for seeing you through the steps. They can help you plan out the project, stay on task, and see it to conclusion.

Backlog Blues

Review

- Observe the gather–keep–discard cycle.
- Use gathering guidelines.
- Read your reading materials.
- Use a speed reading app.
- Learn to skim.
- Go digital!
- Use Google Alerts or other "push" technology.
- Use the Kurzweil Reader to improve academic reading and study skills.
- Focus and rotate your interests.
- Use a Body Double.
- Hire a crew
- Try the Paper Tiger software.
- Head for the cloud.
- Scan your documents.
- Create something from your papers.

Part 6

Organizing Finances

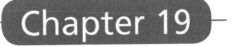

ADD-Friendly Money Management

Eric is a middle-aged divorced father of two teens who has ADD. As a married man he never was a good money manager, but his wife took care of bill paying and, with two incomes, his impulsive spending habits were a source of irritation but hadn't caused financial ruin. Now, Eric is on his own, with significant child support payments. Bills are often paid late because he never developed the habit of regularly managing his finances. His credit card debt skyrocketed as he continued to frequently go out for lunch with colleagues. Eric often ordered the latest electronic gadget online. Several years after his divorce, Eric was on the verge of financial disaster, barely meeting his monthly expenses and making minimum payments on his several credit cards.

Vera is in her early sixties. She had been briefly married in her thirties, but was single for most of her adult life. Although she made quite a decent salary for much of her career working in design and marketing, her champagne taste always placed a strain on her budget and she never seriously saved for retirement. An attractive woman, Vera always vaguely assumed she'd remarry one day and imagined that this fantasy husband would take care of her in her later years. Like many adults with ADD, Vera is always caught up in the "now," for instance buying designer clothes on sale even if she really can't afford them or doesn't really need them. She spends her monthly income, and sometimes more, keeping up with the social life of more affluent friends.

Good money management, like good time management, doesn't come naturally to adults with ADD. Executive functioning skills such as making a financial plan and following it, self-monitoring, attention to detail, and impulse control are all part of the picture. It's a "perfect storm" of challenges. One of the key messages that you've read again and again in this book is that ADD-friendly strategies must be accompanied by structure and support to be successful. And nowhere is this ADD maxim truer than when you're dealing with money management issues. There is much you can do yourself to organize your finances and manage your money, but don't be surprised if you find yourself needing help from friends, family, or professionals.

Spending Habits

Good money management all starts with good spending habits. Let's take a look at where Eric, Vera, and many other adults with ADD struggle with poor spending habits.

1. **Piggy bank thinking**—A young child asked her mother why she said they couldn't "afford" to purchase something the child wanted. "Do you mean that you don't have $25.00 in the piggy bank?" the child asked. This young child had a very literal and concrete notion of what "afford" meant. When the child could "afford" something, it meant that she had that much money in her piggy bank. As adults, we need to get out of piggy bank thinking. Unlike young children, adults have many, many other things to consider beyond how much money happens to be in our bank account at the moment. For example, we need to consider regular monthly bills and savings for short-term emergencies, mid-term needs that may arise such as a house down-payment, longer term needs like college tuition for our children, and even longer-term needs such as retirement.

    Adults with ADD all too often get caught up in piggy bank thinking—more focused on the new car, the vacation, or the restaurant meal they want now, and neglecting to prioritize for longer term needs by putting money aside.
2. **Impulse spending**—Many adults, especially those with ADD, spend money recreation-ally. One woman with ADD became a compulsive gambler, heading to the local casino mid-day and often losing significant amounts of money in the process. Vera's weakness was clothing and home decoration. As a designer, she worked for clients with lots of disposable income and it was hard for her to live within her more modest budget when she shopped for clothing or home furnishings.
3. **Shopping in response to understimulation**—The Internet has put the world at our finger-tips; when adults with ADD are home in the evening after a hard day at work, followed by the round of family responsibilities, the lure of Internet shopping can be hard to resist. And online credit card payments make the spending seem less "real" than if they were at the local mall handing over hard-earned cash to purchase "wants" in contrast to "needs."
4. **Leaking money for immediate gratification**—Many adults with ADD "leak" money even while thinking of themselves as frugal. They may not ever go for big-ticket items such as new cars or vacations, yet they are spending as much money each month on smaller items as they might spend on a big-ticket item. A Starbucks coffee daily, buying lunch rather than packing it, and picking up a DVD or some unnecessary make-up when running into the drugstore for ibuprofen can easily amount to $10 to $20 per day ($300 to $600 per month!) without being noticed.

Money Management Habits

In addition to spending, other important aspects of monthly money management are saving, bill paying, and financial paperwork. Those with ADD often end up paying much more than their base bills because they are paying overdraft fees (forgetting to check balances before using the debit card), increased parking fines (forgetting to pay the original fine before a penalty is added), and penalties on rent or mortgage payments because they are paid several days late each month.

Savings Habits

Studies of savings habits show two clear realities:

1. We're more likely to save when it's automatic and requires no action on our part.
2. We're more likely to save when we "pay ourselves first" rather than waiting to see what might be "left" at the end of the month.

Adults with ADD are much more tuned in to daily wants and needs and much less likely to put themselves on a tighter budget in order to save for the future. Vera, for example, found herself nearing retirement with very little set aside to live comfortably. And Eric's daily spending habits meant that he couldn't even pay his monthly bills, much less set aside money for the future.

Is This Your Story?

It is if you:

- have never developed good habits for bill paying, financial paperwork, and savings;
- tend to spend as much or more than you earn each month;
- have minimal savings set aside for emergencies, a rainy day, or retirement.

LEVEL ONE SOLUTIONS: WAYS TO HELP YOURSELF

Create a Budget

ADD-Friendly Manual Budget System

Budgets tend not to work well for adults with ADD because they are complex, detail-oriented, and require consistent use. A much more ADD-friendly budgeting system is to add up all of your standard monthly expenses, estimate the monthly average of your irregular expenses, and then subtract the total of these two figures from your take-home monthly income. This leaves you with your maximum discretionary spending figure for the month. Divide this figure by four and you'll have a weekly spending budget for ALL of your "wants" (in contrast to "needs"). Wants include entertainment, eating out, clothing, random purchases, gifts, coffee at your local coffee shop, snacks at work, etc. Going on a cash basis will help you to become suddenly realistic. Take the preset amount of cash from your checking account every Friday (so you'll have cash over the weekend) and then DON'T go back to the ATM until the following Friday. You'll find that you suddenly stop and think before putting down hard cash for a purchase, any purchase. You'll find that you start bringing lunch and snacks to work so that you can save your spending money for a purchase or for going out with friends. Looking at how much cash you have in your wallet will help you become much more realistic about spending habits. Of course, you'll need to recalculate your weekly allowance when other expenses change in your life, and you'll need to make a solemn vow to yourself *never* to take out more money until the following Friday.

Automated Budget System

There are dozens of software programs you can use to set up and automatically monitor your budget so you can stay out of the red. Two that are popular with ADD adults are Mint.com and Quicken.com. Both programs have categories of income and expenses that are easy to set up and customize. You can set spending limits for any category and receive e-mail alerts or text messages when you spend more than you've budgeted. Automatic bill paying and online banking are also standard features of the programs. To help you decide whether to move from a manual system to automated personal finance software, and to determine which is best for you, watch a video about each at YouTube.com/Mint.com and YouTube.com/Quicken.com.

Avoid Using Shopping as Recreation

If you don't want to spend money, don't hang out at the mall! And these days, "the mall" is just as likely to be a virtual mall as a brick-and-mortar mall. Online shopping is a real source of financial disaster, and Amazon's one-click purchases make it all too easy to "see it—want it—buy it" with one easy click. And it goes on your credit card, so you don't even feel the pain. If you already owe $6,000 on your credit card, and now you owe $6,078, what's the difference, you ask yourself, as you casually make your next online purchase. And the problem is you can't "cut up your credit card" when all you need is your credit card number for online purchases.

Reduce Impulse Purchases

If you are an impulse shopper, you'll need to develop a two-fold plan. First, limit your exposure to places where impulse shopping can occur. In other words, stop shopping as a form of entertainment. Second, you'll need to introduce other forms of stimulation into your life so that you don't fall back into impulse shopping when you're feeling bored or restless.

1. **Limit your shopping days.** Start by limiting your shopping trips to one or two specified days each week.
2. **Try the "wait a day" approach.** Don't take your credit card with you! If you see something you truly need—or something that is a great bargain—ask to have it set aside for you. Then wait until the next day to return and make your purchase. You'll find that in

many cases you'll decide by the next day that you really don't want to return to the store to make the purchase.

3. **Try the "deep freeze" if waiting a day doesn't help.** If the "wait a day" approach doesn't put the brakes on, try the "deep freeze"—put your credit card in the freezer (frozen into a block of ice).

4. **Make a "cash only" rule.** That way, unless you have the cash in your pocket, you can't make an impulse purchase.

5. **Tape your receipt to an impulse purchase** and leave it in the trunk of your car for 48 hours. Often the impulse will disappear and you'll feel fine about returning the stuff.

6. **Most important of all—look for other recreational activities** to fill your days that are stimulating for you. Consider volunteer activities, book clubs, or classes.

Leaking Money

Laura is a recently divorced mother of two young girls. Although she received child support from her ex-husband, her salary, as is so often the case, is much lower than her husband's, so even with child support she is much worse off financially than she had been during the marriage. Vacations were out of the question, and finding money for birthdays and Christmas was really hard. Laura's credit card was charged to the max, and she had to turn to her parents to borrow money when her car needed an expensive repair. What Laura didn't realize is that she was constantly "leaking" money. She was never extravagant, spent little on clothes for herself, and had no obvious vices, but on a daily basis she spent $10 to $15 or more on unnecessary expenses—which added up to hundreds of dollars over the course of the month.

At a financial management seminar at her church, Laura decided to take on the challenge of "leaking money." The financial advisor suggested that everyone start tracking small daily purchases that were discretionary (wanted but not needed)—the Starbucks coffee, the soda, or candy bar from the snack machine at work, the magazine picked up in the cash register aisle at the grocery, the Kindle book ordered online. Each time, instead of giving in to the impulse, set the money aside in your "rainy day" fund, the financial advisor counseled. Laura was amazed at how much money began to accumulate over the course of several months. Now, she and her girls always pack their lunches and never stop at a fast-food restaurant when they are out running errands. Laura consolidated her errands, running most of them on her way to or from work, to cut down on gas for her car. She got rid of cable TV and explored how to find free shows on the Internet. A year later, Laura felt in much better control of her finances and had a healthy rainy day fund set aside for unexpected bills.

ADD-Friendly Bill Paying

Consistently paying your bills on time is critical for maintaining a good credit rating and avoiding late fees and having to deal with bothersome phone calls from creditors. Online banking and bill paying are a great boon to adults with ADD who have struggled for years with inaccurate record keeping and forgetfulness. With online banking, you never forget to enter the check in your check register—it's done automatically as you pay bills online. And you'll never have to struggle with careless errors in trying to balance your checkbook—this is done automatically as well. All banks offer free online bill paying. All you have to do is go to the bank's website and set up automatic payments for all of your bills that recur each month. Some bills, such as your rent or mortgage payment, can be set up easily to pay the same amount each month.

Other bills, such as phone or utility bills, vary from month to month. These can be set up directly with your phone or utility company to be paid through automatic withdrawals from your bank account.

ADD-Friendly Record Keeping

A well-organized financial record-keeping system is usually a challenge for adults with ADD. You may have repeatedly tried to set up a financial filing system, only to see your system deteriorate back into piles instead of files. If this is the case for you, try this very simple financial filing system that will keep you well-organized despite your ADD.

"Intentional Piles"

If piling your papers is how you naturally tend to function, why not use it to your advantage. You'll need a shelf on which to place a row of sturdy file boxes. These can be purchased at any office supply store. Label each box by year and by category using the following categories:

Tax papers (all papers and receipts you need to save to take to your accountant when preparing your annual tax return)
Financial papers (all monthly and quarterly reports regarding your
investments and savings)
Paid bills and receipts
Insurance
Stuff I want to read about personal finance or money management

Then, when your mail arrives, open and sort it by tossing it into the appropriate "pile" which will be contained for you in the labeled file box. If you receive your statements and other items of financial information electronically, print them out and toss them into the right "pile." You'll have all of your important financial records automatically sorted chronologically, with the latest on top.

The only piles you'll need to keep out on your desk are papers that fall into two categories:

Bills to pay (that are not set up for automatic payment with your bank). Once they're paid, they can be tossed into "paid bills and receipts."
Paperwork to complete, which includes financial forms you may need to fill out, sign, and return to sender.

Schedule a Paperwork Time Each Week

Think about the flow of your week and choose a particular evening each week when you will take care of bills and paperwork. This task will take MUCH less time if you set up automatic bill payment through your bank.

LEVEL TWO SOLUTIONS: HELP FROM FRIENDS AND FAMILY

A friend or family member can be your Paper Partner and lend support as you dig through piles of paperwork to create the ADD-friendly paper "piling" system described above.

Some adults with ADD who are in retirement today grew up before computers became the widespread phenomenon they are today. If you are fearful of online bill paying and banking because you don't know your way around a computer, it's easy to get help.

- Some banks are happy to do this as a service to customers, and many local senior services offices also offer this kind of support.
- If you live in an active 55 and older community, there may also be assistance available through one of your community programs. Your local AARP (American Association of Retired Persons) chapter can help.
- Another option is your Tech Tamer, who can be a friend or family member (or a professional) that sits by your side and guides you through the whole process.

So don't shy away from online banking and bill paying because you're not comfortable using a computer. These systems are simple, and, once you get the knack of it, your banking and bill paying will be on its way to becoming error free—maybe for the first time in your life!

- Use a Body Double: Financial organizing chores are hard to focus on. A friend or family member who assumes the role of Body Double can be a great help. A Body Double sits quietly with you while you balance your checkbook, analyze your statements, or pay your bills.

LEVEL THREE SOLUTIONS: HELP FROM PROFESSIONALS

ADD Coaches

At times, you may need more assistance with money management than can be provided by a friend or family member. If you seek professional help, make sure it's someone that is *very* familiar with ADD, in all of its challenging aspects. One of the best sources of support as you work to set new goals and break old habits is an ADD coach—someone who is very skilled in helping adults with ADD set and meet do-able goals. When you contact ADD coaches, share with them that a particular challenge of yours is money management and ask them if they have experience with that.

Use a Tech Tamer

If you choose to utilize a software program to manage your personal finances, your Tech Tamer can be of great assistance. Two programs popular with ADD adults are Quicken.com and Mint.com.

Professional Organizers

POs are also strong when it comes to paperwork systems. Reach one at the Institute for Challenging Disorganization who is also experienced with ADD (www.challengingdisorganization.net).

Use a Body Double

If you don't have a friend or family member to serve as a Body Double (see Level Two Solutions above), you can ask an ADD coach to be your Body Double while you get your financial paperwork in order. A Body Double often works best for people who are uncomfortable letting someone handle their financial paperwork and make decisions for them. If you're working with an ADD coach, you can work with them to decide on the type of assistance that you desire. In some cases, you may want them to function as a Body Double; in other cases, you may want more hands-on help.

Credit Counseling

If your credit card debt is more than 20 percent of your income, it's time to get help. Contact a consumer credit counseling service. They can help put you on a budget, make regular payments, and protect your credit rating.

If you are behind on your taxes even one year, contact the IRS Taxpayer Advocate Services at www.irs.gov/Advocate.

> ### Review
> - Keep your systems simple.
> - Keep temptations at a distance.
> - Boredom can be very expensive—keep busy with friends and activities.
> - Don't shop for entertainment.
> - Keep cash not charge cards in your wallet.
> - Get help when you need it.

Part 7

Getting Organized in the Digital World

Chapter 20

Managing Digital Distractions

Maya is a 35-year-old single woman. A digital native, Maya is extremely comfortable with all things digital. Her job as Director of Training at a technical college is an "always on, always connected" lifestyle she finds pretty compatible with her ADD. "My days are never boring and I have a lot of freedom to do my work without a lot of micromanagement," Maya says. On a jaunt to a nearby coffee shop for an espresso to pump her up after her usual 3:00 p.m. dip in energy, Maya was looking down at her cell phone and BAM! She slipped on gravel left on the sidewalk during a recent repair. Her ankle, twisted in an unnatural position, caused passers-by to stop and aid her as she sat in pain and embarrassment on the sidewalk. One called 911, another reached her boyfriend by text, a third called her boss, and a fourth generously accompanied Maya in the ambulance to the emergency room. "I am so grateful to my good Samaritans," Maya told her boyfriend, now at her bedside posting photos of Maya and her cast on Facebook. "Maybe one of them will see the post and contact me so I can thank them," Maya said hopefully.

Maya's boss told her to relax and take all the time she needed to heal. "You can work virtually on the important stuff," she said. Easier said than done. Maya found it very difficult to relax. Lying on the couch with her laptop nearby, her tablet in reach, her phone tethered to her by ear buds, and the TV gaming remote on her lap, she could not recall the last time that she had been disconnected from screens and devices. Trying to work from home as she recovered from her digitally induced fall, she was continually distracted by texts on her phone from friends and relatives, by the TV, which she kept on at low volume in the background, and by personal e-mails that distracted her from work. She had to admit, however, that even at work she had difficulty staying on track. Whenever she felt a little bored, she reflexively went online checking Facebook to see what her friends were up to or trolling the Internet for shoes to wear to the upcoming high school reunion.

Maya found herself reflecting that she'd been more and more distracted over the past few months. She had lost her phone recently and last month it was her keys. She noticed lately that when she was introduced to important visitors at work she tended to promptly forget their names. Yesterday she bumped into a colleague in the hall who reminded her of a meeting and Maya showed up late because she had forgotten. "In one ear, out the other," her mother often said to her as a child, but now as an adult the consequences were more profound. Maya needed to pay attention to the constant digital distraction that she was exposing herself to and learn to manage it before her work performance really began to suffer.

Mark's digital distractions almost cost him his job. He is a very bright, restless, easily bored individual who felt trapped in an understimulating job. His efforts to focus on work were constantly interrupted as he checked his favorite news blogs, looked up sports scores, texted his girlfriend 15 to 20 times each day, and did online research for the vacation he was planning in the spring. Mark's productivity had been declining for several months. His boss finally confronted him, saying that his Internet use was going to be monitored because it seemed clear that although he was at his desk, his mind wasn't on his work. This was a real wake-up call for Mark. First, he needed to seriously think about looking for work that would be more engaging for him. But also he needed to break his habits of constantly seeking relief from boredom by checking text messages and digital media throughout the day.

Extraneous Distractions

Maya's and Mark's attention is constantly divided, leaving them in a chronic state of distraction. Emergency room practitioners nationwide report a spike in distraction-related accidents such as people walking into poles, falling down manholes, and crashing into each other while texting and walking since the advent of the smartphone. While everyone today lives in a more distracted state, Maya's and Mark's tendencies are amplified by their ADD.

The compulsions to check Facebook, comment on blogs, follow a LinkedIn conversation, post to Instagram, and generate and respond to tweets, texts, and e-mails are constant external distractions that disrupt one's train of thought or the task at hand. Internally, Maya's brain is always preoccupied, thinking about what to do next, remembering this or that, generating ideas, worrying about something she may have forgotten, and trying to keep up on "what's new." Mark's digital distractions are fueled by his stimulation-seeking triggered by his boredom at work and intensified by his ADD.

POP! (Potential, Opportunity, and Possibility)

People with ADD have a penchant for POP, which stands for potential, opportunity, and possibility. Every new text message holds the potential to be important, interesting, or stimulating. An e-mail might be a new opportunity, and a tweet a positive possibility. Being excited about the future potential, opportunity, or possibility promised in every single digital message that comes Maya's or Mark's way is not a bad thing. It does, however, keep them in a state of high alert. Maya craves the stimulation of social media. She's always "Popping." Even in the early morning, through sleepy eyes and fuzzy brain, she wakes to the alarm on her smartphone, checks the time, and immediately checks Facebook, e-mail, Instagram, and Snapchat before she's even brushed her teeth! Mark's ADD impulsivity, combined with boredom, leads him to text his girlfriend throughout the day. She's had to talk to him about stopping the texts before she gets in trouble with *her* boss.

The War on Working Memory

Digital distractions are creating a war on working memory. Working memory is a kind of scratch pad. "It holds information in the moment either generating a response or tucking it away in long-term memory for later. Our working memory is constantly taking in information, doing something with it and clearing it out to make room for the next incoming information," according to Ari Tuckman, a psychologist specializing in ADD. For ADDers, all sorts of information meant for the working memory is lost, such as names of people that have been introduced, verbal instructions, casual comments, and requests from loved ones to do this or that task. We all need to hold things in our working memories on and off all day long to complete tasks at hand and follow a train of thought. For people with ADD, the flood of information crowds out working memory throughout the day. This digital information overflow makes it even more difficult to retain important information in working memory until it can be acted upon or transferred to longer-term memory for later reference. Our working memory has limited capacity and we need to be careful how much incoming information we're exposed to. A world of digital distractions is like a war on working memory, explaining why so much information "goes in one ear and out the other" for Maya and Mark.

Impulsivity in the Digital World

Maya writes the college's training blog. Thinking this might be an easy virtual task she could accomplish while her ankle healed, she powered up her tablet. "The tablet with its fast Internet connection, cheap e-books, funny YouTube videos, and thousands of iTunes was a bit too much for me," she confessed. "All I needed to do was a little research and 500 words of writing. Instead I watched a short video, bought an e-book, checked out Facebook, and downloaded an app that monitors my prescriptions for drug interactions. All cool, but that blog took me probably twice as long to write as when I do it on my laptop at my desk."

ADD affects each person differently, but a shared symptom is the inability to inhibit impulsive behavior. For ADD adults, impulsivity can come in the form of blurting things out or interrupting conversations. Saying "yes" to every request before thinking through the consequences is another ADD trait, resulting in overcommitment. The digital age introduces many new impulsivity buttons that can be pushed. The impulse to check e-mail all day long is hard to resist and, with mobile apps, very easy to do. Studies show that 80 percent of people check work e-mail on weekends and 60 percent check work e-mails on vacation. In a 24/7 digital world, there is a constant blurring of the line between work and personal life. But the blurring goes both ways, as both Mark and Maya engage in personal texting and social media during work hours.

As we're all learning, digital distraction can be deadly. Digital natives find it incredibly hard to ignore a text, even when driving! Even drivers who use hands-free commands for phone calls in the car remain distracted for 27 seconds *after they make a call*, according to the AAA Foundation for Traffic Safety. In 27 seconds a car at 25 mph can cover the length of nearly three football fields, potentially overlooking stop signs, pedestrians, and other vehicles.

Managing Digital Distractions

Work Creep

Digital distractions can have other detrimental effects for those with ADD. Bob is a health inspector. He gets a barrage of e-mails, texts, and calls, sometimes until 9 p.m. The expectation is that Bob will respond to them within an hour. He answers his phone while at his son's soccer game and checks his e-mail at a restaurant with his elderly parents. "I feel like I work all the time and yet I don't finish anything," Bob despairs. Bob's wife complains, "He takes his laptop to bed with him."

It's a phenomenon called "work creep," the tendency for work to creep into nonwork areas like family time, vacations, and even our bedrooms! The fallout from work creep affects all of us, ADD or not, but two aspects of it hit ADDers particularly hard. The first is the blurring of the line between work and leisure. The second is the issue of task completion. Many with ADD find that they are working longer and longer hours with decreasing productivity. Cognitive fatigue sets in so that they become less and less able to think clearly, write clearly, and complete tasks consistently. Rest from work is essential to reduce cognitive fatigue and to consolidate information, storing it in long-term memory. Adequate, restful sleep is also critical to good cognitive functioning, and yet the blurred lines between work and personal life often mean that people feel stressed, may rise in the middle of the night to write an e-mail that was forgotten the day before, and may experience fractured, inadequate sleep as a result. Without clear boundaries between work life and leisure time, the ADD brain is always overtaxed and overworked.

Finishing Things/Task Completion

Finishing tasks, thoughts, and even sentences is challenging for people with ADD. Now add the fact that we may encounter as many as 100 digital messages by lunchtime, and you can see why getting things done from beginning to end is even more elusive. Finishing things is very important for one's productivity. But it's also important for our mental health, especially since we live in an increasingly distracting world. Due to digital distractions and information overload, Bob is rarely able to complete a task without being constantly interrupted. Over the long term this makes a job he once enjoyed a source of stress, and it can cause physical ailments such as elevated cortisol levels and high blood pressure.

LEVEL ONE SOLUTIONS: WAYS TO HELP YOURSELF

Chunk Your Digital Distractions

Social media has great positive potential as a way to connect, a platform for interaction, a tool for community building, a marketing vehicle, a means of communication, and a disseminator of information. But it can also be a huge time-suck, so it's worth figuring out how to cope with it. Just as limiting and prioritizing print-based information is important, digital information and social media interaction must also have limits and priorities. The more you can chunk your social media interactions together in a clump, the less disruptive they are to your working memory. If you jump from Facebook to Web search, from e-mail to calls, from Pinterest to Twitter, it weakens your working memory. Chunking is less disruptive.

- Try to make a few uninterrupted calls in a row.
- Check your e-mail several times a day and process e-mails in a clump rather than every few minutes.
- Chunk your social media interactions with a tool like HootSuite, TweetDeck, Buffer, or Socialoomph. These tools allow you to schedule posts, tweets, and status updates across several platforms at once at whatever intervals you choose.
- Dedicate regular time for responding to deserving replies and comments. That is the social part of social media. However, you cannot—and should not—respond to all replies and comments.
- Turn off automatic notifications of new e-mails. By leaving the notification on, you're training yourself, like Pavlov's dogs, to automatically respond each time you hear it.

Combat Work Creep

Make yourself unavailable by leaving your devices and phone elsewhere or at least turning them off during family time, vacations, bedtime, and other times meant for rest. If you don't respect your own time, nobody else will.

Create Digital Device-Free Zones

In your personal space and in your family or personal life, create rules to build in digital-free zones. Always being "on" your devices has huge negative impact on your personal interactions, your quality of down time, and your nightly sleep. Suggestions for digital-free zones include:

- no phones, tablets, or laptops at mealtimes with others;
- no digital devices while spending time with kids;
- no digital devices at any social event;
- no digital devices at or after bedtime (many studies demonstrate that using digital devices at night significantly interferes with falling asleep).

You need to be honest with yourself about what steps you need to take to honor these digital-free zones. One man with ADD recognized how addictive the TV and Internet are for him and finally resorted to having no TV in his apartment, and to locking his phone and laptop in the trunk of his car each night. The more tempted you are to break the digital ban, the further away and less accessible your devices should be.

Develop a Personal Technology Policy

A personal technology policy is basically a set of boundaries around the use of technology that sharpens the distinction between work and leisure. An ADD client drafted one after he was late to his daughter's wedding because he felt compelled to answer just one more call. Here are some highlights:

- Live conversation, eye contact, and physical proximity will always be more important to me than virtual communication.
- I will never text and drive.
- If my children or grandchildren are nearby, they'll always have my attention over devices.
- I will not use my cell phone within 10 feet of water, whether it's the ocean, a pool, the bathtub, or the toilet.
- My mother deserves my attention. I won't text in front of her.
- All the screens in my home will be turned off after 8 p.m.

Engage in Nondigital Leisure

There are over 775,000 apps that are all meant in one way or another to help us be more productive. A new app comes out every three minutes. The point of all this productivity is to generate leisure, extra time not meant for work but for rest. Digital leisure, such as games and online videos, has its place. Think Angry Birds or Candy Crush. They do provide relaxation and help us destress. But the effects of nondigital leisure are more profound and long term, according to physicians, psychologists, and educators. Nondigital leisure improves memory, attention, focus, and decision-making, perfect for any adult with ADD. Examples of nondigital leisure include:

- socializing with friends;
- physical exercise;
- being in nature;
- sleeping;
- real-time dating;
- sex with a real person.

Sometimes your work situation is a culture of "always on." Try responding to texts, calls, and e-mails every half hour instead of as they come in. This will help to adjust the expectation of the person trying to reach you and give you at least 30 minutes of uninterrupted time to get things done.

Don't Go Looking for Digital Distractions!

Julie Morgenstern, an organization guru, says, "Don't read e-mail first thing in the morning." It's excellent advice for people with ADD. Your attraction to POP makes it difficult to discern the most important, urgent e-mails. To you, all of them seem like potential, opportunity, and possibility. E-mail is an "opener," not a closer. Open it up first thing in the morning and you're off on a dozen different tasks. Instead, close something from the day before. Finish something first before you open something new.

Fight Fire with Fire: Use the Digital World to Combat Digital Distractions

Lost and Found!

The single most common cause for losing things is being distracted. You can use your smartphone to track down stuff you've lost: www.theTrackR.com and www.thetileapp.com are great apps. A small tile or coin-shaped device attaches to your keys, glasses, phone, or any other item you're prone to losing. Ring up the item on your phone just like you would call a person, and the device uses Bluetooth technology to home in on the lost item. It plays a tune or a sound louder and louder until you find the item, a bit like an audio version of the game "Hot and Cold" you might have played as a child to find hidden items.

Getting Things Done

Digital distractions can keep us from finishing stuff. Consider using an app like carrot.com to keep you on task. You win rewards for completing things on your to-do list and hilarious reprimands for falling behind. Sometimes the game-like quality of an app can really be fun and effective, especially for people with ADD who thrive on stimulation.

Lists You Won't Lose

You already know that to-do lists are a great way to keep you focused on your priorities even as you are bombarded with new things to remember. Use the notes function on your smartphone to create all of your lists—your grocery list, your stubby to-do list for the day, your goals for the week, even your errand list. That way you won't be searching through a pocket or purse for that scrap of paper on which you wrote the list, which is quite possibly still on your kitchen counter at home. You're much less likely to forget your phone than a small piece of paper.

Digital Reminders

How often do we think of something we need to remember to do, but it's not handy to write ourselves a note? And with distractions all around us, it's very easy to forget or lose the note even if we write our reminder down on a random napkin or slip of paper. Use digital reminders instead.

- Use digital sticky notes. They can be positioned on any screen any way you like, are colorful, can be scaled to the size you need, and you can even embed alarms in them. See www.zhornsoftware.co.uk/stickies/ or stickies.com.
- Send yourself e-mails or text messages. Not only are these great digital reminders, but they can also serve to document communication. "I know I told you." "No, you didn't! This is the first time I've heard of it." Does this exchange sound familiar between you and your spouse? With digital communication there is a permanent record of the communication—no more possibility of "you didn't tell me."
- Make a quick recorded message right on your smartphone with an app like Instacorder. Simply push the record button and record a voice memo. When you release the button, the message is sent textually to you via e-mail.

- Leave a message for yourself on Google Voice and it will automatically transcribe and e-mail or text the voicemail to you. Dragon Dictation will also perform this function.
- Use the camera on your phone. Let's say you're comparison-shopping. Instead of trying to remember who has the best deal, take a picture of the product and the price.
- Set alarms! They are everywhere: on all your devices, on your phone, on many wrist-watches, on your oven, and of course on alarm clocks.

Digital Social Connections

One advantage of e-mail or texting is that it can be done at any time that is convenient for us without concern for interrupting others with a phone call. And arranging for group activities such as car pools, group volunteer activities, and social meetings can be done very efficiently with a group e-mail—*much* less work than the old-school approach of making multiple phone calls.

LEVEL TWO SOLUTIONS: HELP FROM FRIENDS AND FAMILY

Strive for Balance

Take a cue from friends and family who seem to lead a balanced life; they make the best of what our digital society has to offer but also engage in real-time, live activities like exercise. Joining a gym to exercise alone can be hard to do and preys on your moods, but signing up with a personal trainer, joining a walking club, or making a commitment to play tennis with a friend every week ratchets exercise up a notch because it involves other people, time, and money.

Get Outdoors!

Initiation and follow-through are executive functions people with ADD find challenging. Sometimes this can hold you back from planning activities like hiking, camping, biking, or hitting the beach, all excellent doses of nature great for burning off excess ADD energy, slowing down a racing mind, or just idling the brain away from digital distractions. It often doesn't take more than expressing enthusiasm for the *idea* of an outdoor activity to get a family member or friend to get the ball rolling. Everybody enjoys being in nature. You're role can be enthusiastic cheerleader. Let someone else make the plan. Keep it simple so you can plug into the plan without a lot of preparation. One ADD businessman goes to one State park within 60 miles (one hour) of his home each Saturday or Sunday in the spring, bringing different friends or family members with him. "State parks are easy to travel to, inexpensive and offer a variety of outdoor things to do," he cheerfully observes. They just choose a park, figure out a date, power up the GPS, and go.

It's great to combine technology with nature. Download that app that tells you what poison ivy looks like or how sedimentary rock was formed. Take a lot of pictures. Use all the gadgets and gizmos you want to avoid getting lost. But be sure to slow down, look around, and take it all in.

Know When You Are in a No Interruptions Zone

Machines, even computerized ones, are dumb. Your smartphone, tablet, apps, and social media do not know the value or importance of a task you are already engaged in. They don't know if what you're doing now is worth putting aside, even for just a moment, in order to respond to a ping of a text, a ring of a phone, or an e-mail alert. Only you can assess that. Once you do ascertain that you need to be in a No Interruptions Zone, friends and family can help you maintain that. But they can't be supportive unless you tell them you need their help. Here are some No Interruptions scenarios when your friends and family may need to be more sensitive to their tendency to interrupt you, whether that's in-person, by sending text messages, or by calling you. Yes, you can ignore those messages, but you might have a brand of ADD that makes that difficult to do, so ask for their support by not interrupting you.

- If your current task or project is time-sensitive, you're in a No Interruptions Zone.
- If what you are doing now is holding up someone else's work, and you simply must get it done, you are in a No Interruptions Zone.
- If what you are doing is complex or requires a highly focused learning curve, you are in a No Interruptions Zone.
- If dividing your attention is hazardous or dangerous, you are in a No Interruptions Zone.

LEVEL THREE SOLUTIONS: HELP FROM PROFESSIONALS

There are signs when an impulsive behavior has become risky or crossed a line into addictive behavior. If you exhibit any of these signs, it's best to discuss your behavior with a counselor.

- Neglecting in-person face time with family and friends.
- Your body can also give you clues. If you feel in an almost trancelike state, oblivious to children crying, the smell of a burning roast, or other environmental hazards, something is up.
- If you feel depressed when you are not on a device, that might be something to pay attention to.
- If you are agitated and impatient with live interactions, get that checked out.
- If you find it hard to sleep because you are preoccupied with FOMO (Fear of Missing Out), speak to a counselor.

Plan a Time Management Session with a PO

If you're not successful in dealing with digital distractions alone, consider planning a time management session with a professional organizer (PO). You can use it to achieve a wide variety of anti-distraction goals, including:

- making lists to supplement your working memory;
- breaking down projects into smaller steps or adjusting your level of focus upward to take in the big picture;

- scheduling your chunked social media activities;
- planning nondigital leisure.

Use Your Tech Tamer

Ironically, the very technology tools that can sometimes cause digital distractions are the same ones that can reduce them! Your Tech Tamer can help you research and test all the apps mentioned in this chapter or find others so that you choose the ones that help you limit the excesses of digital distractions while reaping all the benefits of digital life.

Review

- Chunk your digital distractions.
- Make yourself less available by phone and devices during family time, vacations, and bedtime.
- Create device-free zones.
- Develop a personal technology policy.
- Engage in nondigital leisure.
- Use apps, devices, and the best of the digital world to combat digital distractions.
- Strive for balance between real-time live interactions and virtual, digital interactions.
- Get outdoors!
- Know when you are in a No Interruptions Zone.
- See a counselor if you have impulsive behaviors that are risky or addictive.
- Plan a time management session with a professional organizer.
- Use a Tech Tamer to help you find the right apps and technology tools.

Chapter 21

The Internet Black Hole

My client Ann calls her ADD husband Joe "an information junkie." Joe loves the pursuit of information. New information excites him. In fact, Joe can get so involved in an Internet search that the information he finds can be useless because it's often too late. Ann says, "My car became so unreliable that I wanted another one pretty quickly. Joe, bless his heart, was very eager to help. We discussed a price we could afford and a few features I wanted, and then I let Joe loose on the Internet to do research. BIG mistake." It's not that Joe did anything wrong. He just did not know when to stop. Joe researched automobile performance reports in *Consumer Reports* online. He posted messages on his Facebook page asking his "friends" to tell him their experiences with certain vehicles. He watched YouTube videos of cars in action for hours and hours. "The house could've caught on fire and Joe wouldn't have noticed. I worry because he sits at the computer for hours on end and he needs to be exercising," Ann explains.

Joe's research went on for one month and then two. Meanwhile Ann's car was in and out of the shop, which caused all kinds of difficulties such as having to coordinate errands so Joe could drive her. "Joe keeps thinking there is just a little bit more information 'out there' and we'll find the perfect car to buy." Joe might be correct. The problem is we live in a world of endless information. Joe could literally search the Internet forever and there would still be 'just a little bit more information out there.' Not great news for ADD information junkies like Joe who seek not only an abundance of information, but also the perfect information.

The Thrill of the Hunt

Traditionally, the hours the library was open, the fact that information was paper-based, and the body of knowledge that existed on a topic limited the pursuit of information. But the Internet has no body, walls, hours of operation, or physical limits. It can be scaled infinitely. So, there is no end to the information that can be found to answer a question, solve a problem, make a point, or satisfy a curiosity. People with ADD can be particularly vulnerable to the black hole that is the Internet. Internet searches are extraordinarily stimulating and engaging. The thrill of the hunt plays right to Joe's neurology. Neurologists have found that seeking information on the Internet can release a neurochemical called dopamine. Dopamine is released in the brain when new things are learned, effectively causing a burst of pleasure. It is the same chemical that is released when a person gambles or uses cocaine, according to neuroscientists.

Novelty Is an ADD Turn-On

We also know that the ADD brain is attuned to anything novel. A link to one interesting article leads to another and to another, until the original subject of a search can send people like Joe into tangents and side roads. Along the informational road, Joe encounters serendipitous information, information he didn't even know he wanted or needed. Joe could not resist reading about flying cars of the future and cars that will run on water. Serendipitous information, though accidental or incidental to his main goal, stimulates Joe and extends the information search even longer.

Hyperfocus

As you may recall from Chapter 6, people with ADD are prone to hyperfocus. At one end of the attention spectrum, there is distractibility. At the other end is an inability to shift attention away from something very engaging, which we call "hyperfocus."

Compulsive Perfectionism

Many people with ADD have difficulty shifting from one activity to another. They become so intensely involved in what they are doing, even a relatively unimportant activity, that they have enormous difficulty pulling away and moving on to something else. Sometimes this driven behavior morphs into perfectionism, which is what happened to Joe. He was never satisfied that he had amassed enough information. Laura fell into a similar black hole when doing research on her dissertation. Unfortunately, her dissertation supervisor did not set any parameters for her, and two years later she was still collecting, reading, and organizing research articles that filled multiple five-drawer file cabinets! Instead of moving ahead with her own research, she was stuck in conducting an endless literature review.

> ## Is This Your Story?
>
> It is if you:
>
> - get lost for hours on the Internet;
> - are turned on by the thrill of an Internet search;
> - can't seem to stop when it comes to finding information;
> - might be prone to Internet addiction.

LEVEL ONE SOLUTIONS: WAYS TO HELP YOURSELF

Tips for Stopping

In an era of endless information, we have to develop new ways to stop.

1. Go for quality not quantity: Joe amassed a huge amount of information. Printed out, it is a wad of paper nearly three inches thick. "Sorting through it to find the most relevant information is time-consuming. I'm overwhelmed," Joe confesses. Stop your search when it is well rounded, containing a wide range of sources from authoritative websites, blogs, videos, and live experts, plus people you trust.
2. Observe the law of diminishing returns: Stop when you hit the law of diminishing returns. This is the tendency for continuing effort toward a particular goal to decline in effectiveness after a certain level of result has been achieved. Or, as a client puts it, "After a while, the lemonade ain't worth the squeeze."
3. Stop when you've honored your promise: When you've met people's expectations, come through, or been someone people can count on, you can stop.
4. Stop when you have formed your own opinion, conclusion, or decision.

Don't Get Sidetracked by Serendipitous Information

You're always going to find wonderful, interesting information that is not directly relevant to your search. And that's fine. Just have a place to put it so it doesn't distract you from your major goal.

- Open up a Word document and copy and paste the Web page URL to it and save it to your computer.
- Create an electronic file such as Car Stuff in which to put your extraneous information.
- Or open a digital notebook in Evernote.com and file URLs, Web pages, text, photos, and just about anything else.
- Or you can print out the serendipitous information, set up a tangible file folder for it, and file it away.

Use Apps to Help Control Your Internet Habits

Self-Control is an app that allows you to set an amount of time during which you want to be unable to access the Internet. Once you set the time, you can't access the Internet through restarts or reboots. If this idea of total Internet blocking creates too much anxiety for you, you have the option of setting up sites that are "white-listed" and you are allowed to access. Alternatively, you can "blacklist" certain sites but continue to have access to all other parts of the Internet.

StayFocusd is designed to help you limit the time you spend on time-wasting sites on the Internet. It works in the reverse manner of Self-Control. Instead of deciding how much time you *can't* spend on certain websites, you set the amount of time you want to allow yourself to spend on those websites.

Anti-Social blocks the social websites that are killing your focus. It is an app designed to keep you safe from the best known time-sinks, including Twitter, Facebook, Flickr, Digg, Reddit, YouTube, Hulu, and all standard Web e-mail programs. Unlike Self-Control, Anti-Social has a preset blacklist to which you can add other sites that tend to lure you away from what you want to be doing. Also unlike Self-Control, you can override its site blocking by simply rebooting your computer.

Block Access to Your Digital Devices

Some adults with ADD learn that they need to physically limit their access to their digital devices in order to manage their information junkie habit, for example locking laptops, smartphones, and tablets in a highly inconvenient, relatively inaccessible place like the trunk of a car, inside a credenza, or in a dresser drawer.

Snap out of Hyperfocus

Check out www.dejal.com/timeout/ or www.Timer.com to set up a time-out when you're on the Internet. Or schedule a digital sticky note to pop up to remind you to take a break (see stickies.com). For more information about hyperfocus, see Chapter 6.

LEVEL TWO SOLUTIONS: HELP FROM FRIENDS AND FAMILY

Get Clarity on What Is Expected of You

Information junkies need boundaries! If you're working on an information-dense project that you know will take you into the Internet black hole, ask family members, friends, or coworkers for parameters. Ask for a deadline, a word count, or a defined number of choices. For instance, Ann could have told Joe to narrow his search to ten cars rather than the 25 he researched. "I should have told him to put in maybe three weeks on the project rather than keeping it open ended. My bad," Ann commented.

Joe, for his part, needs to be self-aware that the Internet is a hyperfocus trap for him. Anticipating this, he can take some proactive steps to mitigate hyperfocus mentioned above.

Enough Is Enough

Family and friends can often be better judges of "enough is enough" than you can. If you do research, a report, a writing project, or any other Internet project, do your best and then hand it over to someone else to look over. You might be done and not know it!

Get an Online Buddy

If you are prone to "go down the rabbit hole" when searching online for a purchase or for information, consider asking a family member to sit with you and keep you on track.

Turn over Your Digital Devices

Many parents of kids and teens have learned they need to require them to turn over their digital devices at a specific time each evening in order to prevent them from staying online late into the night. Sometimes, even as adults, we may benefit from turning over our devices to a spouse, other family member, or roommate. The more barriers you place between yourself and the Internet black hole, the more successful you will be in managing your online excesses.

LEVEL THREE SOLUTIONS: HELP FROM PROFESSIONALS

There truly is a phenomenon called "Internet addiction." If you or someone you know displays these signs, a counseling session with a mental health practitioner might be in order.

Signs of Internet Addiction

- Losing track of time, resulting in chronic lateness.
- Becoming irritated or defensive when interrupted on the Internet.
- Neglecting chores, tasks, or responsibilities at home.
- Neglect of live time with family and friends to the extent that your social life suffers.
- A sense of euphoria that is sought again and again as a means to alleviate boredom, stress, sadness, or isolation.
- A feeling of restlessness, boredom, and craving to go online when you are temporarily unable to get on the Internet.

A mental health professional specializing in Internet addiction may draw you down gradually or take more drastic steps to change your Internet behaviors. If you see a counselor for your ADD, ask them for a referral. An ADD coach can also help you research the appropriate assistance.

Review

- Go for quality not quantity.
- Observe the law of diminishing returns.
- Stop when you've honored your promise.
- Stop when you've formed an opinion, conclusion, or decision.
- Don't get sidetracked by serendipitous information.
- Use apps that can help limit time spent on Internet time-sinks.
- Consider blocking access to devices or even turning them over to others temporarily.
- Set timers to snap out of Internet hyperfocus.
- Get clarity on what is expected of you information-wise so you know when enough is enough.
- Get an online buddy.
- Get professional help if you exhibit signs of Internet addiction.

Part 8

Conclusion

Putting Organizing Ideas into Action

Many issues have been covered in the preceding chapters, and many more organizing issues have been set aside. As authors, we chose the issues that we believe are most pressing for adults with ADD. We had to prioritize; we couldn't do it all. And that's exactly what you need to do as you begin to put the ideas in this book to work for you.

Structure, Support, and Strategies

As you think about how to begin to put strategies we've taught you into action, remember that the critical underpinnings of all strategies are adequate structure and support. First, develop a structure for your organizing ventures. What will you work on first? Second? What level of support will you need? You might start off on a solo plan, but it's important to have a backup plan—someone to help you if your solo efforts aren't working well.

Start Small

A typical pitfall that many adults with ADD experience is trying to do everything at once. Often, an adult seeks help for ADD, saying that they want to get control of their life. A laudable goal, but unreachable unless it is broken down into discrete parts that can be tackled one at a time. So take heart as you begin to organize. Set small, do-able goals. You'll build up steam by meeting those small goals. Success leads to confidence, and confidence leads to success.

Don't choose your most overwhelming organizing task as a starting point. If your entire house is in disorder, choose a place to start that will bring the greatest satisfaction in the shortest amount of time. For example, if your feeling upon arriving home is one of being overwhelmed as you walk into a cluttered foyer, that may be a good place to begin. Probably, with a little focused effort, you can clear out your foyer in short order. Then, every time you come home, you'll feel heartened. "Doesn't this look nice!" That boost will encourage you to take on other organizing activities.

Remember, Organizing Is a Process, Not an Event

Consider your newly organized foyer, for example. Clearing it out may be a single, focused task, but keeping it that way is a process. Your foyer will start to become cluttered again, probably the very next day. At this point, you can begin a process of problem-solving. What's causing the clutter? Is the hall table too enticing a place to dump items as you enter the house with full hands? Maybe something as simple as removing the table will induce you to carry items to where they belong—or at least farther than the front foyer. Is the hall closet overfilled, leading you to hang your coat and scarf on the banister or tossed over the chair? Would you be more likely to hang coats in the closet if there were a greater supply of sturdy, accessible hangers? Problem-solving and taking action on the solutions you reach are part of the ongoing *process* of organizing.

Approach Organizing as You Would Juggling

When juggling, your goal is to juggle one ball, then two, then three, and so on. A juggler adds another ball only when he is capable of keeping all of them in the air. If your goal is to eventually have a clean, well-ordered home, start by juggling one ball (the foyer project). Don't pick up a second ball, such as organizing the family room, until you've got the first one down pat. You're not getting anywhere if you're juggling balls three, four, and five, but balls one and two have fallen back to the floor.

Can't Do It Alone? Then Do It Together!

Planning, initiating, and following through on good intentions are the types of activities that are difficult when you have ADD. This is not due to laziness or poor motivation. These tasks are difficult because, when you have ADD, the parts of the brain that are involved in planning and organizing are often unreliable and underaroused. Stimulant medication can help, but the structuring influence of other people cannot be overstated. The physical presence of another person, even if they are not lifting a finger to help you, can keep you focused on your task. Don't apologize for this need. Instead, recognize it and arrange your life accordingly. If you don't have friends or family members who can serve as organizing partners, use a PO or an ADD coach.

You might also consider finding an ADD organizing buddy; you can support one another in your organizing efforts. Although each of you may have difficulty organizing your own environment, you'll probably find that you're much more focused and effective in seeing what needs to be done in one another's cluttered environments. It's always easier to keep going when you have company and encouragement. Some adult ADD support groups are now organizing "dig-outs" of each other's home space. Many hands make light work, and being able to laugh over ADD foibles with others who *really do* understand can move you from self-criticism to self-acceptance.

Invest in the Professional Help You Need

Throughout this book, we write about ways to help yourself. We don't mean to imply, however, that you should *always* try to help yourself first. In fact, it may be best to begin with help from others—friends, family, or professionals.

In certain organizing or maintenance tasks, it may be best to routinely involve others. This is a critical aspect of creating an ADD-friendly lifestyle. Assess your strengths and weaknesses realistically, and engage the assistance of others, whenever possible, on tasks that are your areas of weakness. For example, consider having a professional organizer come into your home on a quarterly basis to organize your files and papers with you; or plan to have an accountant's assistant balance your checkbook and pay your bills on a monthly basis. Many people with ADD resist such advice, protesting, "I can't afford it." For some, this may be true, but perhaps you can barter services with a friend. When deciding whether support is affordable, it's essential to consider the cost of *not* enlisting support. The cost of going it alone may come in the form of missed deadlines, late fees on bills, a poor credit rating, missed deductions on tax returns, and time spent hunting for misplaced papers that could be spent earning money.

Reserve the "Crisis Mode" for Real Emergencies

Many people with ADD routinely create crises as motivators. As a daily mode of operation, this is exhausting and ineffective. A crisis mode of operation may be necessary from time to time, and may be necessary on a more frequent basis until you are further along in taking charge of your ADD. If your in-laws are arriving for a visit in three days, or the IRS has sent you an ominous letter, then perhaps your crisis mode is appropriate in the short run. But, as much as you can, return to the "start small" maxim in your organizing efforts and stick to the *process* of building order in your life.

Be Realistic, Not Perfectionist

Disorganization is one of the greatest and most universal challenges for adults with ADD. While there are adults with ADD who are extremely organized, they typically pay a very high price, expending most of their waking energy to establish and maintain very rigid systems of organization. Many such people may appear to have obsessive compulsive disorder because they are hyperfocused on doing everything in a prescribed manner. Without this rigidity, their organizing systems fall apart.

Don't set such hyperorganization as your goal. It's a bit like becoming anorexic because you have a weight problem—a huge overcorrection that creates other problems. Perfectionism, like anorexia, can take over your life. Instead, aim for a level of organization that allows you to comfortably function in your daily life.

Maintain the "Right" Level of Focus

Adults with ADD can become caught in the "ant's view," concentrating on a single, sometimes unimportant, organizing activity while the rest of their world is falling apart. Often this hyperfocusing results from a need to reduce feelings of being overwhelmed. You may be able to manage "this one thing," but when you look at the whole mess you feel paralyzed. Others take a big-picture view, but can't focus on where to get started. Get familiar with your focusing tendencies, and try to become aware of when your level of focus is an organizing obstacle. The more flexible your level of focus, the greater your organizing success. Most organizing tasks require that you take a big-picture approach, set priorities, and move from one level to another, depending upon the demands of the task.

Don't Bite off More Than You Can Chew

Many, if not most, adults with ADD have "eyes that are bigger than their bellies." They start off with the best intentions, and with great enthusiasm, underestimating how long things will take and how tiring the task will be. Then, when they become fatigued and discouraged, mid-task, they are likely to abandon the project, resolving to finish it "later." Rather than surrounding yourself with discouraging, half-completed, or never-completed projects, try to "underdo it." Pick only a portion of your closet to organize. If you still have energy after you have reorganized the shelves at one end of your closet, there's nothing to stop you from taking on another mini-task, such as sorting and organizing the shoes on your closet floor.

Remind Yourself

Throughout this book, we have introduced many tips, ADD-friendly strategies, and maxims. You've probably tried to build new habits in the past without much success. Instead, try reminding yourself about the new habit you're trying to develop. If there is a particular idea or strategy that you're trying to build as a habit, write it large on a piece of paper and place it where you'll see it often. That's a good way to work *with* your ADD as you organize your life.

Be a Model for Your Children

You may not have had the benefit of knowing that you had ADD when you were growing up. As you work hard to better understand yourself and ways to take charge of your life, you can help your children to avoid many of the struggles that you have experienced. One invaluable gift that you can give your children is to serve as a role model, teaching them by example how to create an ADD-friendly life that allows you to take charge of your ADD and live up to your potential.

You can show them, by example, how to lower the stress level in their lives and how to manage the many activities and responsibilities of life. Time management skills are among the most important skills to develop, but they are rarely taught in school. At home, however, your children can *see* you learning how to better manage your time—writing a to-do list, consulting your calendar, and keeping an ongoing list of projects.

If you are an adult with ADD who is raising a child with ADD, learning the time management skills described in Part 4 and implementing these skills in your daily life will teach your child that these are the habits that people develop to manage their lives well. Our children are much more apt to imitate what we *do* than what we *say*. So instead of nagging your child to write down homework assignments and remember to do chores, show your child, by example, how you manage the same issues in your own life. Better yet, why not work on developing new habits together? Allowing your child to see you set goals, make mistakes, try again, and make progress—even allowing your child to help you track your own progress toward your goal—can make habit development an ADD-friendly family activity.

In Conclusion

Choose a do-able task to begin your reorganization and use the maxims and instructions you've chosen as your guidelines for getting started. Remember, start small and finish what you start. Organizing is an ongoing process, not a time-limited activity. Build habits, solve organizing problems creatively, and give yourself permission to get the help you need from others. You'll get there, creating an organized ADD-friendly life one step at a time!

Index